Linking
and Literacy
Technology

A Guide for K–8 Classrooms

Shelley B. Wepner
Center for Education, Widener University
Chester, Pennsylvania, USA

William J. Valmont
The University of Arizona
Tucson, Arizona, USA

Richard Thurlow
Center for Education, Widener University
Chester, Pennsylvania, USA

Editors

INTERNATIONAL
Reading Association

800 Barksdale Road, PO Box 8139
Newark, Delaware 19714-8139, USA
www.reading.org

The International Reading Association attempts, through its publications, to provide a forum for a wide spectrum of opinions on reading. This policy permits divergent viewpoints without implying the endorsement of the Association.

Director of Publications   Joan M. Irwin
Assistant Director of Publications   Jeanette K. Moss
Editor in Chief, Books   Matthew W. Baker
Permissions Editor   Janet S. Parrack
Associate Editor   Tori Mello
Assistant Editor   Sarah Rutigliano
Acquisitions and Communications Coordinator   Amy T. Roff
Publications Coordinator   Beth Doughty
Association Editor   David K. Roberts
Production Department Manager   Iona Sauscermen
Art Director   Boni Nash
Senior Electronic Publishing Specialist   Anette Schütz-Ruff
Electronic Publishing Specialist   Cheryl J. Strum
Electronic Publishing Assistant   Jeanine K. McGann

Project Editor   Christian A. Kempers

Photo Credits   Comstock Stock Photography

Every effort has been made to ensure correctness of Web site addresses. However, readers are warned that Web pages often change location at a site, and that entire sites sometimes are discontinued.

Library of Congress Cataloging in Publication Data
    Linking literacy and technology : a guide for K–8 classrooms / Shelley B. Wepner, William J. Valmont, Richard Thurlow, editors.
        p.   cm.
    Includes bibliographical references and index.
ISBN 0-87207-258-4
    1. Language arts (Elementary)—Computer-assisted instruction.   2. Computers and literacy.   3. Educational technology.   I. Wepner, Shelley B., 1951–   II. Valmont, William J. III. Thurlow, Richard.
LB1576.7.L56   2000   99-086755

Second Printing, May 2001

Contents

SECTION 1

The Heart of the Matter:
Technology in the Literacy Curriculum

SECTION 2

Into the CyberWoods:
Finding Your Way With Technology

SECTION 3
A Marriage Made
in Cyberspace

Foreword

Many books are published each year, but few books really matter. This is a book that matters. It matters for our children and for their future. It is a book for every person concerned about children, schools, and literacy instruction.

As with any important book that challenges our thinking, *Linking Literacy and Technology: A Guide for K–8 Classrooms* is about change. Shelley Wepner, William Valmont, Richard Thurlow, and their colleagues take us on a journey, exploring the changes in literacy classrooms as new technologies create new opportunities for teaching reading and writing. They show us new instructional practices to prepare children for their literacy futures.

This work fills a critical need in the literacy community. I expect it will be the first of many books from the International Reading Association that will support teachers in the new literacies of information and communication technologies.

Why must we help children develop new literacies? Consider several observations about the changing worlds of literacy and literacy instruction. First, in 1999, 63% of K–12 classrooms in the United States had at least one Internet computer according to the National Center for Education Statistics of the U.S. Department of Education (see http://nces.ed.gov/pubsearch/pubsinfo.asp?pubid=2000086). At the end of 2000, statistics are expected to show that at least 75% of K–12 classrooms will have at least one Internet computer.

Second, in the United States, a branch of the Federal Communications Commission provides over $2 billion annually to schools and libraries to pay for the costs of Internet access (see http://www.sl.universalservice.org).

In addition, countries around the world are developing national Web sites to support teachers and children in the new literacies of their future. See, for example,

Australia (http://www.edna.edu.au/EdNA)
Ireland (http://www.scoilnet.ie)
United Kingdom (http://www.ngfl.gov.uk/ngfl/index.html)
New Zealand (http://www.tki.org.nz)
Canada (http://www.schoolnet.ca)

The technologies of literacy are changing rapidly and so is literacy instruction. As the contributors to this book demonstrate, classrooms now have access to massive amounts of information generated by individuals with many different interpretive stances. Yet many of us in the field of reading hesitate to begin our journey into these new worlds.

"Books?" you ask. "What will happen to books, the touchstone of our field?"

Books will not soon disappear; they will continue to be an important part of our literacy lives. There is nothing as pleasurable as opening a good book and entering another world as you curl up on a couch in front of a fireplace, as you relax on the sand during a warm day at the beach, or as you while away the time during a lengthy journey.

New literacies build on previous literacies; they do not replace them. After reading a book, for example, many teachers engage students in a literature discussion group via e-mail with other classrooms around the world, experiencing different cultural interpretations of a common literary work. Pay a visit to Book Raps (http://rite.ed.qut.edu.au/oz-teachernet/projects/book-rap), a Web site in Australia, to see these discussions in action. Or, after reading and writing books of fall poetry, many teachers now exchange their responses and writing via Web pages, following the wonderful model developed by Susan Silverman. Pay a visit to Online Autumn (http://comsewogue.k12.ny.us/~ssilverman/autumn/index.html) to see how Susan and her colleagues accomplish this. Other teachers, whose students are reading books about Harriet Tubman, have their classes visit the site developed by Patty Taverna and Terry Hongell to enrich their reading experiences. Pay a visit to Harriet Tubman and the Underground Railroad (http://www2.lhric.org/pocantico/tubman/tubman.html). As these teachers demonstrate and the authors in this book suggest, we must begin to prepare children for new literacies that include, but go beyond, the literacy of book technologies. Our children require it; their futures demand it.

Unfortunately, as teachers we confront serious challenges to developing the instructional skills that new literacies require. Despite the fact that states and school districts are setting higher standards for our students, teachers are not always adequately supported in their efforts to accomplish these goals. A recent survey by the U.S. Department of Education found that 80% of K–12 teachers in the United States did not feel well prepared to use technology in their classrooms, perhaps because school districts spend, on average, only 20% of the recommended amount of their technology budget on staff development. The data on teacher education are just as discouraging; these statistics reveal that only half the states in the United States require preparation in computer education.

This book will help meet these challenges, supporting teachers in a world of changing technologies for literacy and changing instructional practices. It is a bold book, taking a broad definition of the new literacies. It includes many ideas for immediate use in the classroom with the many different literacy technologies: CD-ROM, word processing, Integrated Learning Systems, e-mail, Web pages, and many more.

It is also a book that focuses on the needs of the classroom teacher. Almost every chapter begins with a classroom vignette, describing how a teacher uses new technologies for reading and writing instruction. In very practical ways, each chapter shows how to integrate these technologies into literacy lessons. The authors focus on teaching, discussing technology only as it supports classroom instruction. Technology is a tool, the authors remind us, not an end in itself.

Finally, this book is very readable. The authors and editors have worked carefully to make the seemingly complex easy to understand and enjoyable to read. Writing like this is a special art. You will appreciate the authors' and the editors' efforts on every page.

Reading this book reminded me that change has always defined literacy. As a result, change should be familiar to every literacy educator. Reading a book or writing a message, even with traditional technologies, changes us forever; we return from the worlds we inhabit during our literacy journeys with new insights about our surroundings and ourselves. Change also defines literacy instruction. Teaching a child to read and write opens new windows to the world, creating a lifetime of opportunities. Change will always be central to our work as literacy educators. By teaching a child to read and write, we change the world. This book will show you new ways to accomplish this important objective, preparing children for their literacy futures. It provides new resources and tools for the most important role any of us can hope to play, teaching a child to read and write.

Donald J. Leu, Jr.
Syracuse University
Syracuse, New York, USA

Preface

> The revolution I envision is of ideas, not of technology. It consists of new understandings of specific subject domains and in new understandings of the process of learning itself. It consists of a new and much more ambitious setting of the sights of educational aspiration. (p. 186)
>
> Seymour Papert (1980)

Papert expressed this view at a time when educational technologies were disjointed in applicability. Video, computers, and print media were separate entities that were difficult to use in concert. Thus, an emphasis at that time was often placed on the new technologies rather than on the learning those technologies were supposed to evoke. The availability of a video, a computer program, or a textbook was the driving force behind instructional choices. The idea of connecting these technologies was only a dream. Not only was it difficult to combine computers with other media, but even connecting computers within a classroom was rare. Connections among classrooms were not conceivable, let alone connections around the world.

Today, computers and other media are well integrated and becoming more so daily. Not only can a computer select and display full motion video, but that video can be accessed from most parts of the globe. The computer itself can be taken to remote locations and still offer capabilities and connectivity not imagined by teachers in 1980. We stand on the verge of fully integrated classrooms where technology is taken for granted and the emphasis is placed on new ways to learn. Some teachers are adjusting almost as quickly as the technology is developing, while many teachers continue to wonder what technology can do that they cannot do. They have not yet seen Papert's vision of the ways in which technology can alter how we learn. This is especially true for those responsible for literacy instruction. Often, and because of the lack of a discrete hierarchy of skills that lead to reading acquisition, it is difficult to assess the validity of the technological tools offered. Those involved with technology in the schools often are unaware of the complex nature of the reading act. They are not able to help teachers make viable technology connections with instructional needs.

Linking Literacy and Technology: A Guide for K–8 Classrooms recognizes that teachers responsible for literacy instruction are unique. In using as its theme the idea that instruction should drive technology, and not vice versa, this book shares ideas, options, and opportunities for using technology. It is intended to be practical for preservice and inservice teachers, reading teachers, curriculum consultants, and curriculum supervisors whose focus is to help children develop and use literacy for content-area learning in the K–8 classroom. Amidst the array of instructional technology possibilities in this book, especially as they relate to our understanding of literacy development, are lesson strategies that can be used with one or multiple computers in the classroom, or in computer labs. In fact, five of the eight chapters include lesson and unit ideas and plans with the appropriate technological resources that can be used immediately in the classroom.

Three major points about literacy and technology anchor this book:

- Communication and comprehension are two of the most important outcomes of using technology;

- Computers should be used to enhance literacy in the classroom; and

- The basics of working with computers must be mastered so that students can concentrate more on literacy tasks than on technology.

Underlying the use of technology presented in this book is our commitment that students need to be active seekers of knowledge. In other words, they need to construct for themselves the meaning of what they learn. This takes place in an environment that reaches out to where students are functioning, both cognitively and affectively, and motivates them to link ideas, images, and words. Both skills and strategies are part of the instructional landscape for assisting students in the learning process.

Linking Literacy and Technology has three sections:

- Section 1, "The Heart of the Matter: Technology in the Literacy Curriculum," attempts to answer two questions: Why should technology be used to support literacy learning? and How can I begin to use technology in my classroom?

- Section 2, "Into the CyberWoods: Finding Your Way With Technology," presents concrete ideas for using technology to support word-recognition development, reading development, writing development, and content area learning. Different types of software and communication options are highlighted within the context of lesson and unit plans.

- Section 3, "A Marriage Made in Cyberspace," describes ways in which technology is being integrated into the literacy curriculum and outlines strategies for meeting the challenges of integrating technology in the new millennium.

Vignettes and examples of classroom uses of technology are used throughout the book to highlight concepts and ideas, and to help you find your niche in using technology to support your literacy goals. Each of the lesson and unit plans includes objectives, materials, activities, and assessment so that, if they suit your needs, you can readily adopt the plans for your classroom. Additional informational aides include side commentaries (textboxes) to explain concepts and ideas, software publisher addresses to locate the software described, and Web site addresses to locate the sites identified and described. Even if you do not have access to the specific products mentioned, you may discover ideas that work with other resources that are available to you.

A unique feature of this book is the cross-section of authors who bring their messages and ideas to you. All the authors began as teachers, but all are now in positions—as teachers, administrators, and software publishers—to promote change for students. Their varied areas of expertise and interest with technology and literacy instruction offer a collective perspective that is balanced in both theory and practice. We invite you to travel with us to experience the wonders of technology for literacy instruction.

Reference

Papert, S. (1980). *Mindstorms: Children, computers, and powerful ideas*. New York: Basic Books.

Acknowledgments

The idea for this book began during a conference call among four members of the International Reading Association's (IRA) Technology, Communication, and Literacy (TCL) Committee. As these members were creating the committee's 3- to 5-year plan, they realized that achieving a goal of outreach to the membership meant producing some type of publication about technology and literacy.

Four years later, we are grateful to the committee for encouraging us to pursue an outlet to promote technology for literacy instruction. Special thanks are extended to Ann Watts Pailliotet for her extra nudge along the way.

We are particularly grateful to IRA's then president-elect Kathy Ransom for attending our midyear committee meeting to help us appreciate the need for a practical book with down-to-earth ideas and unassuming writing. Comfortable in admitting her own technological insecurities and dedicated to highlighting technology during her term, she helped us establish a tone that would speak to the IRA membership. We are equally indebted to Director of Publications Joan Irwin for believing in the need for this book, and for having faith in our ability to deliver. We do not know many academic editors who will take the time to travel to the authors to coach them through the process. And without Matt Baker, Editor in Chief, Books, we know that this book simply would not be in the form that it is today. He pushed us to rethink, reorganize, and restate so that our ideas would be more coherent, more understandable, and better expressed.

We especially thank the contributing authors of this volume for their knowledge, professionalism, and congeniality. No deadline was too short, and no request was too onerous. Graduate students James German and Stephanie Hoskins also deserve acknowledgment for their willingness to conduct a search at a moment's notice.

A special thanks to our families—husband Roy and daughters Leslie and Meredith Wepner, wife Sharon Valmont, and wife Nancy and son Paul Thurlow—for understanding our need to spend our leisure time offline from family and friends and online with the computer.

About the
Authors

Ernest Balajthy is an associate professor in the School of Education at State University of New York at Geneseo. He is the author of two books and more than 80 articles on computers and education in journals such as *The Computing Teacher*; *The Reading Teacher*; *Electronic Learning*; *Journal of Reading, Writing, and Learning Disabilities, International*; and *Computers in the Schools*. He is currently editor of "Issues in Technology," a regular column in *Reading and Writing Quarterly*.

Barbara J. Fox teaches reading education courses and directs the reading clinic in the Department of Curriculum and Instruction at North Carolina State University, Raleigh. She has taught elementary school, has given many presentations, and has been a consultant for the design and use of word-identification programs within the context of balanced reading instruction. She is interested in how children learn to read, how technology affects learning, and how children develop the ability to identify and learn new words while reading. She has written two books on the teaching of phonics, as well as numerous articles on the reading process.

Mary Jane Mitchell is a reading specialist and Reading Recovery teacher at Cleveland Elementary School in Clayton, North Carolina. In addition to teaching at-risk first and second graders, she provides staff development for elementary school teachers in the area of early literacy instruction and assessment, and she conducts workshops for parents of emergent and developing readers. She is currently conducting a research study to investigate and compare the effectiveness of computer-administered instruction with teacher-delivered instruction on the phonemic awareness of low-progress kindergarten and first-grade students.

Lucinda C. Ray is Director of Curriculum Development for IntelliTools, Inc. She was formerly the Group Product Marketing Manager at TLC School, a division of The Learning Company, and the Education Product Manager at Broderbund Software, Inc. She was a classroom teacher for 25 years, teaching language arts, reading, English, speech, theater, and composition primarily to middle and high school students, but she also has taught at the university level. She holds one master's degree in theater education and another in English literature. Her responsibilities as Group Product Marketing Manager include conceptualizing and planning teacher-support material for software products. She is also instrumental in locating talented teachers as contributors and writers, editing, and working with print materials through the page design and print process. Ray is a strong advocate for educationally important features in software, and is a key player in managing the development and production of software titles specifically designed for the school market.

Betty D. Roe is a professor of curriculum and instruction at Tennessee Technological University in Cookeville, Tennessee, where she teaches reading, language arts, and library science methods courses. She developed and taught a course on the use of computers in reading and language arts instruction, which she is currently turning into a Web-based course. After earning her doctorate from the University of Tennessee, Knoxville, she taught elementary school before she took a university position. Roe is author or coauthor of 36 college textbooks in the areas of reading, language arts, storytelling, technology, and student teaching, as well as numerous professional articles. She has given presentations at professional meetings across the United States and in Canada from local to international levels.

Jean Sharp has an extensive background in teaching and training, instructional design and development, and project management. She holds a bachelor's degree in elementary education from Illinois State University and a master's degree in educational technology from the University of Oklahoma. She has 7 years of classroom teaching experience and 10 years of experience in product development with MECC and The Learning Company. She has been involved directly in the design and development of more than 25 award-winning software programs for children, among them *The Art Lesson* with children's author and illustrator Tomie dePaola, the Storybook Weaver series, *Opening Night*, and *The American Girls Premiere*. Sharp is currently Vice President, Product Development, for wwwrrr.net.

Jane E. Sullivan is a professor emeritus of reading at Rowan University, Glassboro, New Jersey, where she teaches courses in reading methods, including using children's literature in the reading/writing classroom. She also has taught courses in using technology to enhance teaching. She has written about and given presentations at state and national conferences on using technology in classroom instruction. Sullivan is currently collaborating with classroom teachers in studying strategies for teaching writing.

Richard Thurlow is an assistant professor of educational psychology and coordinator of technology for the Center for Education at Widener University in

Chester, Pennsylvania. He teaches graduate courses in educational psychology, theories of reading comprehension, educational research, and statistics. His doctorate is from the University of Minnesota. Before he began teaching at the university level, he taught music in elementary through high school in a suburb of St. Paul, Minnesota. There, he served as chair of the school district's computer committee and coauthored the district's first computer curriculum.

William J. Valmont has been Director of Technology in the College of Education at The University of Arizona in Tucson since 1993. In addition, he leads the technology focus area in the Department of Language, Reading, and Culture, where he develops and implements technology courses, including the college's first online undergraduate course. In addition, he has authored a spelling series, two reading programs, and a textbook about using video for school use. He has written numerous articles and has made presentations for such organizations as the Society for Information Technology and Teacher Education (SITE), the Arizona Educational Media Association (AEMA), and the Arizona Distance Learning Association (AZDLA), of which he is the founding president. A reviewer for the online journal *Reading Online*, he chaired IRA's Technology, Communication, and Literacy Committee, 1998–2000.

Shelley B. Wepner is the Director of the Center for Education, Associate Dean of the School of Human Service Professions, and professor of education at Widener University, Chester, Pennsylvania. She has coauthored or coedited 5 books, authored or coauthored more than 80 articles and chapters, and has authored or coauthored 3 award-winning software products. A former column editor of "Technology Links to Literacy" for *The Reading Teacher*, and a former cocolumnist on technology for *Reading Today*, she chaired IRA's Technology, Communication, and Literacy Committee, 1996–1998. She has been studying the benefits of technology for literacy development since the early 1980s.

SECTION 1

The Heart of the Matter:
Technology in the
Literacy Curriculum

■ This section contains two chapters to get you started thinking about technology as a natural next step for your classroom. Chapter 1 uses comparisons of children's past and present learning contexts to convince you to use technology as an effective instructional tool in today's high-tech culture. Chapter 2 helps you assess your current technology capabilities on a continuum of development in order to set an appropriate and affordable direction for your future growth. Both chapters set the stage for Section 2, which contains specific uses of technology for the literacy curriculum.

CHAPTER 1

Using Technology to Support Literacy Learning

WILLIAM J. VALMONT AND SHELLEY B. WEPNER

How We Learned to Read

Take a moment to visualize this situation. Dick and Jane are the main characters. They have a dog Spot and a sister Sally. They live in a white, suburban community in a perfectly coifed house surrounded by a white picket fence. Earth-shattering events of the day are certainly not about world crises. This is the basal reader of the 1950s, using its portrayal of the American family as the springboard for introducing emerging readers to the printed page. With three reading groups created—the red group, the green group, or the blue group—children in primary classrooms across the United States knew to take their progressively more difficult Dick and Jane stories to their small groups so that they could take turns reading aloud to their same-ability grouped peers and their teacher. Students' progress with reading was demonstrated by their ability to read quickly and in isolation the words that were listed in the back of the book.

Although exaggerated slightly and not the same for everyone during the 1950s, this situation typifies how reading was taught. Debates about the whole-word method and the phonics method for introducing students to Dick and Jane persisted then. Not debated was the value of the idea of repetition and practice to help with what is now referred to as automaticity. Not challenged either was the type of material to which students were exposed. Racial, gender, age, and disability sensitivity was not part of the vernacular for those creating the reading materials or for those instructing with the materials. Rather, the image of living harmoniously and productively was used by many teachers to bring students into the world of literacy.

Advances in technology were startling during this era. Television's impact on leisure life and school life was beginning to be felt. Black and white television sets were entering more and more homes, and color television was soon to arrive, with many predicting its effects on students and adults. Record players with 78 rpm were being supplanted by 45 rpm as favorites for teenagers. And airplanes were beginning to help passengers weave in and out of major cities and towns that were heretofore inaccessible. Automobiles, a major technological revolution, liberated people to inhabit those suburban communities portrayed in the Dick and Jane stories.

Of greatest significance were the feelings of advancement that people living in this era felt. After all, the Dick and Jane basal readers of the 1950s and 1960s replaced the readers of the preceding decades and centuries, including the paddle-shaped hornbook with its alphabet, its syllabary, and its religious-oriented reading passages. For writing, lead pencils with attached erasers replaced pens with ink bottles and slate pencils. Images of events and topics now came from television and the movies, and not just from one's imagination while listening to the radio. People no longer had to depend on the still images placed in newspapers and magazines to experience major events in history; rather, they could see events about the world or the arts unfold in front of their eyes.

People of this generation were excited, nervous, and challenged by the vast technological advances that they were experiencing. Air flight, although increasingly second nature to some, was considered daring to many. Color television originally was an unnecessary frill for the average household. And, mainframe computers the size of a building were used by scientists who needed to calculate numbers about esoteric subjects. Indeed, it was an era that had many weary and wary about the future of the next generation.

Modern-Day Literacy Classroom

Here we are in a classroom in the 21st century. Basal readers still are around, but Dick and Jane no longer are the main characters. People of all races, colors, ages, and abilities appear in the massive sets of materials that are offered to students. The white picket fence has been replaced by a diversity of living situations: for instance, high-rise buildings, igloos, reservations, and nursing homes. Reading groups still exist but with less permanence. Whole-group instruction, cooperative learning groups, and individual learning centers do find their way into literacy instruction. Sight reading is not nearly as important as comprehension with the whole language versus phonics debate simmering to an agreement across philosophical camps about the value of balanced instruction.

And the people of this generation are as excited, challenged, and nervous as they were years ago about the technological advances they are experiencing. Witness this cellular phone generation in which anyone at anytime can be phoned or paged. Everyone uses wireless devices to communicate by land, sea, and air. Technologically, everything is faster, cheaper, and better. Access to information and opportunities is the hallmark of this era.

By the time children enter school, they have had access to multisensory instruction, have seen the world through various media, and have been introduced to many animated characters who have shared with them important lessons in life. These children's classrooms are not the classrooms of past generations. Rather, they are equipped to talk to the world and bring the world to the classroom through the Internet, CD-ROM (compact disc), DVD-ROM (digital video disc), laserdisc technology, and interactive television.

Children in kindergarten and first-grade classrooms are creating electronic books with multimedia packages and making spreadsheets of class surveys. Children in second grade are using electronic encyclopedias to look up information about places across the globe, and they are using the Internet to study different types of animals (Holzberg, 1997). In addition to computers and printers, scanners and digital cameras are some of the hardware found in primary classrooms. Indeed, children in today's classrooms find themselves working with technology to communicate with others, searching for information online—whether through the Internet or other electronic tools—and recording their discoveries in multimedia format.

Unlike children in the learning environment of the 1950s and 1960s, children today are not as regimented to follow a precise schedule of instruction. Rather, they are invited to explore and discover the many avenues available for acquiring knowledge. In other words, much more knowledge is available to them through multiple media sources (Mann, 1998). The teacher no longer is the sole source of information and inspiration. The teacher now serves to facilitate students' acquisition and processing of information, which, in many ways, is liberating and frightening at the same time. And, given what we know about how children learn, we are realizing that the literacy classroom is becoming a place for exploring the world.

What We Know About Literacy Learning

As literacy educators, we know that the most important purpose of a basic education is to teach children to read so that they can use written language to learn more about the world (Boyer, 1996). We use our intuition to create balanced and eclectic instructional approaches to help students emerge and develop as readers. Whatever we use—basal readers or trade books, phonics or sight words, whole-group instruction or paired reading, Directed Reading–Thinking Activities or K-W-Ls—we work hard at preparing comprehensive reading plans that move students to more complex levels of text processing. As students develop to read more complex narrative and expository text, we continue to use our repertoire of instructional strategies (for example, webbing, mapping, and reflective discussions) to help them continue to construct meaning for themselves. We know that our students respond differently to our instructional practices because of their various abilities, experiential backgrounds, and levels of motivation. Although this book does not address reasons for students' varying responses to our efforts, it does explore ways that we can use technology to expand and deepen our array of instructional practices. We believe that technology opens doors to teaching literacy skills in ways not available to us from only books and other traditional print sources.

Rationale for Using Technology for Literacy Learning

Why use technology to support literacy learning? In truth, we do not have a choice if we want our students to succeed in the world in which they find themselves. Functional literacy as we know it means that people are able to process print in their environment, whether it be, for example, newspapers, train schedules, or official government documents. Now included in this array of materials for which people must have functional literacy is information technology. Everywhere one goes there is reference to an online address. Radio and television advertisements send their listeners and viewers to Web sites to get additional information about the many items advertised. Retail stores and local services boast about their 24-hour accessibility through their specialized Web sites. We are fast approaching a time when online activity is the only activity accepted by major institutions and service providers. Some colleges and universities already accept only online registration for course schedules. It quickly becomes obvious that one's ability to function online must be considered an essential element of functional literacy.

Federal, state, and local governments are placing thousands of public documents on the Internet. Museums are placing images of artwork treasures online. Libraries are digitizing rare books and papers from private collections and putting them online. People with expertise about thousands of topics are sharing their knowledge on the Internet. People who would never be able to publish their ideas through standard publishing channels are able to do so through new technology. Information has never been as readily available as it is now. As a result, equity in education has never been as possible as it is now. For instance, children in rural areas can access the same artwork as children in major cities. Children in small towns can read about topics and ideas that they might never have been able to read about before because the materials were not available in their schools or libraries—if they even had a library. Children literally are able to bring the world and beyond to their desks. Once they access such information, they can use it in any number of ways with the various technological tools available to them.

Technology not only has made reading materials easily available, but it also is changing the way in which reading takes place. Although there are similarities between reading traditional printed text and reading electronic text, there are some differences that need to be addressed (Leu, 1997). Hypertext, a computer capability that links information on the screen to stacks of related information, calls for different reading skills than traditional printed text. Because hypertext enables readers to move quickly between large chunks or small portions of text, they need to know where they have been and where they are going. When the World Wide Web (WWW) was new, writers placed large segments of text on it that already had been designed for other printed sources. Some people call this "dead" text. At that point in the evolution of the World Wide Web, most adults preferred to read the traditional printed version rather than the version on the Internet. Then, electronic text started to become different from printed text: Sound, video, animation, photos, and graphics were used to illuminate the text. The multimedia format of electronic text in which text and graphics are combined has brought about the interdependence of the language arts and the visual arts (Flood & Lapp, 1998). Because electronic text now is seen as a highly effective form of linguistic and visual communication for young and old alike, it has become an integral part of a person's functional literacy. As with other components of functional literacy, the intelligent processing of multimedia-based elec-

Linear Versus Hypertext Reading

If we are speaking about reading English text, conventions dictate that we generally read a page from left to right and top to bottom. Most print text, then, is linear. After reading page one, most of us turn to page two and continue reading. We work our way through an extended print text, usually from its first to its last page. Text on a given Web page is also linear, but when many hyperlinks to other Web site pages are placed within electronic texts, readers can click on those links in a sequence that can be dictated entirely by the person holding the mouse at the computer. Hypertext is nonlinear in the sense that readers can, at will, move to another piece of electronic text created by the same author in the same Web site; or readers can be led to entirely new Web sites written by others, thereby creating a variety of paths that readers can take in their search for meaning.

The conventions of reading print text typically encourage readers to begin on page one and read to the last page, although many people enjoy peeking at the ending or leafing through books before they start on page one. The possibilities of moving about in electronic hypertext constructions are determined by both the author's web of connections and the readers' choices about which part of a site they want to encounter first, second, and so forth. Researchers are interested in discovering how interacting with hypertext is affecting students' ability to read and comprehend print. Easy answers will be hard to find in the near future because few readers today have a very long history of dealing with hypertext.

tronic text must be part of the array of skills that students acquire as they progress through school. Today's reading teachers are especially poised for helping students use the technology available to them to help produce meaning.

What Technology Can Do That Teachers Can't to Support Literacy Learning

Using computer technology in the schools has several advantages. Computers offer drill activities that can repeat until students give correct responses. Computers can help teachers and students find old information (for example, from the Library of Congress Web site) and new information from thousands of sites on the Internet that are updated daily. Computers enable students to view live, synchronous events happening almost anywhere in the world (e.g., MayaQuest) or from space (e.g., the current weather as seen from a satellite). Computers can be used to manipulate data so that students can grasp quickly how a change in one variable in a system affects other variables. Computers enable students to assemble and create new information. Computers enable students to have text, audio, and graphic information that they might not have access to in some less densely populated areas. Computers allow students to communicate with just about anyone, anywhere, and anytime.

Most important for literacy instruction and development, computers enable students to navigate their own learning. With the advent of hypermedia, students have immediate, continuous, and repeatable access to information and ideas about content, concepts, and skills. Computers bring to students the world of knowledge unavailable through traditional print. Forms of hypermedia through the WWW and through software products enable students from all socioeconomic strata, and with varying intellectual capacities, to have access to individualized learning opportunities on just about any topic. Try as they might, teachers simply cannot bring to each student what computers can bring by offering learning platforms with large reservoirs of information that branch back and forth between topics in many media forms, and that can be used at will. Many people—teachers, psychologists, learning specialists, linguists, artists, and software designers—are involved in creating electronic learning opportunities that can be brought to students' desks. In sum, technology allows teachers to open their classroom doors to many other additional teachers who are all in the business of providing multiple forums for helping students develop their literacy skills as fully as possible.

What Teachers Can Do That Technology Can't to Support Literacy Learning

Teachers can think! Computers can be loaded with information that is manipulated in a variety of ways. However, contrary to the wisdom of the most fanatical technologists, computers do not think, initiate, or react the way teachers do. Although some people believe that information equals education, teachers know that understanding is not automatic with the acquisition or memorization of facts. Knowing how to apply information, how to use ideas in new ways, how to evaluate information, and how to extrapolate or go beyond basic information are important aspects of learning. Today's students must learn how to think and how to use the vast amount of unfiltered information that is available to them through the Internet and other technological forms.

The teacher, who has always been the most important variable in the classroom, will continue to be the one to guide students throughout their education. Teachers know when the teachable moment is at hand. They know when students need a little extra attention because of some personal or other problem. They know when to step aside and allow a student to pursue an exciting project.

Teachers deal with the psychosocial aspect of education as well. Part of learning in school means learning how to socialize and how to cope with all types of cognitive, affective, and psychomotor issues. Teachers foster intelligent thinking about these issues by serving as role models through their own language and actions. Although computers can simulate real-life experiences, they are not true to life the way teachers are. We are convinced that teachers will not be replaced by computers, and we are equally convinced that teachers' roles in the way in which they organize their classrooms for instruction will change over time because of the way today's children are learning.

How Today's Children Are Learning

Children today are growing up in the digital age. The change from analog to digital production has revolutionized technology, in general, and communications products, in particular. This revolution has changed the context of children's lives. Many of today's teachers may remember playing outdoor games, going on hikes, talking with friends, playing sports, reading, or just staring at the sky. We simply did not have the many gadgets to beckon us away from nontechnological pastimes. Today's children, however, are surrounded by information and opportunities that affect what they learn and how they learn. New electronic toys and information devices capture children's attention and imagination and compete for their time. With the introduction of electronic gadgets over the past few years, it is useful to take a closer look at what many children are exposed to in their daily lives.

Preschool and Out-of-School Experiences

Today's children are stimulated to learn—sometimes even before they are born. Some parents, for instance, play music to their unborn children to soothe them and to help them gain music appreciation. Toddlers often stop and look at the television set as some sound, color, or event catches their attention momentarily, and a few months later they will sit glued to the television watching videos. Some of the major out-of-school influences on children are radio, videocassette recorders (VCRs), television, electronic games, home computers, and several other high-tech devices.

Radio

Although radio lost popularity as a storyteller when television became widespread, today's teenagers listen to popular music on the radio. Few seem interested in radio news or talk shows. Limited opportunities exist for children to hear stories that would enable them to create images of characters and settings in their minds the way previous generations did when they listened to *The Shadow*, *Fibber McGee and Molly*, and other radio shows of yesteryear. Newly emerging digital radio stations that can be heard from one end of the United States to the other will provide opportunities for people to listen to extended stories without interference or signal loss, but no plans have been announced to indicate that such stories will be told (Rozansky, 1998). The main influence of radio today is not so much the technology of the radio, but rather the technology used to create the sound of the songs. As with previous generations, today's culture-driven lyrics influence young people's attitudes about many things—including learning.

VCRs

VCRs are almost ubiquitous, and it is not an uncommon sight to see children—some as young as one year old—staring intently at a television screen, oblivious to anything else happening around them. The packaging of Disney classics for home viewing such as *The Fox and The Hound*, *Dumbo*, *Toy Story*, *The Lion King*, and *Pocahontas* has had an impact on the viewing habits of children. Some of us remember going to the local theater to see Disney movies such as *Bambi* and *Snow White* one or two times. A year later when the movie would be shown again, we might go to see it another time. Then the movie might not have been shown for several years until it was "revived." Today's children can watch *The Return of Jafar* or *Jumanji* one or more times a day for weeks if they so choose. It is not unusual for children to know all the dialogue in their favorite videos because they know every frame, when to anticipate scary events, and when to anticipate the laughs. They process entertainment quite differently from their older family members who saw a movie once or twice. The ability of students to replay and relive the same video over and over, in effect, enables them to have control as they process the literary elements of the stories that they watch. In a sense, they quickly develop into autonomous learners who control what they view and how frequently they view it. Children learn quite early to help themselves as learners.

Television

Blue's Clues, *Barney & Friends*, *Sesame Street*, *Teletubbies*, and other shows designed for children are available on local television stations, while the Nickelodeon, Toon, and Disney channels are available on cable television constantly throughout the year. Cable systems and satellites deliver hundreds of channels to homes across the United States. Many stations show news programs that often contain violent scenes and talk shows that frequently contain topics that are not meant for young listeners. Within a few years, television will change dramatically with the advent of high-density television (HDTV). Not only will the images on a television screen be more clear and lifelike, but screens will become bigger. HDTV uses digital signals, allowing new features to be added to television broadcast signals. Along with the main image, it will be possible to display additional text and graphics. Multiple screens will be able to be viewed simultaneously, permitting viewers to deal with two or more information sources at one time. Unlike many previous generations, children will be able to interact with the auditory and visual information on their television screens.

Electronic games

A major revolution occurred when arcades opened and were filled with noisy, interactive games that children could play for a quarter. Mall arcades became social centers for thousands of teenagers and preteens. Nintendo, Gameboy, and a variety of other electronic games soon became part of many home environments. Although these game systems were not inexpensive, they were so refreshingly portable that they allowed children to play electronic games at will. Home electronic games are usually fast paced, repetitive, and often violent. These games appear to have an effect on children's eye-hand coordination, and they capture children's attention for hours at a time. Children will play these games again and again as they try to reach the games' highest possible levels of achievement. It is unclear whether such persistence carries over into academic pursuits, but electronic games are out-of-school experiences with modern technology that occupy a great deal of children's time. Their action-oriented and sometimes violence-laden genre needs to be studied in relation to children's learning experiences.

Home computers

Teachers report that more and more students have access to home computers, because computers became less expensive and because more parents recognize that they, too, must become computer enabled in order to obtain or keep jobs. Computers are rapidly becoming a necessity for almost everyone. Word processing was a major reason to buy a home computer originally, but with the advent of multimedia computers and CD-ROMs, home computers have become a source of information (encyclopedias), training (typing programs), and entertainment (solitaire and other games). In truth, home computers became even more popular with the advent of the Internet. The ability to get and send e-mail to people all around the world was irresistible. The World Wide Web changed everything again when it became possible for people to place text, graphics, video, music and other sounds, animations, and photo images on Web pages for everyone to see.

The growth of the Internet (the total interconnected computer system) and the WWW (the text, graphics, audio, etc. accessed through browsers) has been phenomenal. The Internet started as a way to connect scientists' computers together so they could calculate data and communicate with one another. It was soon determined that creating a system that permitted others (businesses, libraries, etc.) to communicate was a solid idea. In the early 1990s, *Mosaic* was developed and enabled images to be viewed easily via the Internet. Soon *Netscape* and *Internet Explorer* became giant systems for accessing text and images as well as sound, video, and animations. Millions of people today communicate through e-mail and Web sites as if these fantastic communications tools have been around for decades instead of a few years.

The World Wide Web has had another major impact on people, young and old alike. There is an old saying that everyone has a story to tell. Today people want to put their stories on the Web, which allows access to millions of pages of information. Gutenberg move over! With a little knowledge of HTML (Hypertext Markup Language), or a word-processing program that converts documents into Web format, or a specialized Web site production tool, anyone can create a presence on the Web. Depending on a family's circumstances, children's experiences with computers may be greater out of school than in school where they might have only 50 minutes each week of computer instruction in a lab.

Other high-tech devices

The digital revolution has prompted the production of many other products to which school-aged children are exposed. A common image is to see parents turn down the car CD player so they can talk on their digital cellular phones as they drive into the bank to make a deposit at an automated teller machine (ATM). Children and parents walk around with pagers so they can be reached anytime for just about any reason. Those so inclined already have videophones so they see their family and friends as they talk to them from the next town or across the country.

Times certainly have changed from just a decade or two ago when many of today's teachers were students themselves. The current context of life experiences must be kept in mind as we find ways to make technology work in a positive way to help students learn. We need not only to learn to cope with today's technology and its products, but also to prepare to grapple with the technologies of the future—technologies that will include virtual realities and other experiences we cannot yet imagine. We can think about those low-tech times when our ancestors churned butter and put clothes through wringers on their washing machines, but we do not live that life. Rather, we have lived with several generations of electronic wizardry that continues to alter the way we live our lives at work and at home. Although each of us has had one or more anxious moments with such changes, we owe our students the opportunity to learn with the technologies available to them.

Elementary School Experiences

Computer technology has made its way into the schools slowly and steadily. Initially, schools acquired a few computers that were put into school offices and computer labs. Students were instructed in these labs once or twice a week. These computers were not connected to the Internet. Gradually, however, more and more schools became networked, and faculty and staff members were introduced to e-mail. In 1993, teachers were introduced to *Mosaic* and the beginnings of the World Wide Web. Most students, however, still went to labs that were not networked. Since 1996 there has been a major thrust to connect all schools and classrooms to the Web, but much work remains. Many students throughout the United States are unable to have sustained access to the Internet. Some cannot use the Internet because there is only one computer in the classroom capable of accessing the Net, and some cannot access it because there are no Internet-ready computers in their classrooms. Most students still go to computer labs to work, and many of the labs are now network enabled.

Within elementary classrooms, a variety of software programs run on computers. The following is a sample of the kinds of programs found in many elementary schools: *Kid Pix Studio Deluxe*, *AppleWorks*, *Storybook Weaver*, *Word Munchers Deluxe*, *The Print Shop Deluxe*, *WiggleWorks Plus*, and *HyperStudio*. These programs are used with students to read stories, write stories, add artwork to their original stories, and produce presentations to share with other students. CD-ROMS are available in some classrooms and libraries so that students can read and listen to stories such as *Arthur's Teacher Trouble* and *Odell Down Under*. Many multimedia software packages in classrooms promote reading, writing, and listening. Speaking is fostered in students' efforts to present to teachers and other students that which they have created with the help of a computer.

Most children accept computers as a way of classroom and home life. However, in a typical classroom there still may be a few students who have little experience with computers. There also are many astute students who can access a computer's operating system and change the settings that control the computer's programs. Computers are as natural in children's environments as television was to the last generation, movies and radio were to the generation before that, and stage shows were to the generation before that. The task facing elementary school teachers is to help beginning readers and writers become literate, using computer programs as tools to that end.

One of the foremost tasks in elementary schools today is to help students acquire keyboarding skills. Kindergartners and first graders may need adults to transcribe their thoughts, or they might be able to copy a few words themselves. Some people suggest that formal keyboard instruction should wait until the end of second grade or the first part of third grade. Some contend that teaching keyboarding strengthens letter naming and letter recognition, and that this will help students learn to read earlier. Learning to keyboard (type) at early ages may have an effect on students' handwriting skills, but that is still undetermined (Ellsworth, 1998). At any rate, learning to type has now become an elementary school requisite. (See Chapter 5 for additional information and ideas about keyboarding.)

Current practices with technology build on keyboarding and include the introduction of electronic stories on CD-ROMs and other applications for producing projects. It is becoming commonplace to see students accessing the Internet to run a search in order to gather ideas and facts for their class projects. These same students are illustrating their ideas with the help of a digital camera or a paint program, producing a slide show, and posting their projects to the school's Web site. Technology is a great enabler for authentic learning activities. No longer must students work on a project that only their teachers or a few other students see. Now, they can share their projects with the world.

Anecdotal evidence indicates that many children are motivated to spend a great deal of time at a computer in order to play games, to read text, and to enjoy hearing words and other sounds (Glasgow, 1996–1997; Goldstein, Olivares, & Valmont, 1996). They also enjoy the animation that multimedia CD-ROM programs and Internet sites provide. As teachers expand their knowledge of ways to help students deal with both electronic text and traditional printed text, it is certain that the motivating aspects of computers will help students become literate.

Middle School Experiences and Beyond

Computer technology now is having a major impact on what and how middle and high school students learn. There is a growing sense that students need to master the basics of computers to obtain better jobs. Thus, beginning in middle school, students now are dealing with major computer applications such as *Microsoft Office 2000*, consisting of *Word*, a basic word-processing program; *Excel*, a spreadsheet program; *Access*, a database program; and *PowerPoint*, a presentation program. These applications, and similar programs, are fairly standard tools in the business world. In schools, after mastering the basics of such programs, students use them to assemble information into research findings and reports. On a visit to a middle school classroom, one of us observed a group of students planning menus for imaginary submarine sandwich shops their teacher had asked them to design. They used word-processing and graphics programs to create their menus (ten types of subs, five beverages, five side items, three special combos or value meals, five toppings for subs, three bread selections, and prices for everything). They kept lists of the necessary ingredients in a database, used a spreadsheet to keep track of the projected income and expenses, and presented their sub-shop project to their classmates using computer-generated images shown on a screen via an LCD projector.

In another classroom, one of us observed students creating videos and editing the morning announcements for the school. They used equipment for both analog and digital editing of videos. Other students used *Adobe Page-Maker 6.5 Plus* and *PowerPoint* to create a story told in 20 frames. Students in vocational education courses use technology in many ways to prepare for future employment. Computers are used to analyze automobile problems, create plans for building models, plan food services, and so forth.

Students in middle school and beyond search the Internet for countless topics. Students in one classroom can be found downloading images of the night sky from Kitt Peak, a renowned scientific observatory located near Tucson, Arizona. They are looking for novae using images from satellites. Their teacher reports that they really like using live data in their schoolwork. Another class uses live data that they create. They keep temperature and rainfall records and upload their findings to the GLOBE Project.

At another school, students use a digital audio editor to create the morning's voice news that follows the morning's video news created by another group of students. After the audio news is edited and played for the school through the speaker system, it is placed on the school's home page on the In-

The GLOBE Project

GLOBE is the acronym for Global Learning and Observations to Benefit the Environment (see the GLOBE Web site at http://globe.fsl.noaa.gov). Students and teachers from more than 7,000 schools in over 80 countries are participating in this worldwide project that enables students to report measurements and observations of phenomena in their localities and send them to a database that is accessed by scientists who then provide feedback to the students. Students at Ft. Lowell Elementary School in Tucson, Arizona, measure rainfall and soil and take other readings that they contribute to the GLOBE Web site. Those students became so conscious of the environment that they started recycling and kept records of how many pounds of recyclable materials they retained. Mary Bouley, their teacher, reports that the GLOBE project has helped students see that they can be part of real-life investigations and can make a difference.

ternet and can be downloaded as streaming audio. Students are proud of the home page that they have designed and placed on the Internet.

These are just a few examples of how the context of teaching and learning has changed education beyond the elementary school years. Many computer-savvy students are already graduating from high schools. However, much work needs to be done before all students gain sufficient competencies with modern computer technology. Not only is learning changing because of new technologies, but also teaching practices must change and take advantage of these technologies, too.

Concluding Remarks

Even as today's process for teaching reading changes, there are many aspects of the literacy classroom that probably will not change. Reading teachers historically have been the first teachers to help students learn to think logically and actively while reading. Reading teachers have helped students understand an author's purpose for writing, learn more about an author's background, and be able to tell the difference between fact and fiction in writing. Reading teachers typically have alerted students to authors' uses of propaganda. Reading teachers, in other words, have helped develop critical thinkers who know how to think before, during, and after reading. Reading teachers have been the ones to teach students how to locate information, how to collate that information, and how to use recursive writing procedures to get ideas ready to share with others. Reading teachers are the ones who entice students to read exceptional literature, to play word games and to develop vocabulary, and to use various types of resources to expand their vocabularies. Reading teachers, as academic bellwethers of effective instructional practices, will continue to play a major role in helping students learn and live in the 21st century. It is for this reason that reading teachers simply need to discover which facets of instructional technology work best for them in the classroom. The remainder of this book is dedicated to helping with this journey.

References

Adobe PageMaker 6.5 Plus [Computer software]. (1999). San Jose, CA: Adobe Systems.
AppleWorks [Computer software]. (1999). Cupertino, CA: Apple Computer.
Arthur's Teacher Trouble [Computer software]. (1993). Cambridge, MA: Brøderbund/ The Learning Company.

Boyer, E. (1996). Literacy and learning. In M.F. Graves, P. van den Broek, and B.M. Taylor (Eds.), *The First R: Every child's right to read* (pp. 1–12). New York: Teachers College Press; Newark, DE: International Reading Association.

Ellsworth, B.G. (1998, June). *Keyboarding for kids on the computer*. Paper presented at the 6th Annual Arizona Technology Conference, Mesa, AZ.

Flood, J., & Lapp, D. (1998). Broadening conceptualizations of literacy: The visual and communicative arts. *The Reading Teacher*, *51*, 342–344.

Glasgow, J. (1996–1997, December/January). Motivating young readers using CD-ROM storybooks. *Learning and Leading with Technology*, *24*(4), 17–22.

Goldstein, B., Olivares, E., & Valmont, W. (1996). CD-ROM storybooks: Children's interactions. In B. Robin, J. Price, J. Willis, & K. Willis (Eds.), *Technology and teacher education annual* (pp. 110–111). Charlottesville, VA: Association for the Advancement of Computing in Education.

Holzberg, C.S. (1997). Little kids, big projects. *Technology & Learning*, *18*(3), 42–46.

HyperStudio [Computer software]. (1999). El Cajon, CA: Roger Wagner Publishing.

Kid Pix Studio Deluxe [Computer software]. (1998). Cambridge, MA: Brøderbund/The Learning Company.

Leu, D.J. (1997). Caity's question: Literacy as deixis on the Internet. *The Reading Teacher*, *51*, 62–67.

Mann, D. (1998, May). *Using telecommunications to link homes and schools*. Paper presented at the 43rd Annual Convention of the International Reading Association, Orlando, FL.

Microsoft Office 2000 [Computer software]. (1999). Redmond, WA: Microsoft.

Odell Down Under [Computer software]. (1994). Cambridge, MA: MECC/The Learning Company.

The Print Shop Deluxe [Computer software]. (1999). Cambridge, MA: Brøderbund/The Learning Company.

Rozansky, M.L. (1998, June 8). Outer space radio. *The Arizona Daily Star*, pp. ST 8–9.

Storybook Weaver [Computer software]. (1996). Cambridge, MA: The Learning Company.

WiggleWorks Plus [Computer software]. (1999). New York: Scholastic.

Word Munchers Deluxe [Computer software]. (1996). Cambridge, MA: MECC/The Learning Company.

CHAPTER 2

How Do I Begin to Use Technology in My Classroom?

RICHARD THURLOW

Mr. Adams sits at his desk reading book reports his third-grade students handed in that day. He notes, once again, that several students have turned in typed papers. They are much easier to read than the cursive writing he usually receives, but he is wondering whether he should insist on cursive for these assignments. Not only is he worried that the students with word processors will not develop proper handwriting, but also he wonders how much help these students are getting with their work. For one thing, the spelling is almost perfect on each of these papers, and there are not as many of the typical third-grade grammatical errors. He is also worried that the children who can afford computers at home are gaining an advantage in grading because of the homework's neatness. Resources in his school are not available for all the children to use a computer, and he would not be able to teach them how.

Mrs. Bashir sits at her computer, reading her students' daily journal entries. As she types responses into the word-processed computer file containing progress notes of one student, a chime from her computer informs her that an e-mail message has arrived. Switching programs quickly she reads the note from a parent that confirms their meeting next week. The parent wants Mrs. Bashir to send a copy of an assignment her son misplaced and promises to fax a permission form for the upcoming field trip. A quick sequence of keystrokes sends the assignment off, and Mrs. Bashir again switches programs to update her calendar that the conference next week is confirmed.

Introduction—Am I Too Far Behind?

One result of the increasing presence of technology in society is that many children now have access at home to word processors and laser printers that enable them to create typed papers and projects for school. They are able to use copiers and printers to include full-color illustrations within their assignments. In addition, their reference lists can now include materials that are often unavailable at the school library such as CD-ROMs (compact discs), video discs, and sites on the World Wide Web.

Some teachers such as Mr. Adams are concerned that tools such as spelling and grammar checkers and other electronic resources might hamper the development of children's writing and research skills. Others also are concerned about the technological advantage enjoyed by children of affluence. However, there also should be concern about the gap that is growing between students with high degrees of technological literacy and the teachers who are supposed to be guiding them through their education.

Teachers may feel left behind or even intimidated by the skills students have with modern technologies such as computers. Even very young children are so comfortable and have such speed with a computer keyboard and mouse that inexperienced adults are rightfully amazed. Add to that the fluency chil-

 ## Understanding Computer Terms and Acronyms

One of the first acronyms that a novice should learn is the one they are most likely to need, which is FAQ. FAQ stands for Frequently Asked Questions. This acronym is used on the Internet to help beginners find answers to the questions most asked by other novices. The creation of FAQ files originated with computer bulletin boards where visitors could enter into discussions with other people on topics of interest. FAQ files were documents that stored the most commonly asked questions and the appropriate answers. Newcomers to a discussion group could read the file and not clutter up the bulletin board with questions that had been asked and answered many times before. The term now is used on Web sites and even in books. A teacher might even want to create such a document to hand out on parents' night. A good introduction to acronyms such as this one and other technical jargon can be found in an introductory book such as The Computer Learning Foundation's *Everything You Need to Know (But Were Afraid to Ask Kids) About the Information Highway* (Marsh, 1999). (The Computer Learning Foundation's Web site at http://computerlearning.org has many resources for teachers, students, and parents.)

dren have with computer jargon (words such as *modem* or *scanner*), fancy acronyms such as ISP (Internet Service Provider) or SCSI (Small Computer System Interface, pronounced *scuzzy*), and a growing lexicon of slang terms and phrases (such as "hacker," "logon," or the chatroom abbreviation "who r u?"), and it is easy to understand why novices might just give up on technology, believing they will never catch up.

However, the experience that helps these children develop their skills is only that: experience. It is difficult for a beginner to recognize, but most of the people who seem comfortable with technology are not that far ahead, and many are not particularly skilled or knowledgeable. Their advantages, generally, are the very things that can be so intimidating: speed, which comes only with practice, and an unfamiliar vocabulary. If you challenge them, you might find they do not know the meaning of all the words and phrases they use.

As with any other area of learning, no matter your particular skill level, there will be others with higher skills. That cannot be a factor that scares you away from using computers. Each teacher will come to instructional technology with different capabilities. The only way to improve yours is to commit to learning and get started.

The purpose of this chapter is to help you examine your skills and the resources that may already be available to you, with the following two goals in mind: First, you should realize that familiarity and comfort with technology are not difficult to achieve. Determination and practice are the main resources required. A moderate budget can help, but even that is not essential. Second, you can formulate and implement a reasonable plan for improving your computer skills in order to begin infusing technology into your literacy classroom.

How to Proceed and Use This Chapter

You will be asked to answer several questions throughout this chapter and design some possible plans of action to take in the future. A useful tool for completing these tasks is a journal or other record of your assessment of your areas of strength and the many resources available to you in your school and community. Figure 1 on pages 22–25 presents an example of what such a journal might look like. If you keep a record of your responses to the questions in the first part of this chapter, the information you collect can be used later in the chapter to guide you in formulating a plan for future action.

Figure 1
Hypothetical Journal Entries for Mr. Adams

Personal Resources

1. Commitment
   I will find time for an hour on the computer
   - at least three weekdays and either Saturday or Sunday, maybe both.
   - one entire evening if I enroll in a computer class.

   Main uses in classroom:
   - vocabulary acquisition
   - writing skills
   - searching electronic resources

   I am very committed to learning to use computers in my classroom.

2. Technological Skills
   Familiarity with computers
   - some word processing
   - searching the Internet
   - a few educational programs
   - can use a keyboard and mouse, but typing is hunt and peck

   Other technology
   - a VCR in the classroom
   - take pictures of classroom activities and field trips
   - not comfortable with cables and connections!

   My comfort level with technology is moderate.

3. Budget
   Training
   - one or two graduate classes each year—maybe $2,500 including supplies

   Equipment
   - NEED a new system—$2,000

   Other
   - continue the $20 a month for Internet service from home

Summary
My personal resources are good, especially commitment and budget. I will need to work the most on my technology skills.

Hardware and Software Available

4. Hardware
   Home
   PC computer

(continued)

Figure 1
Hypothetical Journal Entries for Mr. Adams *(continued)*

- 486 processor, 16 megabytes RAM
- 640 meg harddrive
- inkjet printer, black & white
- modem
- no CD-ROM or speakers

School
Classroom with 20 Macintosh computers
- CD-ROMs and speakers
- connected to a laser printer
- one is connected to the Internet
- full-time aide
- first-come, first-served
- supposedly a good classroom for schools in this area

5. Software
   Home
   - *Microsoft Windows 3.1*
   - *Microsoft Works*
   - a few games
   - used for connecting to America Online to send e-mail
   - very slow for surfing the Web—boring

   School
   - *ClarisWorks*
   - *Print Artist*
   - *HyperStudio*
   - computer room aide—teaches keyboarding and word-processing skills; helps with *Print Artist*

Summary
The computer and software I have at home is inadequate to keep me motivated, but the equipment at school is good. I would like a computer in my classroom and more educational software available at school.

Support

6. Friends and Relatives
   - Jack (my brother)—has a new, fast PC—sends me e-mail twice a week
   - Andre (neighbor)—avid computer user—tracks the stock market, manages his budget
   - Andre's daughter uses it for chatrooms; is learning to make her own Web page

(continued)

Figure 1
Hypothetical Journal Entries for Mr. Adams *(continued)*

7. People in the School District
   My building
   • Betty (computer room aide) is main resource
   • Mrs. Clark (third-grade teacher) helps her a great deal
   • Mrs. Clark started an after-school class on computers for kids and parents

   District's Computer Coordinator
   • if building principal approves—can request a classroom computer in next year's budget
   • district is increasing the budget for instructional software—looking for ideas!!

8. Community
   My college
   • new courses in educational technology

   My library
   • Internet connections—can be reserved for up to 30 minutes
   • free classes on searching the Web and creating Web pages

   Jackie (my student) pushes technology
   • has a computer at home
   • is always asking to use the school's computers during the day

   International Reading Association
   • Main Web page—http://www.reading.org
   • Publications Web page—http://www.reading.org/publications

Summary
There are more resources available to me than I realized. My brother and neighbor are willing to help me learn about computers, and the parents of two students will volunteer in the computer room. Mrs. Clark has agreed to let me get involved with her after-school class. My support resources are high.

Plan of Action

Hardware/Software
1. I will buy a computer that runs the same software used at school in order to speed my learning and keep my costs down. For home software I will buy a word processor, graphics package, and some role-playing strategy games that my students like (that will help me talk with them about computers).
2. I will request a computer for my classroom and try to increase that number in the future. I will request several software packages to use in the computer classroom, including electronic books, encyclopedias, multimedia, and Web page software.

(continued)

Figure 1
Hypothetical Journal Entries for Mr. Adams *(continued)*

3. I will start asking now for an Internet connection in my classroom. This might take some time, but it will really help my plans to use the World Wide Web.

Personal Resources
1. I will use the computer every day to check my e-mail (my brother and a teacher in my school will be my first contacts), play a game, and practice my typing skills.
2. I will immediately start taking a course at my library on creating Web pages.
3. I will talk to a technology instructor at my college to see what technology course would be best for meeting my goals.

Support Groups
1. I am going to join the after-school computer class run by my colleague to learn more about the computers at our school.
2. I will join the users group for teachers and parents that has been created by our parent-teacher organization.
3. I have reserved a time in the school's computer classroom when my two parent volunteers are available. They will help me manage the class and learn even more about the computers.

Instructional Uses
1. I want to start my students using the Web to collect information and then prepare presentations (see Chapters 6 and 7).
2. I will have my students find keypals and eventually create a Web page to share their ideas with other kids around the world (see Chapters 4, 6, and 7).
3. I hope that this will help them improve their vocabulary, writing, spelling, and presentation skills (see Chapter 5).
4. I'm also going to work with the other teachers on my team to see if they want to try a thematic unit that includes computer resources (see Chapters 3 and 4).

Summary
My plan might be a bit ambitious, but I already have some skills and I have a lot of help available. Because my home computer is my weakest link, I will start by getting a new computer. I also have just two major areas of interest at school: using Web resources and literacy unit plans. My colleagues will help with the unit plans, and the kids will definitely help with using the Web. I'm going to create a notebook to keep track of what my students and I learn, and I will ask my students to start their own computer journal.

Use Your Journal to Create a "Haves Assessment"

An important way to start when moving into the technical world is to take stock of the resources around you. Some of these will reside in your school or community, but many will be personal skills you already possess. Rather than conducting the typical "needs assessment" that points out what is missing, you should start by looking at the resources that are available to you. That is, you will first create a "haves assessment."

We will examine your "haves" in three sets, or groups, of resources: personal resources available to you, hardware and software resources to which you have access, and school or community resources that can help you.

Personal Resources

Resource 1: Commitment (essential)

By far, the most important resource you must have is commitment. As is true for any new learning experience, you must dedicate time to master the skills needed and apply yourself to regular practice of those skills. Getting comfortable with technology is not just an academic exercise of learning facts and taking a test. Even at a basic level there are psychomotor skills required that will improve only with practice. Also, the vocabulary is much easier to learn when working in an authentic context. In words you may have heard before, "You learn best by doing." Finally, your personal beliefs about the role of electronic media in literacy will play a critical role in determining the ways and the extent to which you bring technology into your classroom (see Reinking, 1998, for more discussion of this issue).

The first entry in your journal should be labeled "commitment." Write down the amount of time each day that you will be willing to set aside to work on a computer; examine and read books on technology; try software, CD-ROMs, and video materials; or search the Internet for curriculum ideas that use technology. Then write down the number of days per week that you will pursue one of these activities for that length of time. Certainly flexibility will be required, but this is an indication of the average time you are willing to devote to this area.

Keep in mind that the time investment will be diminished if you have a computer available to you at home, at work, or both. You will save on travel and set-up time if you are not borrowing or sharing equipment.

In addition, you should make a list of areas in literacy instruction that you feel will benefit from inclusion of electronic media such as word recognition, vocabulary acquisition, comprehension, writing, or content learning.

Resource 2: Technological skills (whatever you have will do for a start)

No matter how inexperienced with computers you may feel, you have some technical knowledge that will help you. For instance, most people are comfortable with one or more appliances. You may use a toaster, a microwave oven, or a cassette tape recorder. If so, then you know about electrical cords and outlets, and push buttons that control devices. If you ever used a record player or, even better, a CD player, then you know about taking care of delicate equipment and the media they use. If you are able to hook up the components of your stereo system or a videocassette recorder (VCR), you have experience in following directions to prepare electronic equipment for home use.

A skill possessed by many teachers that they take for granted is typing. Most computer activities involve typing, so skill in this area is quite valuable. The computer keyboard is, however, somewhat different from the typewriter. It has extra keys with unusual labels such as "Ctrl" (Control) or "Esc" (Escape) and many keys that serve different functions at different times. In addition, using a computer mouse is a separate skill that is very different from using a keyboard. But, if you know how to use a typewriter, or even better, if you are a touch typist, you have an advantage over those who have not developed that skill.

Your second journal entry should describe your familiarity with technical and electrical appliances. Under a heading "technological skills," first write down your familiarity with computers. If you use a computer at home or school you have some familiarity with them. For what purpose do you use a computer? Do you use a word-processing program, a spreadsheet, a grading program? Do you use educational programs or games in the classroom? Do you use home or business applications such as a budget, checkbook, or tax preparation program?

In addition, note any other technical equipment you use either at home or at school. Do you use a VCR or a slide projector? Have you used a laminating machine or a label maker? Do you use a still or video camera at home, on vacation, or in your classroom?

If you still do not have many skills listed, write down all the home appliances or tools that you use. From a power saw to a blender, from a fax machine to an automated teller machine (ATM), everyone deals with technology in some form.

At the end of this journal entry, give yourself a rating (low, medium, high) on how comfortable you are with technology. If you mostly use home appliances, your comfort level with more technical devices is probably low. If you use a computer on occasion and are able to handle a VCR for play and record, you might consider yourself moderately comfortable with technology. But, if you take new products out of the box and hook them up yourself, you probably have a high degree of comfort with technology.

One last personal attribute to keep in mind that will help you in advancing your technical skills is that, like most of us, you are probably comfortable with admitting that you do not know everything. Willingness to ask questions and seek assistance will be critical to your progress.

Resource 3: Budget (helpful)

An area that is related to commitment, but not as essential, is budget. This is, of course, an area that keeps many people away from technology. They are afraid that it will be too expensive. Although it is true that high-end equipment can be very expensive, the cost of computing has dropped dramatically over the

---

Emerging Technologies

Many devices other than computers are also part of technological literacy. Some of these are familiar household devices such as videocassette recorders (VCRs), compact disc (CD) players, and tape recorders. However, new technologies continue to emerge offering greater capacities and enhanced features. For example, digital video disc (DVD) players that can include massive amounts of video information are supplanting compact disc read only memory (CD-ROM) readers in computers, and traditional CD players are competing with technologies such as MPeg3 (MP3) players that allow recording as well as playback. On occasion the new technologies are easier to use as well. For example, difficult-to-program VCRs may be a thing of the past as computers are teamed with cable television to create automated recorders that will find your favorite programs by name and store them without tapes or cassettes for later viewing. Keeping up with new technologies is as easy as a trip to your library. Computer magazines such as *MacWorld* (http://macworld.zdnet.com) or *PC Magazine* (http://www.pcmag.com), and educational technology magazines such as *T.H.E. Journal* (http://www.thejournal.com) explore a variety of technologies that can be used in classrooms.

years, and it should continue to do so. If you are postponing your purchase of a computer fearing that the machine you buy will be out of date by the time you get it home, rest assured that in some sense it is obsolete before you buy it. This is a practical view, not a cynical one. There is always a more expensive model with features that you might not be able to afford now, but that will be much less expensive next year. However, by holding off on a purchase, you are only prolonging the delay in getting yourself started using the computer.

It is possible to begin working with computers without a major expenditure, by using equipment that you simply borrow. For example, the school where you work might own several computers you can borrow. Your county or city library also might have computers that are available for public use. Libraries, in particular, are more and more likely to have computers that are connected to the Internet. However, if you can afford your own equipment, your efforts to learn will be much more convenient and efficient.

One possible drawback to borrowing hardware is that you will have available only the software installed on that machine. For example, your school may have only drill-and-practice software for the students. This may not motivate you to practice using the computer, especially if it does not fit with the approach to literacy instruction that you use in your classroom. If you are just beginning to work with computers, you may not need a variety of software. But, as soon as your skills begin to develop, you will want to include money in your budget to purchase additional software that (1) allows you to explore your own interests (for example, you might wish to own a program that helps chart your genealogy or a game that simulates flying a plane), or (2) matches your beliefs about literacy instruction (for example, one teacher might wish to keep a computerized record of students' reading of trade books, whereas another might wish to use a CD-ROM program to develop students' rhyming skills).

It is easy to think that hardware and software will be the only major expenses for which you need to plan. However, another item that is worthy of investment is professional training. If your school district offers inservice training on using computers that matches your skill level and interests, this will offset the need for spending your own money on training. However, you might want to investigate learning opportunities available through other avenues, such as courses offered by computer retailers, professional organizations, community education programs, or colleges.

There also will be several less expensive, but important, items to purchase, even if you are borrowing a computer and getting free training. These consumable items, such as floppy disks, paper, and printer supplies, will not ruin

Self-Guided Training Materials

Your local library or bookstore is a treasure house of materials that can guide you in the use of computers. There are many books, videotapes, and CD-ROMs available to help people learn particular hardware or software. In particular, there are two popular series of books designed for beginners. Que Publications (http://www.mcp.com/publishers/que) uses the provocative start to its titles: *Complete Idiot's Guide to* _____. IDG Books (http://www.dummies.com) uses a similar style in its books called _____ *for Dummies*. The blanks are filled with the topic of that particular book. Beginners might want to start with a book about the Internet or their Web browser software such as *Complete Idiot's Guide to the Internet*, Sixth Edition (1999) by Peter Kent, or *Netscape Communicator 4.5 for Dummies* (1998) by Paul Hoffman. Instruction tailored to teachers is also available. For instance, Allyn & Bacon provides a CD-ROM book called *Teaching with Technology* by Desberg and Fisher that allows hands-on experience as you learn about classroom technologies.

your budget, but you should plan for them. You might also want to purchase books or other self-training materials.

Journal entry three, budget, should be your best estimate of what you can afford to invest toward any or all of the items mentioned. Whatever you are able to spend will help you move toward your goals. Yet, the amount you ultimately will need to invest will depend on variables such as your starting skill level, your ability to borrow equipment, and the level of involvement with technology to which you aspire. So you need to ask yourself some questions: How much can I afford, per month, to apply toward owning computer equipment? How much can I spend to buy software and supplies? How much am I willing to spend for connecting to the Internet? How much can I afford to spend on learning how to use the equipment?

Once you have finished these three journal entries, you can step back and make a general assessment of your personal resources. If you have very little time to invest in practicing computer skills, have low starting skills, and can afford only a small budget, you have few personal resources available. But you should see that you are not void of resources. Having few resources does not mean you should delay; it means only that you may have to be more creative in your plan for bringing technology into your classroom.

Hardware and Software Available

Another general area to assess, in terms of resources, is the equipment that will be available to you for both practice and application. As mentioned, you may not need to expend a great deal of money to get started with computers, but it is essential that you actually are in contact with one in order to learn how to use it. In this group of resources, you may need to explore your school and community to find all the avenues available to you. You may find a machine for making color copies at a local print shop, or a scanner may be available at your high school. You might even find a local company that will donate used computer equipment to your school.

Resource 4: Hardware (essential)

If you are new to computers, you probably are wondering what kind of equipment you will need to get started. Even if you own a computer at home, you may not know if it has adequate capabilities. The accompanying textbox ("What Do I Need to Get Started?") gives a description of a minimum configuration to run the sophisticated software available today. Unfortunately, many teachers have outdated computers in their classrooms. Some of these will run only outdated software that may be useful only for practicing the most basic

What Do I Need to Get Started?

To take advantage of the current class of interactive software with color graphics and stereo sound, you need a computer that is fast enough, has enough storage capacity, and has some important peripheral devices such as a printer. In addition to the processor unit (typically the box with the main components) you will need a color monitor, keyboard, mouse, floppy disk, fixed disk, high-capacity removable disk (e.g., Zip drive), CD-ROM, sound card, speakers, and printer. It is also important to have a modem (which often includes faxing capabilities) or another method to connect to the Internet.

An exciting development for novices is the decision by a growing number of Internet Service Providers (ISPs) to provide a computer at no charge to any customer that makes use of their connection service. These are high-quality machines that allow the user to send and receive e-mail and to have full access to the World Wide Web. Check whether they include some desirable accessories, such as a color printer or a CD-ROM. They should also include a minimum of software, such as a word processor.

of computer skills. However, they will not be able to run the software currently available for the literacy classroom. Some are also not capable of accessing the Internet because they lack a modem. If it is possible, try to match or exceed the configuration described here as you search for hardware resources.

For the fourth entry in your journal, take stock of any computers and peripherals that are available to you for personal and classroom use. If you own a computer, write down the major components and any attached peripheral devices. Peripherals are equipment such as printers and scanners that attach to the computer and extend its capabilities. Compare what you have to the list of equipment in the accompanying textbox to determine the level of your system. Do the same for any computers available to you at work. Are they available in your classroom or the teachers' workroom? Are they available only in a separate computer classroom or a computer lab? Will you have to go to the school library?

If you do not have personal access to a computer, make a list of computers accessible to you outside of school. Check with your school to see if equipment can be borrowed for home use, especially over the summer months. Also check your public library. As mentioned, libraries likely have computers that are available for public use, at least on a limited basis. Another often overlooked resource is your local college. If you happen to be taking a graduate course in any area, your tuition dollars might entitle you to use computer labs and resource rooms on campus. You even may be able to get an e-mail account on the college's computer system. Check with an instructor, your advisor, or the college library as to what resources are available.

Resource 5: Software (essential)

Software is needed for you to accomplish anything with a computer, and not all computers will have the same software. Therefore you need to assess separately the computer programs available at home, at school, and at any other location that you or your students will be using computers. One way of developing such a list is to organize the items by categories. The accompanying textbox mentions different software types that you might already own or have access to at your school.

Create a journal entry number five to list the software you find by location and category. Because new versions of programs are constantly being developed, you should note the version of each software package you find to be sure it is current. It is not always easy to determine which software packages are installed on a computer, so you may need to ask for assistance from the people who maintain the computers you are checking.

Varieties of Software

Software is available for many specialized applications such as budget management or second-language instruction, and for general purpose functions such as word processing or data storage. Most beginners will want to learn how to use a Web browser (*Netscape* or *Internet Explorer*) and a word processor such as *Microsoft Word* or *ClarisWorks*. There are several books available to help you learn the most popular brands of programs, such as the Que and IDG books mentioned earlier. However, if you need to learn more about the various types of educational software available, you might try *Essentials of Educational Technology* (1999) by Schwartz and Beichner, *The Computer as an Educational Tool* (1999) by Forcier, or *Using Technology in the Classroom* (1999) by Bitter and Pierson. These are introductory textbooks that describe various software programs with a perspective on their educational applications.

Once again, wrap up this group of resources with a general assessment of what you found. Do you have minimal resources available, or have you found out that computers and software are plentiful in your environment? This can be a difficult assessment for a novice, because a person new to computers may not know what to look for, or which questions to ask. You might need to enlist the help of the support people available to you. In addition, keep in mind that as you learn about the capabilities of computer hardware and software, you will develop more sophisticated ideas about what you would like to do with them. The need to meet your own goals will be strong motivation to keep looking for more resources.

Support

One aspect of the computer-literate community is that it is just that—a community. Computer skills are very difficult to develop in isolation. If you have seen students working together with computers, you have probably seen the high level of interaction and mutual support that is almost essential for developing their skills. Working with others certainly speeds up the learning process. For the next section of your journal, you need to seek out the people who can help you meet your technology goals. You need to find out who controls the resources, who has the expertise, and who will spend some time helping others. Even the efforts to find these people and let them know of your interest will ease your entry into that community.

Resource 6: Friends and relatives who use computers (helpful)

If you have a friend, relative, or neighbor who uses a computer, that person will very likely be eager to share his or her enthusiasm and knowledge with you. A person close to you who has a common interest is a valuable resource in most endeavors, such as diet or exercise.

For your sixth journal entry, write down the names of those friends and relatives that you might even wildly consider talking to about their experiences with computers. If you know what they use their computers for, write those uses after their name. If you do not know what they use the computer for, ask them. Find out if they would be willing to help you learn to do the same things. As mentioned, most people are willing to share what they have learned. In addition, they, too, might like to know that someone shares their interests.

Resource 7: People in your school district (very helpful)

Unless there are no computers in your school and nobody else has the slightest interest in them, you are likely to find some support in your building or another building in your district. For your seventh journal entry you should find and list the computer users around you at work and the ways they use computers. If you have never asked, you may be surprised at the number of colleagues who already use computers at home if not at school.

When interacting with your colleagues, you will have to deal with your own comfort level in asking for assistance. But, as mentioned, you will need to admit your lack of knowledge at some time in order to improve your abilities. You also will have to deal with colleagues who might not know as much as they think. This is not something to worry about. As your understanding improves and your circle of support increases, you will come to know the people on whom you can rely.

There are particular people you will want to identify. Is there an expert in your building or district, a computer guru, so to speak? This is often a person who has skills with the computer and is available to help others. Sometimes this person has an official position of technology or computer coordinator. Just as often, the "guru" will be another classroom teacher or reading specialist who uses computers at home, in the classroom, or both. People with assigned responsibility for computers, coordinators or supervisors, will also be assets, and you should record their names and areas of expertise in your journal. Building principals and district office personnel can easily identify people with official technology positions. Once you identify them, talk to them yourself to find the ways they can help you meet your goals. Don't forget to talk to supervisors of literacy instruction: Even if they do not use technology in the classroom themselves, they should be aware of teachers who are using technology in your district.

In addition, you may have an intermediate unit or consortium of school districts that offers inservice training and other support for technology. Call these groups to learn about resources that they have or can help you find.

Resource 8: Community support (helpful)

Already a number of community resources for equipment have been discussed including libraries, colleges, and businesses. These resources also may employ people who are willing, or assigned, to support computer users. It can be worthwhile to inquire about any such support from these and other community organizations. Make a final entry in your journal that records support resources in your community. These will vary from items such as the hours of support offered by the computer center at your local college to the name of a reference librarian who helps people with Internet access.

A frequently unknown community of computer users that is often willing to help others is called a users group. These are groups of people (many with technical careers) who meet regularly to discuss and explore issues in computers and technology. You can find local users groups by checking at computer retailers for newsletters or lists of groups. You can also check community bulletin boards for announcements of their meetings.

Two other community resources that you should explore are parents and even students from your own school. The applications children are learning at home are part of the driving force behind school districts' involvement in technology. If you are willing to learn from your students, or to include parent volunteers in your classroom, you might find the most valuable resource right in your classroom.

You also should be aware that professional organizations, such as the International Reading Association, are excellent resources for finding support from other teachers with similar interests. State, regional, and national conferences provide workshops and interest-group sessions where you can learn about technology and evaluate products from many hardware and software vendors.

Use Your Journal to Create a Plan of Action

With your haves assessment in hand, you can determine personal goals, set priorities, and create a general plan of action. First, examine the groups of

Improving Your Keyboarding and Mouse Skills

If you are not familiar with the standard computer keyboard and mouse, you should look for ways to improve your comfort level. Asking a family member, friend, or co-worker with computer skills to spend some time showing you how to get around on the keyboard and select items with a mouse is a nonthreatening way to get started. Once you have started, computer software also can assist you in learning how to get around the keyboard. Programs such as *Mavis Beacon Teaches Typing* are designed to improve your computing skills (see Chapter 5 for more information on developing keyboarding skills). A terrific way to gain familiarity with the mouse is by exploring an electronic book, such as *Arthur's Teacher Trouble* (see Chapter 4). Many electronic books have interactive features that require using the mouse to see the hidden actions and activities.

resources discussed: personal resources, hardware and software, and support. If you are weak in any of these three areas, you should address the weakest as your highest priority. Figure 1 on pages 22–25 includes a hypothetical plan based on the sample haves assessment.

The quality of the hardware and the utility of the software available to you will affect your persistence. Slow computers that lack essential capacities and run only outdated software can frustrate even the most dedicated professional. The cost of quality hardware is dropping so low that acquiring a new computer with educational and productivity software can reasonably be part of your plan of action.

Once you have a quality computer, either at home or work (preferably both), then finding applications of technology that fit your personal and professional goals can help with your motivation. There are many computer programs that support home finances and other record keeping. Computer programs or instructional videos increasingly can enhance hobbies such as genealogical research. The Internet is now one of the best sources for tracing family histories. Include a personal goal for using technology in your plan of action.

Arguably, the best software tool for a teacher to learn today is a Web browser. Several Web browsers are available, but the two most popular are *Netscape Navigator* and *Microsoft Internet Explorer*. A browser allows you to access (browse) the millions of pages of information made available on the Internet and the World Wide Web. Each page is accessed by entering a URL (Uniform Resource Locator—often called a "Web address") into a window in the program's screen. Figure 2 shows a screen from the browser *Netscape Navigator* with a Web page about International Reading Association (IRA) publications. The URL for this Web page (http://www.reading.org/publications) is near the top of the page. You can move from page to page by entering addresses, or by clicking the mouse on links (text or pictures that will enter the URL for you) built into Web pages, or on navigation buttons, which are part of the browser. Figure 2 shows several links that are included in the Web page (the links are the underlined words). The browser's navigation buttons can be seen at the top of the screen (clicking the mouse on the button labeled "Back" will return you to the Web page previously visited).

Figure 2
Sample Screen From *Netscape Navigator*

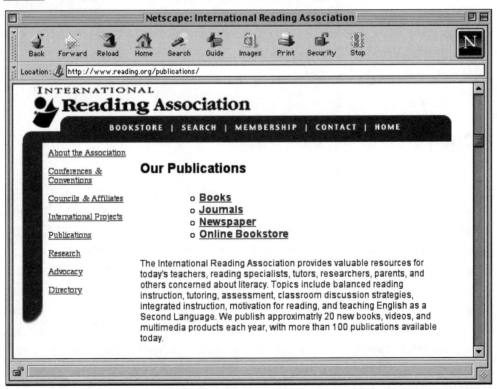

You must be connected to the Internet to use a browser in this way. For home use this means paying a fee to an Internet Service Provider (ISP). The fee will usually include an e-mail account, which will allow you to send electronic mail to (and receive it from) other people with an e-mail address. For example, if you want to learn more than is posted on the IRA Web site about upcoming IRA conferences, you can send a message to "conferences@reading.org." Schools are creating permanent connections to the Internet for teachers to use for e-mail and WWW access, but if this is not available, check your local library.

Include in your plan a collection of educational software as part of your professional library. The cost of software is decreasing, and many excellent programs are very affordable. The educational software you select to integrate technology into your literacy classroom will depend on your teaching goals and the grade level you teach. Later chapters in this book give numerous examples of CD-ROMs, such as electronic books and learning adventures, and other software, such as writing and multimedia tools, that are available for teachers concerned with emerging and developing literacy.

Create a support group as another part of your plan. This can be as simple as working regularly with a friend or family member, or it can involve joining or creating an after-school computer club for children or teachers. Remember that people are proud of their accomplishments and are usually willing to share their knowledge. This is especially true when they have an eager student who is willing to share in return.

Concluding Remarks

The best way to improve your skills with computers is to use them. If you have created a journal of self-assessment and planning, as is suggested here, you must now take the next step and begin to carry out your plan. The plan you have created is just a sketch, or guide, for ways to bring technology into your personal life and classroom activities. You will help yourself if you use your journal to keep track of your progress and modify your plan as your skills improve or your circumstances change. For instance, if you initially plan to take a class to meet a particular goal but the class is canceled, try to find an alternative route to achieve the same goal. Or, if you change some of your priorities, do not set aside your plan for a later date. Rather, change the plan to accommodate your new priorities. Do not let a change in your budget stop you from making progress. If your school makes curriculum changes, do not let those demands on your time stop your efforts. Try to advocate for technology to be part of those changes.

Another way to modify your plan is to keep a record of your attitudes and responses to this new learning situation. Note the things that interest you as well as those that annoy you. If, for instance, you plan to keep a home checkbook on the computer but find that such an application does not really interest you, drop it in favor of another computer activity.

One final note about your journal is to use it to follow your progress. When you feel good about an accomplishment, write it down. Every achievement that you celebrate is a motivational milestone that you can look back at when you have forgotten to back up an important file or left a disk on your dashboard and lost a day's work. Your journal will be useful to you in a few months when friends ask you to share how you learned so much, so fast. They will be looking to you for help when they are creating their own journal.

References

Arthur's Teacher Trouble [Computer software]. (1993). Cambridge, MA: Brøderbund/ The Learning Company.

Bitter, G.G., & Pierson, M.E. (1999). *Using technology in the classroom* (4th ed.). Boston: Allyn & Bacon.

ClarisWorks [Computer software]. (1999). Santa Clara, CA: Claris.

Desberg, P., & Fisher, F. (1999). *Teaching with technology* [CD-ROM]. Boston: Allyn & Bacon.

Forcier, R.C. (1999). *The computer as an educational tool* (2nd ed.). London: Merrill Prentice Hall.

Hoffman, P. (1998). *Netscape Communicator 4.5 for dummies*. New York: IDG Books Worldwide.

Internet Explorer [Computer software]. (1999). Redmond, WA: Microsoft.

Kent, P. (1999). *Complete idiot's guide to the Internet* (6th ed.). Indianapolis, IN: Que Publications.

Marsh, M. (1999). *Everything you need to know (but were afraid to ask kids) about the Information Highway* (2nd ed.). Palo Alto, CA: The Computer Learning Foundation.

Mavis Beacon Teaches Typing [Computer software]. (1996). Cambridge, MA: Mindscape.

Microsoft Word [Computer software]. (1999). Redmond, WA: Microsoft.

Netscape Navigator [Computer software]. (1999). Mountain View, CA: Netscape Communications.

Reinking, D. (1998). Introduction: Synthesizing technological transformations of literacy in a post-typographic world. In D. Reinking, M.C. McKenna, L.D. Labbo, & R.D. Kieffer (Eds.), *Handbook of literacy and technology: Transformations in a post-typographic world*. Mahwah, NJ: Erlbaum.

Schwartz, J.E., & Beichner, R.J. (1999). *Essentials of educational technology*. Boston: Allyn & Bacon.

SECTION 2

Into the CyberWoods:
Finding Your Way
With Technology

■ This section contains four chapters to help you find your way in using technology for word development, reading development, writing development, and content learning. Chapter 3 describes exemplars of software products and Web sites that support word recognition, spelling, and vocabulary acquisition. Specific lesson plan ideas are offered in each of the areas. Chapter 4 examines technology's usefulness and applicability for reading development. Different types of software products and Web sites are examined for emergent, developing, and independent readers. Also, ideas are given for using software products and Web sites with different types of instructional plans. Chapter 5 demonstrates ways in which technology supports writing development. The issue of keyboarding is addressed before different types of writing tools are described for their value and suitability in literature-based classrooms. E-mail and Web site applications also are described. Chapter 6 describes a multitude of ways in which technology supports content learning. Different types of software products, Web sites, and electronic applications are included for instructing in mathematics, social studies, science, and the arts. These four chapters navigate you into the next section of ideas for integrating technology into all facets of your literacy curriculum.

CHAPTER 3

Using Technology to Support
Word Recognition, Spelling,
and Vocabulary Acquisition

BARBARA J. FOX AND MARY JANE MITCHELL

Eleven-year-old Tyler is an accomplished video game player. After many hours of practice, he skillfully uses the controller to make video characters jump, kick, run, and turn summersaults in mid air. In playing video games, Tyler uses the controller within the context of thoughtful plans of action, or strategies, that he knows will give him an advantage when playing. The combination of skill and strategy that makes Tyler the top player in his neighborhood is not much different from the combination that makes the students you teach good readers.

Just as Tyler skillfully manipulates the video game controller and uses a variety of strategies to advance to more challenging game levels, good readers skillfully use many different types of knowledge and employ a variety of strategies in order to comprehend text. Because it is crucial for students to use graphophonic, semantic, and syntactic cueing systems, much of the technology and all the lessons in this chapter include ways for students to strengthen their ability to use these cueing systems strategically when reading and writing.

Just as video games are an integral part of students' lives, so, too, are computers, scanners, digital cameras, color printers, and the Internet. Encyclopedias are on disk; virtual shopping malls are on the Internet; and lessons and activities for learning about words, sounds, and letters are available through a vast array of educational software and media. Technology is a way to reach students such as Tyler who are accustomed to working with media that taps into their visual, auditory, and kinesthetic modalities. Software and Internet sites with color, animation, and audio clips invite students to use such modalities to interact with the sights and sounds of language. Sound reinforces, extends, or confirms the letter and sound relationships of our English language. Also, in combining the sight of words with the sound of words, technology gives students opportunities to develop their reading vocabulary and to practice reading words in context. When sight and sound are coupled with immediate feedback, students know right away if they have applied a skill or strategy successfully. When you set a purpose for using technology to support skill development in your classroom and identify the content students need to learn, technology is a powerful teaching tool that goes far beyond drill-and-practice exercises in paper-and-pencil workbooks.

Not many years ago, students typed or wrote papers, and thumbed through the card catalog when searching for references in the school library. Although students came to school with varying needs, languages, and abilities, the tools teachers had with which to meet individual (and small-group) differences were limited to print, audiotape, and film technology. Skill development was largely determined by the learning sequence laid out in textbooks and workbooks. Today, technology challenges you to think differently about meeting the skill-development needs of individuals. Each student brings to learning a unique complement of prior knowledge, language, cultural background, and personal characteristics. Though students need to develop skills and strategies, this does not imply that every student in your classroom needs to learn every bit of word- and sound-level knowledge in the same way, in the same sequence, or at the same time.

Types of Software

You will encounter three different types of skill-development software: (1) drill-and-practice, (2) tutorial, and (3) learning games. Drill-and-practice programs provide for the practice of content that has already been taught. Tutorial programs teach new information and principles, as well as provide for practice (Heinich, Molenda, Russell, & Smaldino, 1999). Learning games usually include drill-and-practice in a format that incorporates some sort of challenge specifically designed to motivate students and to capture their interest (Morrison, Lowther, & DeMuelle, 1999). The practical implications are that the use of drill-and-practice and learning-game software should follow classroom instruction, whereas tutorial programs may, at your discretion, be used before information is presented in classroom lessons. All three types of programs have a place in today's classrooms and contribute to skill development when used to meet individual and small-group needs.

Selecting Software

When selecting skill-development software, base your decisions on the following: (1) what the individual students in your classroom need to know (the skills they need to develop), (2) how students need to know it (the strategies they need to apply skill knowledge), and (3) which software programs or Internet sites are the best matches or are the most beneficial for students. For example, students who need to increase their fluency in making letter-sound associations are candidates for drill-and-practice and learning-game software (Torgesen & Barker, 1995). Students who need basic instruction, say in learning the letter-sound associations of phonics, will benefit from tutorial programs that teach this information and provide systematic practice. Alternatively, children in your classroom who respond rapidly and accurately to the skills you have already taught do not need to spend their time using tutorial, drill-and-practice, or gamelike activities that focus on skills they have already mastered. These students benefit from interacting with instructional technology that challenges them to increase or expand their literacy skills. This generalization applies equally to computer software, Internet sites, and paper-and-pencil activities.

Evaluating Software and Internet Sites

When evaluating skill-development software, look for programs that allow for freedom of movement among activities and skill levels, and provide opportunities to apply skills strategically. Because one of the advantages of technology is its ability to maximize learning by providing for individualized skill-development instruction, branching software is a must. Branching, or webbed-design, software allows students to go directly to the program sections that address their individual needs, instead of forcing them to practice skills they have mastered. Likewise, once students are familiar with branching software, it allows them to skip time-consuming introductions and directions and go directly to teaching, drill-and-practice, or gamelike activities.

In our experience, the type of feedback included in skill-development software is extremely important. The feedback our students seem to respond to most positively gives them knowledge of results and does not take too much time. Knowledge of results helps students learn when they are successful and when they need to rethink a response. Yet, we have found that lengthy feedback is counterproductive. Learning or practice should not be put on hold while bells chime, whistles blow, balloons burst, fireworks explode, and characters yell "Hooray, good job!" Though we certainly support enthusiastic, positive feedback, feedback that is overdone disrupts learning and distracts students from the major focus of the software. (See Figure 1 for guidelines for evaluating skill-development software.)

Skill-development software that targets individual needs should include a management component that allows you to monitor student progress and to determine the level, challenge, and complexity of activities. Because it is critical for students to use skills strategically, software also should include opportunities for students to apply skills—to actually use what they know to help them identify unknown words and to spell—when reading and writing. This ensures that students apply skill-based knowledge within the context of strategies. In so doing, skill-based knowledge becomes more than item knowledge; it becomes

Figure 1
Guidelines for Evaluating Skill-Development Software

Does the software:	Yes	No
1. Have a webbed design so that students do not practice skills they have already mastered?	_____	_____
2. Use voices that are clear?	_____	_____
3. Sequence skills from easy to difficult?	_____	_____
4. Allow students to bypass lengthy introductions once they are familiar with the program?	_____	_____
5. Provide for different levels of difficulty within skills?	_____	_____
6. Use pictures that are easy to identify?	_____	_____
7. Provide opportunities to apply skills when reading?	_____	_____
8. Include a management system to help the teacher keep track of the skills students have practiced?	_____	_____
9. Use words in students' speaking vocabularies to illustrate or explain principles?	_____	_____
10. Provide explanations of the principles students are learning and/or practicing?	_____	_____
11. Give students access to a dictionary to help them learn words when spelling or writing?	_____	_____
12. Provide opportunities for students to use skills when writing?	_____	_____

integrated within complex strategies. Application and integration, in turn, provide avenues through which strategies might be further developed and refined.

Internet sites, like software, have the potential to make a significant contribution to skill development. The Internet extends literacy learning beyond the four walls of your classroom, transforming your classroom from a physical space to a worldwide learning laboratory with rich and exciting ways for students to apply word-identification strategies when reading and spelling strategies when writing. Look for sites that are relevant to the skills and strategies your students are learning and using. Bookmark those sites for easy access. You will find many more Internet sites for strategically applying skills than for practicing skills. Examples of activities for enriching and extending the use of strategies include sites that (1) provide technical and factual information for writing reports, journals, or brochures, as described in the vocabulary unit later in this chapter; (2) offer free electronic postcards, as explained in the phonics unit in this chapter; and (3) allow students to ask questions and participate in online chatrooms, as explained in the spelling unit. We also have found that these types of sites are most valuable when they are integrated into large thematic units. (See also the textbox in Chapter 6 "Evaluating Web Sites.")

Leu and Kinzer (1999) say that the effective use of Internet sites depends on assigning a specific activity (or activities) to be completed within a reasonable period of time and then giving students the chance to share their work. We have the greatest success when we carefully structure the use of technology to create a seamless integration of literacy across the curriculum and across various forms of media. Using this framework, technology is a part of the typical learning activities in the classroom. Along with Internet sites, and tutorial, drill-and-practice, and learning-games software, offer your students a variety of experiences with (1) word-processing programs that give them the chance to use skill-based knowledge strategically when writing, and (2) multimedia programs such as *HyperStudio* that allow for the strategic use of skills when creating presentations. (See Figure 2 for more suggestions for designing units.)

Using Technology to Develop Phonemic Awareness and Letter Knowledge

If you teach early emergent, beginning, or low-progress young readers, phonemic awareness is undoubtedly part of the reading program in your classroom. Phonemic awareness is the understanding that spoken language con-

> **Figure 2**
> **Designing Units Using Technology for Skill Development**
>
> Skill-development units using technology should:
> 1. Provide for meeting the skill-development needs of individual students.
> 2. Include opportunities to apply skills strategically when reading.
> 3. Give student opportunities to apply skills strategically when writing.
> 4. Use a variety of technology and print when practicing and applying skills.
> 5. Have a focus or theme that allows students to develop skills within the context of learning about their environment or content subjects.
> 6. Provide multiple ways to practice skills.
> 7. Include activities and themes consistent with students' interests and age.
> 8. Assess skill development through speaking, reading, and writing in a variety of contexts.
> 9. Sequence the unit so that easier skills are learned before more advanced ones.
> 10. Give students guidance when they inappropriately respond to skill-based activities.

sists of words, rhymes, syllables, and sounds (Fox, 2000). Children who are phonemically aware are skilled at recognizing rhyme, identifying sounds in words, and blending sounds into words. Good phonemic awareness has repeatedly been correlated with success in reading and spelling, whereas poor awareness has been found to be one of the underlying causes of reading failure (McBride-Chang, Wagner, & Chang, 1997; Nicholson, 1997; Torgesen, 1998). As young children become aware that the words and syllables of language consist of small units of sound, which we call phonemes, they begin to think analytically about the sounds in spoken words. When children learn the letter-sound relationships of phonics, they use awareness of the sounds of language as a conceptual platform for understanding that the letters in written words represent the sounds in spoken words. In other words, phonemic awareness helps readers make sense of our alphabetic writing system, which, in turn, helps them benefit from the phonics instruction you provide in your classroom (Juel, Griffith, & Gough, 1986).

Selecting Phonemic Awareness Software

In selecting software to develop phonemic awareness, look for programs that include many different phonemic awareness skills. Phonemic awareness develops gradually in a relatively predictable order and consists of a variety of skills, including skill at detecting rhyme and alliteration, identifying sounds in words, sound blending, sound substitution, and sound deletion (Fox, 2000). Interestingly, the students in your classroom who develop one of these skills, for example skill at detecting rhyme or alliteration, may not necessarily and automatically develop the other skills. Effective software, therefore, must include rhyme recognition, sound identification, and blending, and set appropriate limits on the amount of auditory memory students must have to complete the program's activities successfully.

Because phonemic awareness is an oral-aural language skill, there are several other things to consider when selecting phonemic awareness software in addition to rhyme detection, sound detection, and blending. If pictures are used to present words, are the pictures easy to identify? Do students have to bring some knowledge of reading to the program, or can they be successful even if they are in the early emergent phases of learning to read? Are the voices easy to understand? Are words clearly articulated? Is speech normally paced? If sounds are spoken in isolation, is the "uh" added only when necessary (e.g., "s" not "suh")? The "uh" creates confusion and sound blending is made more difficult. For example, there is no need to add an "uh" to the sound we associate with the letter *r*; it can and should be articulated as "r," not "ruh." We advise that you use software in which the digitized speech adds the "uh" only to consonants when necessary (the sound of the letter *b* as "buh" and *d* as "duh") and does not add the "uh" when it is not needed (e.g., the sound of *s* as "s," and *m* as "m").

Examples of Phonemic Awareness Software

We divide phonemic awareness software into two categories: One category, sound-only software, uses sounds and graphics to present phonemic awareness tasks. The other category, sound-with-text software, includes some activities that use a combination of sound, graphics, and print. *DaisyQuest* and *Daisy's Castle* are examples of sound-only phonemic awareness programs that are suitable for emergent readers. These two branching, tutorial programs provide instruction and organized practice in the phonemic awareness skills of rhyme recognition, sound identification, and sound blending. Each has easy-to-understand voices, clearly articulated sounds, colorful graphics, and easy-to-identify pictures. *DaisyQuest*, which has been shown to result in significant improvement in the phonemic awareness of kindergarten children (Foster, Erickson, Foster, Brinkman, & Torgesen, 1994), focuses on identifying rhyme and beginning, middle, and ending sounds. *Daisy's Castle* consists of segmenting words into beginning sounds (e.g., the "l" in *log*), rhyme (e.g., the "og" in *log, dog,* and *hog*), and individual sounds (e.g., the "l," "o," or "g" in *log*), as well as whole-word blending. Because both programs develop different aspects of phonemic awareness, it is not surprising that using them together can result in significant improvement in the word reading and sound identification of low-progress first graders (Barker & Torgesen, 1995).

In *DaisyQuest* and *Daisy's Castle*, explicit instruction is presented for each skill, followed by practice items and feedback via digitized speech. Programs use a gamelike format and allow students to bypass the storyline and go directly to activities, which saves time for students who are familiar with the instructions. Students demonstrate learning and mastery by correctly responding to yes/no and multiple choice questions. There are three skill levels for each activity in these programs, with the response time decreasing at advanced levels in order to develop automatic, rapid responding. Skill mastery is rewarded in *DaisyQuest* with clues to the location of Daisy, a shy, friendly dragon, and in *Daisy's Castle* with clues to the location of Daisy's lost eggs (see Figure 3).

Figure 3
Screen From *DaisyQuest*

Reprinted by permission of Great Wave Software.

Leap Into Phonics, an example of sound-with-text software, includes some activities that use speech as well as print to develop phonemic awareness. We have found this program to be beneficial for kindergartners and beginning first graders who need to develop both phonemic awareness and print knowledge. Unlike sounds, which are ephemeral, letters are fixed in time. Students can, therefore, use letters as visual referents for sound, which has a positive effect on the development of phonemic awareness (Chew, 1997). *Leap Into Phonics* provides instruction and practice in the eight phonemic awareness skills of identifying (1) environmental sounds, (2) words, (3) rhymes, (4) syllables, (5) beginning sounds in words, (6) middle sounds in words, (7) ending sounds in words, and (8) blending word parts together.

Blending is one of the more difficult phonemic awareness skills for many students. In *Leap Into Phonics*, students practice blending by identifying whole words that are pronounced with the first or last sounds separated from the rest of the word. Students see written words, listen to segmented words ("m" and "op"), and then select a picture that represents the word. Sound substitution, another important and challenging skill, is practiced for beginning, middle, and ending sounds. For students who need more practice with letter names, this program includes opportunities to associate letters with their names and sounds. Kindergarten and first-grade teachers tell us that *Leap Into Phonics* is a no-frills program that is beneficial for students who need extra practice manipulating the words, rhymes, and sounds of language. Because it includes opportunities to practice using letter-sound associations, this program provides good scaffolding for connecting awareness of sounds (phonemic awareness) and knowledge of letter-sound relationships (phonics). The carefully sequenced developmental progression ensures that students are exposed only to those activities in which they will be successful.

A Phonemic Awareness Unit

Figure 4 is an example of a unit we use when teaching and reinforcing sensitivity to rhyming words. Because the students who participate in this unit are low-progress learners who have little phonemic awareness and letter knowledge, we use programs such as *DaisyQuest* and *Daisy's Castle*, which offer strictly aural instruction and practice and, therefore, put no demands on letter knowledge. Then, when students begin to be successful with a purely aural technology learning format, we add practice with technology that uses both sound and text. Consistent with our belief in giving students ample opportunities to link knowledge and skills with real reading and writing, we begin by sharing the rhyming books of Dr. Seuss, and end by publishing a rhyming picture book. Our students enjoy print and CD-ROM books, and we use both extensively. Interactive CD-ROM books have the advantage of increasing students' ability to retell stories (Matthew, 1997) and, hence, hold the promise of promoting active learning (Heilman, Blair, & Rupley, 1998). In this lesson, we use a CD-ROM Dr. Seuss book because we want to maximize the conditions under which good story recall might occur. Good story recall then acts as a gateway to discussing and discovering the rhyming words that are found throughout *Green Eggs and Ham* (Seuss, 1973). This interactive book is appropriate for preschool through beginning first-grade students.

Students who are sensitive to rhyme in speech can more readily detect rhyming letter patterns in print (Goswami, 1998). It follows, then, that phonemic awareness instruction is enhanced when combined with opportunities to see and hear rhyming words. Consequently, technology with rhyming words and pictures of rhyming words in gamelike formats helps students transfer a strictly aural skill to print. Therefore, we ensure that children play the two speech and print rhyming games in the *Green Eggs and Ham* CD-ROM, as

Figure 4
Unit Plan for Teaching Rhyme Awareness

Theme:	Dr. Seuss's Birthday
Objectives:	To help kindergarten and beginning first-grade students recognize rhyming words; publish a rhyming picture book; learn the letter names; and appreciate literature.
Materials:	Software programs: CD-ROM book *Green Eggs and Ham*, *DaisyQuest*, *Leap Into Phonics*, *Let's Go Read! An Island Adventure*, or *Kid Works Deluxe*.
Activities:	1. Introduce the concept of rhyme with the *Green Eggs and Ham* CD-ROM. 2. Use *DaisyQuest* to teach rhyme and to give students practice identifying rhyming words. 3. Use the auditory rhyming games in *Leap Into Phonics* for additional practice. 4. Use *Let's Go Read! An Island Adventure* for phonemic awareness and letter-name practice. 5. Publish a rhyming picture book with *Kid Works Deluxe*.
Assessment:	Learning is evident when students recognize rhyming words in stories, poetry, and games; match upper- and lowercase letters; and use lowercase letters when writing.

shown in Figure 5. One game is a spelling activity in which the students click on chickens that lay eggs with beginning letters that are added to common phonograms to spell words. In the second game, students match two rhyming pictures and listen to silly sentences with the rhyming words.

The children we teach enjoy Internet sites that feature rhyme, such as NFBKids (National Film Board of Canada) (http://www.nfb.ca/kids) and Story Hour in the "Reading Zone" area of The Internet Public Library (http://www.ipl.org). Many software programs include rhyme, such as *Sugar & Snails*, which gives kindergarten and first-grade children auditory, visual, and contextual cues to identify rhyme. Included in this program is a riddle game in which students look at and listen to riddles and then click on a picture of a

Figure 5
Screen From *Green Eggs and Ham* CD-ROM

Green Eggs and Ham CD-ROM ©1999 The Learning Company and its licensors. All rights reserved. Dr. Seuss characters, text, and images © and ™ 1996 Dr. Seuss Enterprises, L.P. All rights reserved. *Green Eggs and Ham* book ©1960 Dr. Seuss Enterprises, L.P. All rights reserved.

rhyming object that completes the riddle. Preschool and kindergarten students also enjoy *Elmo's Reading*, which includes a rhyme activity that uses letters and digitized speech to help children build words with onsets (e.g., "cl") and vowel-consonant combinations (e.g., "ock"). Programs like *Elmo's Reading* and *Leap Into Phonics* help children transition from learning phonemic awareness to phonics, and we use them for this purpose.

Phonemic awareness units such as Dr. Seuss's Birthday in Figure 4 (page 51) are more effective when students know something about letter-sound relationships (Lundberg, Frost, & Petersen, 1988). However, the kindergartners for whom this unit was designed came to school unable to name the letters of the alphabet or consistently differentiate one letter from another. Because rhyme recognition is an easier skill than identification of individual sounds in words and blending, we teach rhyme awareness along with the letter names. Once children know letter names, we teach phonemic awareness in conjunction with letter-sound associations.

One of us uses Dr. Seuss's Birthday as a kindergarten and first-grade unit theme in our school. The teachers wear hats like the one from *The Cat in the Hat* (Seuss, 1957); students and their teachers share the works of Dr. Seuss; green eggs and ham are cooked as part of the study of nutrition in the healthful living curriculum; and children write about their favorite Dr. Seuss characters. Students visit the Dr. Seuss's Seussville Web site (http://www.random house.com/seussville) and they participate in a variety of activities, such as writing rhyming words on large cut-out versions of the hat from *The Cat in the Hat* and creating rhyming books. This unit is particularly well suited for kindergarten students and is also appropriate for first graders who do not recognize rhyme or know letter names.

Examples of Letter-Name Learning Software

When students start school without knowing the names of letters, it is important to use a variety of activities to teach letter names. Because many letters are visually similar to emergent readers, look for software programs that give students practice noticing similarities and differences. For example, in *Sugar & Snails*, students identify visually similar and different upper- and lowercase letters as well as words and shapes. The use of sight and sound, easy-to-recognize and uncluttered pictures of common objects, and simple directions makes software programs such as *Sugar & Snails* highly appropriate for young learners. Not surprisingly, the emergent readers we teach enjoy and benefit from software programs with these characteristics.

When you choose software for letter-name learning, look for programs that show upper- and lowercase letters. Though everyone knows the English alphabet has 26 letters, this is not the way it looks to many emergent readers. Some students think that each upper- and lowercase letter is a separate entity and, therefore, should have a different name. In seeing both upper- and lowercase letters together, students come to understand that the 52 symbols represent only 26 letters. Some software programs use only uppercase letters. We do not recommend these programs because the text read by emergent readers consists mainly of lowercase letters. If you are not sure whether lowercase letters are part of a program you are considering, call the publisher before you purchase. Examples of programs that include both upper- and lowercase letters are *Let's Go Read! An Island Adventure*, *Reading Mansion*, and *Bailey's Book House*, which also includes rhyming words and identifying letter sounds at the beginning and end of words.

In teaching letter names, we recommend the use of traditional alphabet books, student-created ABC books, software programs such as *Sugar & Snails* that help emergent readers learn to recognize and name letters, and Internet sites such as Infostuff (http://www.infostuff.com) that feature a colorful online alphabet book. In creating their own ABC books, emergent readers use pictures of words they know. This activity taps into the language base emergent readers bring to reading and increases the possibility of recall. Drawing and painting programs, such as *Paint, Write & Play!* and *Kid Works Deluxe*, are ideal for student publications. For example, *Paint, Write & Play!* has many possibilities for creating ABC books that include familiar pictures, words beginning with each letter of the alphabet, and digitized speech to pronounce words and letter names. Also included are drawing and painting tools that allow students to create their own illustrations and capabilities for publishing their own books.

Letter-name knowledge is a good predictor of later reading success, most probably because learning letter names helps students discriminate among the letters (Adams, 1990; Snow, Burns, & Griffin, 1998). After students are able to differentiate among the letters, introduce them to technology that supports the development of phonics skills.

Using Technology to Develop Phonics

Phonemic awareness pertains to oral-aural language, whereas phonics pertains to the relationship between the sounds of spoken words and the letters of written words (Vandervelden & Siegel, 1995). Though different, phonemic awareness and phonics have a mutually supportive relationship in which improvement in one supports improvement in the other. Consequently, the positive effects of technology are strengthened when you teach both phonemic awareness and phonics to the same group of students.

When Nila Banton Smith wrote a history of reading instruction in 1934, she observed that phonics "has in recent years been one of the most widely questioned and discussed phases of reading instruction…" (p. 271). More than half a century later, phonics is still the center of debate. There are two essentials most teachers agree on, however. One is that learning to read English requires some knowledge of the way letters represent sounds. This view is supported by research showing that letter-sound knowledge significantly contributes to comprehension and vocabulary in the early grades (Rupley & Willson, 1997) and that students who are good word identifiers are good readers throughout the elementary years (Carver, 1998). The other important point about phonics that teachers generally agree on is that the time to teach phonics is in the early grades when students are beginning to read (Baumann, Hoffman, Moon, & Duffy-Hester, 1998).

Phonics software contributes to learning by using both sight and sound to present letter-sound associations. This is a tremendous learning advantage because seeing letters and hearing the sounds associated with them reinforces the connections between the letter sounds of phonics. Phonics software also can give students consistent and immediate feedback, which helps students correct mistakes and solidify letter-sound learning. The branching design of many phonics software programs allows for flexibility of movement within a program, thereby affording some degree of individualization (Moeller & Hupert, 1997). Added to this, colorful graphics, engaging characters, and game-like practice situations are motivational tools particularly well suited for students with Tyler's out-of-school experiences with technology. Tyler, and students like him, relate to software that reflects their everyday experiences with technology and, perhaps more important, bring to your classroom a predilection for high levels of interactivity.

Selecting Phonics Software

If you are looking for software that provides comprehensive phonics instruction, then we recommend that you consider tutorial software. Tutorial programs are more extensive than practice programs and, therefore, are better suited for students who need carefully planned, sequenced instruction and practice. Examples of tutorial software include *SuperSonic Phonics* and *Let's Go Read! An Island Adventure.* The *SuperSonic Phonics* tutorial program has three levels of five gamelike activities for short vowels, long vowels, consonant blends, vowel and consonant digraphs, r-controlled vowels, diphthongs, simple syllabication, and cloze sentences—sentences with words omitted—for applying skills. Because the graphics are age neutral, *SuperSonic Phonics* is appropriate for students in any elementary grade who need extra exposure to the majority of the letter-sound associations.

The two tutorial programs *Let's Go Read! An Island Adventure* and *Let's Go Read! An Ocean Adventure* feature a friendly squirrel and raccoon that have special appeal for kindergartners and first graders. We have found *Let's Go Read! An Island Adventure* to be effective in providing instruction and practice associating letters and sounds, as shown in Figure 6. This engaging software program teaches and reinforces consonant letter sounds, short vowel letter sounds, letter names, and letter forms. It also supports the development of phonemic awareness, provides practice building words, and offers students opportunities to read short books. *Let's Go Read! An Ocean Adventure* teaches first and second graders long vowels, consonant digraphs, and the various sounds represented by the letters *c, g,* and *y.* Students sound out and build words up to five letters long, practice reading books, and add to stories with a speech recognition feature. This program teaches only long vowels. Clear voices, attractive and easy-to-interpret graphics, careful pacing, opportunities for practice, and clear explanations make these two programs good choices for learners who need extra support to develop phonics skills. We particularly like the combination of phonics, word building (which helps with spelling), and book reading in these balanced reading programs. This combination gives students chances to apply their phonics knowledge to spelling and textual reading.

There is a wide selection of drill-and-practice phonics software programs from which to choose. Computer-guided phonics practice software generally is for students who need to develop phonics skill, not for good readers who know phonics and are likely to become disinterested in activities that are too easy for them. It is very important, therefore, to consider the needs of your students and then match phonics drill-and-practice programs to individual learners. We find that many drill-and-practice programs are not applicable to everyone in a class because the range of some of these programs—the scope of phonics skills covered—is not broad enough to be a good match for an entire kindergarten, first-, or second-grade class. We encourage you to analyze carefully

Figure 6
Screen From *Let's Go Read! An Island Adventure*

Reprinted by permission of Edmark.

the specific letter-sound associations practiced and then select the program that is the best match for your students' needs.

Phonics practice programs involve students in learning through use of a game board or quest format. The game board format is a facsimile of traditional board games, and the quest format involves reaching a goal such as finding a hidden treasure. Many programs have organizing themes, such as the wild west in *Kid Phonics 2*, the circus in *Curious George Learns Phonics*, and a trip to France in *Madeline 1st & 2nd Grade Reading*. Most programs use cloze sentences or sentence building as a way of providing for the application of phonics skills at the sentence level. At a minimum, students must be able to differentiate among letters, though in most cases students need to know letter names. And, of course, drill-and-practice software is to be used only after classroom instruction in the letter-sounds included in the programs.

Examples of Phonics Software

Examples of drill-and-practice software include *Reading Mansion*, *Kid Phonics 1*, *Kid Phonics 2*, *Curious George Learns Phonics*, *Madeline 1st & 2nd Grade Reading*, and *JumpStart 1st Grade Reading*. Our kindergarten, first, second, and third graders who are developing phonics skills give high marks to *Reading Mansion*. This is a comprehensive gamelike practice program that includes brief tutorial-type explanations when students make mistakes. This program simulates a scavenger hunt through the rooms of a mansion, a feature our students find intriguing. Unlike many drill-and-practice programs that target only a few skills, *Reading Mansion* provides practice in letter names; phonemic awareness; consonant sounds in the beginning, middle, and end of words; long and short vowel sounds; consonant blends; digraphs; diphthongs; r-controlled vowels; hard and soft *c* and *g*; and simple syllables. In addition, *Reading Mansion* covers synonyms, antonyms, contractions, plurals, and alphabetical order. Students apply phonics skills while reading sentences to follow directions, to identify complete and incomplete sentences, to differentiate between true and false sentences, and to rearrange scrambled sentences. Instead of using only pictures as clues for word completion tasks, as is typical of most phonics practice software, some *Reading Mansion* activities ask students to click on a megaphone icon to hear the words they are to spell. Another feature we endorse is a management tool that allows you to combine various phonics skills and customize curricula to meet individual needs and to support classroom instruction.

We have found that the practice activities in *Curious George Learns Phonics* require that kindergarten and first-grade students carefully analyze the letters and sounds in words. These activities include letter-by-letter word building, thinking about sound as a basis for identifying consonants and vowels in words, and identifying beginning and ending sounds in words. Students benefit from this type of phonics practice when classroom activities support the development of phonemic awareness skills. *JumpStart 1st Grade Reading*, another example of a drill-and-practice gamelike program, includes practice using consonant blends and digraphs, rhyming words, synonyms and antonyms, and vowel sounds, and it asks comprehension questions while students read along with a fortune teller.

Many of the low-progress readers we teach need extra practice recognizing consonant-vowel-consonant (CVC) short vowel words, such as *mop* and *cap*. Examples of CVC short vowel activities are Jungle Bowl and Splatter-the-Batter, both in *JumpStart 1st Grade Reading*. In Jungle Bowl, students use letter-sound knowledge to roll lettered coconuts down a bowling lane so as to build words with short vowel patterns. Splatter-the-Batter is a food fight, always a favorite among our students, in which they have to complete a cloze sentence by correctly selecting CVC short vowel words that make sense. When students make frequent errors, the *JumpStart 1st Grade Reading* program provides explicit explanations of letter-sound patterns. We find this feature quite helpful in that it adds a measure of independence for students who need additional support as they practice.

Practice programs for kindergarten through third grade such as *Richard Scarry's Best Reading Program Ever* and *Reader Rabbit's Interactive Reading Journey* are based on the premise that phonics is best learned when students read and interact with stories. *Richard Scarry's Best Reading Program Ever* includes writing stories, reading, and practicing phonics. *Reader Rabbit's Interactive Reading Journey* focuses on using beginning sounds and word families as a means of learning the sounds that letters represent. As with the *Let's Go Read!* software programs, the letter-sound patterns students practice are present in the books that students read, thereby giving them the opportunity to apply skills immediately.

A Phonics Unit

If computer-guided phonics practice is to have a positive effect on literacy, students must be able to transfer their phonics knowledge in order to identify words that are not in software programs. This is particularly important for students who have fallen behind their classmates in reading. Our circus unit (Figure 7) was designed with such children in mind. Research shows that learning disabled students are able to use the phonics skills developed with computer-guided practice to identify words that are not in the practice program (Jones, Torgesen, & Sexton, 1987). The use of decontextualized drill-and-practice programs or more comprehensive programs that include textual reading depend on how much practice students need, your own teaching philosophy, and the level of reading ability needed to be successful. Both types of practice programs are beneficial.

The unit we describe in Figure 7 uses the circus as a theme and includes activities that are specifically tailored for low-progress first graders who need instruction and practice in recognizing CVC short vowel words. The circus comes to our town in February, which creates an excellent avenue for using technology to improve the phonics skills of our low-progress readers. In particular, we find that students who need more instruction and practice in rec-

Figure 7
Unit Plan for Teaching Phonics to Low-Progress First Graders

Theme:	Circus
Objectives:	To understand the CVC short vowel pattern; recognize and decode CVC short vowel words when reading; and conventionally spell CVC short vowel words when writing.
Materials:	Software programs: *Let's Go Read! An Island Adventure*, *JumpStart 1st Grade Reading*, and *Curious George Learns Phonics*; and electronic postcard Internet sites (for example, http://www.cardcentral.net).
Activities:	1. Read books about the circus, discuss circus performers, visit the circus.
	2. Use *Let's Go Read! An Island Adventure* to learn about and practice identifying vowel and consonant letters and their sounds.
	3. Select activities for additional practice, such as Jungle Bowl and Splatter-the-Batter in *JumpStart 1st Grade Reading*, and Phonics Funhouse and Sammy the Musical Seal in *Curious George Learns Phonics*.
	4. For application, students read books with CVC short vowels and send electronic postcards describing their circus unit experiences.
Assessment:	Learning is demonstrated when students fluently read CVC words in stories and conventionally spell CVC words when writing.

ognizing and decoding the CVC short vowel pattern in words enjoy and benefit from a combination of *Let's Go Read! An Island Adventure* to augment classroom instruction, *JumpStart 1st Grade Reading*, and *Curious George Learns Phonics* for practice. Generally, we would not use so many different software programs in one unit with our normal-progress readers; however, first graders who lack competence using the CVC short vowel pattern as late in the school year as February need many practice and application opportunities. In using a variety of software programs, we offer our students many different practice and application venues. In keeping with our belief that contextualized application is the goal of skill development, this unit combines phonics skill development with reading and writing activities in order to give students ways to strategically apply their knowledge.

The CVC focus of the teaching and learning activities we describe is a portion of a much larger first-grade circus unit. The larger unit includes teaching and learning activities that are appropriate for students of many different abilities, not just low-progress readers. One of the contributions technology makes to the circus unit is to allow teachers to differentiate instruction so as to provide for small-group and individual learning, while still including many large-group activities. One feature of the circus unit that all children enjoy is writing about their circus unit experiences. When spelling, students either write words from memory, consult a dictionary or expert speller, or use their knowledge of phonics to write words the way they sound. It is not surprising, then, that some students gain insight into letter-sound relationships through writing and spelling (Gentry, 1997).

Using Technology to Develop Spelling

Typical classroom spelling activities for grades 1–6 might include a weekly spelling list, a textbook with a prescribed scope and sequence, writing assignments, word study using the dictionary, and a variety of activities and games, such as word sorts, crossword puzzles, and mazes. Writing, dictionary use, sorting, and crossword puzzles, while distinctly different, share two common traits: Each calls for the active involvement of students, and each combines teaching spelling with learning word meaning. Technology, too, requires active involvement and combines learning to spell with learning the meaning of words. In addition, the interactivity of technology adds to learning by including sight, sound, color, animation, rapid knowledge of results, and practice in the context of motivational gamelike formats. From the teacher's perspective, spelling software programs create ways to individualize spelling instruction and practice. Many programs give you the flexibility to create spelling lists for the whole class, to design customized word lists for individual students, and to specify the level of difficulty of the spelling words and activities.

Good spellers know how to match sounds with letters when spelling. Drawing on phonics knowledge, they could spell a phonetically predicable word—a word that is spelled like it sounds—by writing the letters that match the sounds. Not surprisingly, much of the phonics software available today includes spelling activities as a means to practice phonics skills. Phonics software that includes spelling activities takes advantage of the mutually supportive relationship between the phonics skill of associating letters with sounds and the spelling skill of associating sounds with letters. By carefully selecting and using technology in your classroom, you can create learning conditions in which students benefit as both readers and writers from the same software programs.

If each letter represented only one sound, English spelling would be a relatively simple affair. Some of the variations of English spelling are due to the complex nature of our alphabetic writing system, and some are a consequence of foreign-language words that have entered the English language over the years. Take, for example, the spelling of the "j" sound in *jelly*, *gem*, and *ledge*, or the French words *café*, *chaise longue*, and *chenille*. Simply matching letters with sounds does not work for these words. Good spellers understand this and hence use many different strategies when learning to spell the English language. Good spellers learn to (1) associate letters with the sounds they hear in words, (2) develop mental images of words, (3) create mnemonics for spelling tricky words, (4) identify analogous relationships among words (the *oy* in *toy*, *voyage*, and *foyer*), and (5) divide long words into multiletter chunks—prefixes, suffixes, and syllables (Cramer, 1998). Good spellers also have a spelling consciousness, or awareness, of when a word "looks right" and when it does not (Cramer, 1998). These students readily identify misspellings, which is critical for self-monitoring and for correcting spelling during the editing phase of writing. Consequently, when deciding on spelling software for your classroom, look for programs that help children develop a spelling consciousness by asking them to recognize and correct misspellings. Look, too, for programs that give you the option of customizing word lists for the students in your class; this way a single program can be used with the most advanced speller and the least mature speller you teach. Additionally, look for programs that develop students' understanding of the meanings of the words they spell. This ensures that students will make the connection between the spelling of words and the meanings of words, which creates favorable conditions for the use of words in writing and the recognition of word meanings when reading.

Selecting Spelling Software

Most spelling software is drill and practice. When we evaluate drill-and-practice spelling software, we look for software programs that ask students to spell words, recognize and correct misspellings, use words in sentences, and understand word meanings. Our students prefer gamelike formats that are tuned into their interests and consistent with their expectations for the type of interactivity they encounter in many Internet sites, CD-ROM books, and, of course, the video games they play in their leisure time. Therefore, consider your students' interests and then look for gamelike, drill-and-practice spelling software that has an interesting theme and challenges students to accomplish some sort of goal.

Examples of Spelling Software

I Love Spelling is an example of a drill-and-practice program for second through sixth graders (see Figure 8). Drill-and-practice spelling software gives students repeated chances to spell, see, and use words within the framework of motivating games and activities. In this software program, one or two students play an intergalactic game. The option to have two players allows students to learn from each other and also makes efficient use of a limited number of classroom computers. There are three levels of spelling difficulty, and you can select from thematic word lists and skill-based word lists, or students can construct their own customized word lists. Students visit four planets that have spelling practice games, in addition to playing a word-attack game. The word-attack game flashes in rapid succession three versions of a word, only one of which is spelled correctly. Students earn points for identify-

Figure 8
Screen From *I Love Spelling*

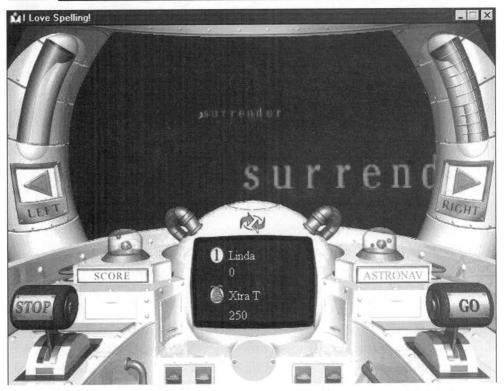

Reprinted by permission of DK Interactive Learning.

ing correctly spelled words and lose points for selecting misspelled words. This activity not only challenges students to recognize conventionally spelled words quickly, but also helps them develop the type of spelling consciousness that is so important for lifelong literacy.

Spellevator Plus is an example of a tutorial software program that is suitable for children in grades 1–6. This program includes direct instruction along with practice recognizing misspellings and using words in cloze sentences. You can add word lists to this program, decide which students will have access to different lists, and even write your own version of cloze sentences. Extra practice is provided in a *Spellevator* game that looks much like the video games Tyler and his friends often play at home. The difference is that here students must spell words, recognize misspellings, and identify word meanings to win the game or to move to the next level of difficulty. In our experience, this type of tutorial software, while not always flashy, is an effective way to extend and enrich basic classroom spelling instruction.

A Spelling Unit

The unit lesson we describe in Figure 9 uses *Spellevator Plus* to support basic classroom instruction and the *I Love Spelling* program for gamelike practice. Other examples of spelling software you may wish to consider are *Spelling ToolKit Plus*, *Spellbound*, *Spelling Spree*, and *Super Solvers Spellbound*. *Spelling ToolKit Plus* is appropriate for students in the first through twelfth grades, and features puzzles, tests, and study sheets with customized spelling words. *Spellbound*, a gamelike practice program for students in the second through sixth grades, features a spelling bee. *Spelling Spree,* for third through sixth graders, offers progress reports, the opportunity to customize lists, definitions, and four spelling games. *Super Solvers Spellbound*, for students in second through sixth grade, has a spelling bee, presents words flashed or scrambled, and includes 1,000 words, with the possibility of adding up to 3,000 more words.

Internet sites offer resources for you and spelling-related activities for your students. Everyday Spelling (http://www.everydayspelling.com) is a good teacher resource that groups spelling words and strategies by grade. The Wild World of Words, which is part of the Challenge Chaser section of the Alphabet SuperHighway (http://www.ash.udel.edu/ash/index.html), includes spelling activities at basic, medium, and advanced levels that are appropriate for students from second grade to middle school. Look at the FunBrain site (http://www.funbrain.com/kidscenter.html) for a game called Word Turtle that lets students create their own downloadable word searches. Using this Inter-

Figure 9
Unit Plan for Teaching Spelling

Theme:	Solar System NASA (National Aeronautics and Space Administration) Internet Project
Objectives:	To teach third-, fourth-, or fifth-grade students to correctly spell words when writing; identify the meaning and use of spelling words by completing cloze sentences and using words conversationally; and learn about our solar system and space travel.
Materials:	Software programs: *Spellevator Plus* and *I Love Spelling*; and Everyday Spelling (http://www.everydayspelling.com) and NASA (http://www.nasa.gov) Internet sites.
Activities:	1. Create customized spelling lists in *Spellevator Plus* and *I Love Spelling*.
	2. Use *Spellevator Plus* as a tutorial program and *I Love Spelling* for practice.
	3. Read and discuss books about the planets and space. Visit the NASA Internet site to communicate in an online chatroom, ask space questions and learn about space exploration.
	4. Have small groups use Internet sites to research a planet, build a planetary model, and write a report to present to the class.
Assessment:	Evidence of learning is demonstrated when students use conventional spelling as they write for a variety of purposes.

net site, students create word searches for their spelling words, download the puzzles, and then trade puzzles with their classmates, thus getting extra practice in a gamelike paper-and-pencil format. For additional activities, look at the Geocities Puzzle Ring site (http://www.geocities.com/WestHollywood/2555/puzzlrng.html) for 155 word search and word puzzle Internet sites.

In a discussion of the reasons some students are good spellers and others are not, Smith and Davies (1996) explain that spelling ability is related to the amount and variety of students' writing. It follows, then, that spelling lessons will be more meaningful when they include some words from students' own writing. In individualizing students' word lists, you ensure that students learn to spell the words they need to communicate as authors. But before students can use words when writing, they need to know word meanings. In fact, the good spellers in your classroom not only know how to spell words conventionally, but they also know the meanings of the words they spell. Hence, skill development in vocabulary, the topic of the next section, has a significant impact on the quality of your classroom literacy program and on students' ability to communicate effectively.

Using Technology to Develop Vocabulary

When Tyler stops playing a video game, he uses a memory card to save his progress, removes the CD, and puts the controller away. Everyday words such as *memory card*, *CD*, *modem*, *e-mail*, and *hypermedia* were not around in the 1950s. As new words have joined our language, others have taken on new meanings. For instance, the mouse that students talk about in your classroom is attached to a computer, and it is not a furry little rodent. As some words gradually make their way into our language, others words fall into disuse and, ultimately, disappear. Any high school student who has read *Macbeth* in Shakespeare's original language has observed this phenomenon firsthand.

The strength of a fluent reading vocabulary and the ability to understand what is being read are interdependent (Ruddell, 1999). For vocabulary to support reading and writing, students need to use words, understand concepts, and appreciate how words are related to the content being studied (Vacca & Vacca, 1998). This type of in-depth vocabulary knowledge develops as a consequence of many opportunities to hear, see, and use words in mind-engaging ways. This is where we see technology making a significant contribution to students' vocabulary growth. Technology brings to your classroom the capability of connecting dynamic, interactive vocabulary learning with reading, writing, spelling, and content area learning.

Graves, Juel, and Graves (1999) say that a solid vocabulary program includes (1) wide reading, (2) teaching individual words, (3) showing students how to learn words on their own, and (4) helping students develop an appreciation of words and the motivation to learn and use them. To this we would add a fifth component: extensive opportunities to interact with words in multiple mediums and in multiple ways. First and foremost, students should read all sorts of material, and they should read everyday. Tyler's fascination with video games does not preclude reading books routinely and often. And, in fact, Tyler is an avid reader who is currently enjoying books in the Goosebumps series.

When Tyler was in the early grades, the words he learned to read were already in his speaking vocabulary, so the goal was to associate known spoken words with unrecognized written words. Now, many of the new words Tyler meets in print on a daily basis are not likely to be in his speaking vocabulary. Phonics is not particularly helpful when identifying totally new words—words that are not known in spoken or written form—because pronunciation does not lead to meaningful recognition.

Examples of Vocabulary Software

As students progress in school, they encounter a plethora of new words in novels, subject-matter textbooks, and magazine articles. Even though most of these new words are not in readers' speaking vocabularies, readers often are able to identify their meaning by using context clues. The strategy of using context clues is extremely important, and, therefore, students benefit from the chance to practice using context clues. Many software programs give students opportunities to use context when determining word identity. This is typically done by the use of cloze sentences that call for the use of context clues to determine the identity of missing words. *Carmen Sandiego Word Detective* is an example of a software program for grades 4–7 that combines cloze sentences with spelling (see Figure 10). In the Carmen Sandiego Spellanyzer activity,

Figure 10
Screen From *Carmen Sandiego Word Detective*

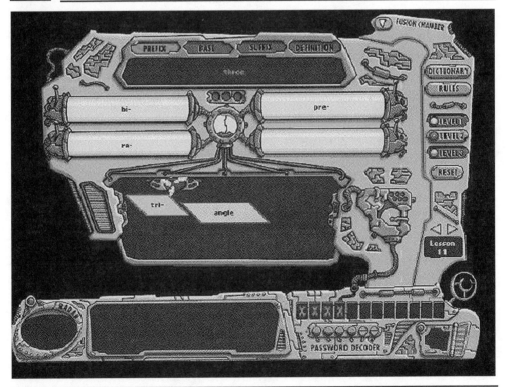

Courtesy of *Carmen Sandiego Word Detective*, ©1999 The Learning Company and its licensors. All rights reserved.

students spell words that are contextualized in cloze sentences and have access to a dictionary for word meaning should they need more word-specific information. This activity, which Vacca and Vacca (1998) call a context puzzle, has the advantage of encouraging students to use two sources of information—context and spelling—to identify and learn new words.

Meaningful multiletter chunks—the prefixes, suffixes, and root words of our language—are another important resource for developing vocabulary, and they are a more efficient way to identify words than sounding out letter sounds (Fox, 2000). As it turns out, many of the new words students encounter are related to known words through prefixes and suffixes (Nagy, Diakidoy, & Anderson, 1993). For example, students who know the word *move*, and who understand how prefixes and suffixes contribute to word meaning, will understand that *move*, *removable*, and *movement* belong to the same family. Even seldom-used words, such as *unceremoniously* and *unconventionally*, are not obstacles for students who know how prefixes and suffixes affect word meaning (Nagy, Diakidoy, & Anderson, 1993). Therefore, it is important to support students as they acquire a full understanding of the way our language uses prefixes and suffixes to augment or change word meaning. The Fusion Chamber activity in *Carmen Sandiego Word Detective* is an example of a software activity to develop knowledge of prefixes and suffixes. In playing this game, students identify the meaning of a root word, "fuse" root words with prefixes or suffixes, and identify the meaning of the new word. For another example, look at the Word Rodeo activity in *Kid Phonics 2*.

Understanding syntax, or grammatical structure, is also important for developing a rich vocabulary. Students who understand the structure of English sentences make logical inferences about word meanings when reading and construct meaningful messages when writing. Typically, this understanding is developed through extensive writing, and we support this approach for gaining insight into word usage. We encourage our students to use word processors whenever possible. Word processing makes editing more accessible and, when programs check grammar, students perceive syntactic inconsistencies. However, when students use grammar checkers, teacher supervision is necessary to ensure that students understand the syntactic structure of language. Even with extensive writing, some students benefit from extra practice in identifying the common parts of speech, and technology is beneficial here, too.

The Micropix activity in *Carmen Sandiego Word Detective* illustrates how technology can increase students' opportunities to identify and use grammatical function when reading. This practice activity requires that students complete cloze passages in which different parts of speech are deleted. Passages pertaining to the storyline are interesting and illustrate how words serve different grammatical functions. The software program *Word Munchers Deluxe* gives students practice in identifying nouns, verbs, adjectives, adverbs, pronouns, and prepositions. Cloze sentences illustrate the use of words in context, thus creating a bridge to meaning. Another way to use technology to reinforce and extend knowledge of the grammatical function of words is to visit Internet sites that ask students to use different parts of speech to create zany stories. In creating zany stories, students write words, such as nouns, verbs, and adjectives, and then the words are integrated into a pre-existing storyline. Look at FunBrain (http://www.funbrain.com/kidscenter.html) for Wacky Tales, a section that gives players a choice of story topics; Games, especially Wacky Words, on the Big Busy House home page (http://harperchildrens.com); and Plaid Libs on the Bill's Games site (http://www.billsgames.com).

A Vocabulary Unit

In our Egypt unit in Figure 11, *Carmen Sandiego Word Detective* and *Word Munchers Deluxe* are used to enhance and extend vocabulary development by giving students practice recognizing meaningful multiletter chunks in words, grammatical function, and spelling. In using the *Carmen Sandiego Word Detective* software, students travel to different sites around the world in search of word clues that will rescue captured secret agents and, ultimately, save the planet from Carmen's scheme to destroy language. Because this software program allows you to customize word lists, it can be adapted to reinforce the word knowledge that is unique to particular teaching units, students, and classrooms. *Word Munchers Deluxe* uses a gamelike practice format that is appropriate for students in first through fifth grades. In grades 3 through 5, the vocabulary activity consists of identifying synonyms and antonyms. Synonyms and antonyms help students understand the connections among words, which in turn helps them comprehend what they read. An added advantage of *Word Munchers Deluxe* is the student option to play with Troggles, creatures that gobble up the Word Munchers character. The presence of Troggles moves the action much faster, which helps students develop fluency—the quick and accurate recognition of words and their parts of speech.

By the time students are in high school, their fluent reading vocabulary numbers somewhere between 25,000 and 50,000 words (Nagy & Anderson, 1984). This impressive number is acquired, in part, through the use of self-teaching strategies that help students identify and remember words. Self-teaching strategies include the use of phonics, spelling, contextual clues, and meaningful multiletter chunks, to mention a few. Having excellent word-identification and vocabulary strategies is one thing; using these strategies is another thing altogether.

Motivation, according to Nagy and Anderson (1984), is as important a factor as any other characteristic of your classroom literacy program. Students are more likely to be motivated to learn words when words (1) are intriguing and used by adults, (2) convey strong emotions or when mispronunciations could be embarrassing, (3) have immediate utility, and (4) are in common use among students' peers (Ruddell, 1999). Learning words in the context of challenging games, as in *Word Munchers Deluxe*, and competitive quests, as in *Carmen Sandiego Word Detective*, holds students' attention while engaging them in learning and using words.

The Egyptian focus of the unit described in Figure 11 is consistent with the study of nations on the African continent, which is part of an intermedi-

Figure 11
Unit Plan for Teaching Vocabulary

Theme:	Egypt
Objectives:	To help fourth and fifth graders develop the vocabulary needed for reading and writing; use new words when speaking and writing; and learn about Egypt and the pyramids.
Materials:	Software programs: *Carmen Sandiego Word Detective*, *Word Munchers Deluxe*, and books on Egypt and *Destination: Pyramids* or print encyclopedias.
Activities:	1. Use reference books, *Destination: Pyramids*, Internet sites, and a CD-ROM encyclopedia to learn about ancient Egypt, pyramids, and mummies.
	2. Customize words lists in *Carmen Sandiego Word Detective* to develop vocabulary.
	3. Review and teach, when appropriate, parts of speech.
	4. Use the games in *Word Munchers Deluxe* for practice recognizing in parts of speech.
	5. Visit Internet sites in which students create crazy stories by writing words representing different parts of speech.
	6. Have students work with a learning partner to create and publish an Egyptian travel brochure.
Assessment:	Learning is evident when students use new words when writing for a variety of purposes, fluently recognize new words when reading, and use new words when speaking.

ate (grades 4–5) social studies curriculum. This unit could be broadened by including Tanzania, a site visited in the Carmen Sandiego program, as well as other African nations. Extend study to other parts of the globe by inviting students and their learning partners to decide for themselves where they would like to travel. In doing this, students might choose a nation (or city) featured in the books they are reading or one of the sites in *Carmen Sandiego Word Detective*—London, Morocco, Tanzania, or the Indian Ocean, for example. When using this unit, the language arts can be integrated with content areas by coordinating sites studied with social studies; customizing spelling lists using words from nations studied; learning about map reading as a part of travel journal writing; and using mathematics when estimating miles traveled, hotel and meal costs, and the exchange rates of foreign currency.

Final Remarks

This chapter describes how to use technology as a mainstay to support skill development. In selecting technology, consider the needs of the students you teach and ways to integrate skill development across the curriculum, as demonstrated in our unit plans. Your school may already have a variety of software from which you can choose. So, before you purchase, look at the resources that are available in your school and use those portions of software programs that meet students' needs and support your classroom literacy program.

Students such as Tyler who are comfortable with computers and video games understand how to interact successfully with skill-development software programs and skills-oriented Internet sites. Technology is such an integral part of the lives of students that they cannot recall a time when interactive video games, learning software, and Internet sites were not available. These same students bring to the instructional uses of technology a curiosity and willingness to learn that evolves from their everyday experiences. Technology has changed the way students get information and the way students communicate. E-mail and chatrooms are replacing the telephone; Web sites for storytelling are resurrecting an important oral tradition. Technology has changed the way we think about teaching, too. In using technology, we can provide a level of individualization for our students that was not possible in years past without long hours of planning; in so doing, we can enhance the student-centered focus of our classrooms.

The power of technology is its ability to bring together all the language arts—speaking, listening, reading, and writing—in a seamless curriculum that flows naturally across the content areas. Now more than ever, we as teachers have choices and options that take us and our students far beyond our classroom walls as we learn about language, develop the skills that support literacy, and become global citizens.

References

Adams, M.J. (1990). *Beginning to read: Thinking and learning about print.* Cambridge, MA: MIT Press.

Barker, T.A., & Torgesen, J.K. (1995). An evaluation of computer assisted instruction in phonological awareness with below average readers. *Journal of Educational Computing Research, 13*(1), 89–103.

Bailey's Book House (Version 2.0) [Computer software]. (1995). Redmond, WA: Edmark.

Baumann, J.F., Hoffman, J.V., Moon, J., & Duffy-Hester, A.M. (1998). Where are teachers' voices in the phonics/whole language debate? Results from a survey of U.S. elementary classroom teachers. *The Reading Teacher, 51,* 636–650.

Carmen Sandiego Word Detective (Version 1.0) [Computer software]. (1997). Cambridge, MA: Brøderbund/The Learning Company.

Carver, R.P. (1998). Predicting reading level in grades 1 and 6 from listening level and decoding level: Testing theory relevant to the simple view of reading. *Reading and Writing: An Interdisciplinary Journal, 10,* 121–154.

Chew, J. (1997). Traditional phonics: What it is and what it is not. *Journal of Research in Reading, 20,* 171–183.

Cramer, R.L. (1998). *The spelling connection: Integrating reading, writing, and spelling instruction.* New York: Guilford Press.

Curious George Learns Phonics (Version 1.0) [Computer software]. (1997). Somerville, MA: Houghton Mifflin.

Daisy's Castle (Version 1.0) [Computer software]. (1993). Scotts Valley, CA: Great Wave Software.

DaisyQuest (Version 1.0) [Computer software]. (1992). Scotts Valley, CA: Great Wave Software.

Destination: Pyramids (Version 1.0) [Computer software]. (1996). Redmond, WA: Edmark.

Elmo's Reading (Version 1.0) [Computer software]. (1998). Cambridge, MA: Creative Wonders/The Learning Company.

Foster, K.C., Erickson, G.C., Foster, D.F., Brinkman, D., & Torgesen, J.K. (1994). Computer administered instruction in phonological awareness: Evaluation of the DaisyQuest program. *Journal of Research and Development in Education, 27,* 126–137.

Fox, B.J. (2000). *Word identification strategies: Phonics from a new perspective* (2nd ed.). Columbus, OH: Merrill.

Gentry, J.R. (1997). *My kid can't spell.* Portsmouth, NH: Heinemann.

Goswami, U. (1998). Rime-based coding in early reading development in English: Orthographic analogies and rime neighborhoods. In C. Hulme & R.M. Joshi (Eds.), *Reading and spelling: Development and disorders* (pp. 69–86). Mahwah, NJ: Erlbaum.

Graves, M.F., Juel, C., & Graves, B.B. (1999). *Teaching reading in the 21st century*. Boston: Allyn & Bacon.

Green Eggs and Ham (Version 1.0) [Computer software]. (1996). Cambridge, MA: Brøderbund/The Learning Company.

Heilman, A.W., Blair, T.R., & Rupley, W.H. (1998). *Principles and practices of teaching reading* (9th ed.). Columbus, OH: Merrill.

Heinich, R., Molenda, M., Russell, J.D., & Smaldino, S.E. (1999). *Instructional media and technology for learning* (6th ed.). Columbus, OH: Merrill.

HyperStudio [Computer software]. (1999). El Cajon, CA: Roger Wagner Publishing.

I Love Spelling (Version 1.01) [Computer software]. (1997). New York: DK Interactive Learning.

Jones, K.M., Torgesen, J.K., & Sexton, M.A. (1987). Using computer guided practice to increase decoding fluency in learning disabled children: A study using the hint and hunt I program. *Journal of Learning Disabilities, 20*, 122–128.

Juel, C., Griffith, P.L., & Gough, P.B. (1986). Acquisition of literacy: A longitudinal study of children in first and second grade. *Journal of Educational Psychology, 78*, 243–255.

JumpStart 1st Grade Reading (Version 1.1) [Computer software]. (1997). Torrance, CA: Knowledge Adventure.

Kid Phonics 1 (Version 1.0) [Computer software]. (1994). Torrance, CA: Davidson & Associates.

Kid Phonics 2 (Version 1.0) [Computer software]. (1996). Torrance, CA: Davidson & Associates.

Kid Works Deluxe [Computer software]. (1997). Torrance, CA: Knowledge Adventure.

Leap Into Phonics (Version 1.0) [Computer software]. (1998). Evanston, IL: Leap Into Learning.

Let's Go Read! An Island Adventure (Version 1.02) [Computer software]. (1998). Redmond, WA: Edmark.

Let's Go Read! An Ocean Adventure (Version 1.0) [Computer software]. (1998). Redmond, WA: Edmark.

Leu, D.J., & Kinzer, C.K. (1999). *Effective literacy instruction: K–8* (4th ed.). Upper Saddle River, NJ: Prentice Hall.

Lundberg, I., Frost, J., & Petersen, O. (1988). Effects of an extensive program for stimulating phonological awareness in preschool children. *Reading Research Quarterly, 23*, 263–284.

Madeline 1st & 2nd Grade Reading (Version 1.0) [Computer software]. (1998). Cambridge, MA: Creative Wonders/The Learning Company.

Matthew, K. (1997). A comparison of the influence of interactive CD-ROM storybooks and traditional print storybooks on reading comprehension. *Journal of Research on Computing in Education, 29*, 263–275.

McBride-Chang, C., Wagner, R.K., & Chang, L. (1997). Growth modeling of phonological awareness. *Journal of Educational Psychology, 89*, 621–630.

Moeller, B., & Hupert, N. (1997). Reading in the age of multimedia. *Electronic Learning, 8*, 80.

Morrison, G.R., Lowther, D.L., & DeMuelle, L. (1999). *Integrating computer technology into the classroom*. Upper Saddle River, NJ: Prentice Hall.

Nagy, W.E., & Anderson, R.C. (1984). How many words are there in printed English? *Reading Research Quarterly, 19,* 304–330.

Nagy, W.E., Diakidoy, I.A.N., & Anderson, R.C. (1993). The acquisition of morphology: Learning the contribution of suffixes to the meanings of derivatives. *Journal of Reading Behavior, 25,* 155–170.

Nicholson, T. (1997). Closing the gap on reading failure: Social background, phonemic awareness, and learning to read. In B. Blachman (Ed.), *Foundations of reading acquisition and dyslexia: Implications for early intervention* (pp. 381–407). Mahwah, NJ: Erlbaum.

Paint, Write & Play! (Version 1.0) [Computer software]. (1996). Cambridge, MA: MECC/The Learning Company.

Reader Rabbit's Interactive Reading Journey (Version 1.1) [Computer software]. (1996). Cambridge, MA: The Learning Company.

Reading Mansion (Version 1.0.2) [Computer software]. (1998). Scotts Valley, CA: Great Wave Software.

Richard Scarry's Best Reading Program Ever (Version 1.0) [Computer software]. (1996). New York: Simon & Schuster Interactive.

Ruddell, R.B. (1999). *Teaching children to read and write: Becoming an influential teacher* (2nd ed.). Boston: Allyn & Bacon.

Rupley, W.H., & Willson, V.L. (1997). Relationship between comprehension and components of word recognition: Support for developmental shifts. *Journal of Research and Development in Education, 30,* 255–260.

Seuss, Dr. (1957). *The cat in the hat.* New York: Random House.

Seuss, Dr. (1973). *Green eggs and ham.* New York: Random House.

Smith, A., & Davies, A. (1996). *Wordsmithing: A spelling program for grades 3–8.* Winnipeg, MB: Peguis.

Smith, N.B. (1934). *American reading instruction.* New York: Silver, Burdett.

Snow, C.E., Burns, M.S., & Griffin, P. (1998). *Preventing reading difficulties in young children.* Washington, DC: National Academy Press.

Spellbound (Version 1.1) [Computer software]. (1996). Cambridge, MA: MECC/The Learning Company.

Spellevator Plus (Version 1.0) [Computer software]. (1996). Cambridge, MA: MECC/The Learning Company.

Spelling Spree (Version 1.0) [Computer software]. (1999). Boston: Houghton Mifflin.

Spelling Toolkit Plus (Version 1.0) [Computer software]. (1997). Cambridge, MA: MECC/The Learning Company.

Sugar & Snails (Version 2.0) [Computer software]. (1994). Victoria, BC: Entrex Software.

Super Solvers Spellbound (Version 1.1) [Computer software]. (1994). Cambridge, MA: MECC/The Learning Company.

SuperSonic Phonics (Version 1.0) [Computer software]. (1997) North Billerica, MA: Curriculum Associates.

Torgesen, G.E. (1998). Instructional interventions for children with reading disabilities. In B.K. Shapiro, P.J. Accardo, & A.J. Capute (Eds.), *Specific reading disability: A view of the spectrum.* Timonium, MD: York Press.

Torgesen, J.K., & Barker, T.A. (1995). Computers as aids in the prevention and remediation of reading disabilities. *Learning Disabilities Quarterly, 18,* 76–87.

Vacca, R.T., & Vacca, J.L. (1998). *Content area reading: Literacy and learning across the curriculum* (6th ed.). New York: Longman.

Vandervelden, M.C., & Siegel, L.S. (1995). Phonological recoding and phoneme awareness in early literacy: A developmental approach. *Reading Research Quarterly, 30,* 854–875.

Word Munchers Deluxe (Version 1.02) [Computer software]. (1996). Cambridge, MA: MECC/The Learning Company.

CHAPTER 4

Using Technology
for Reading Development

SHELLEY B. WEPNER AND LUCINDA C. RAY

irst-grade teacher Mrs. Kinsey is a collector who constantly brings all types of new materials to her classroom. When you walk into her classroom, you immediately see her collection of books, magazines, audiotapes, videotapes, and software. Her use of technology for instructional activities is evident because of the visual display of directions for working with different software packages and the number of students working at the computers. Because of her persistent requests for technology to her building administrator, she has five computers placed permanently in her classroom. Her classroom has become a model for the administrators and board members in a position to make decisions about additional technological acquisitions for other teachers in the district. Thus, Mrs. Kinsey is very careful to document her use of computers with her students. She is equally conscientious about documenting students' responses to their computer activities.

With the five computers placed in her reading center, Mrs. Kinsey is able to have students read and work with an electronic book each day. Five CD-ROM books, loaded into the computers, are two of Marc Brown's books, *Arthur's Teacher Trouble* and *Arthur's Reading Race*; a Dr. Seuss book, *Green Eggs and Ham*; a Mercer Mayer book, *Just Grandma and Me Deluxe*, and a Tomie dePaola book, *The Art Lesson*. Students follow the procedure Mrs. Kinsey has established. First, they read the book as is; then they read the book in animated fashion; next, they complete the activities that accompany the book or that Mrs. Kinsey has created to build comprehension. Finally, students know that any book read electronically must be taken home in printed form to read to a parent or guardian for the next day. Mrs. Kinsey has students work with a new book every week or two.

Mrs. Kinsey's whole-group instruction with the district's basal series is similar to other teachers'. She uses a motivational strategy to introduce the story, has students read silently and then orally in pairs, and then uses questions and activities to promote students' comprehension of the story. Her small-group instruction differs, though. Rather than have students work with printed worksheets, she has a full collection of software that focuses on vocabulary, phonics, and other reading skills (see Chapter 3 for examples of such software). Five pairs of students go to their computers and log on for skill development. They work for one week at a time on a specific skill they need to develop. Mrs. Kinsey works with the other groups of students to teach new skills or to reinforce the skills developed with the software.

Mrs. Kinsey's growing integration of technology into her instruction is having an impact on both students and parents. Parents are beginning to request Mrs. Kinsey's class for their sons and daughters because her students' standardized achievement test scores are the highest in the first grade. She attributes the test score improvement to her students' increased engagement with reading, both with electronic and traditional text.

Fifth-grade teacher Mr. Xavier is revising some of his lesson plans for an upcoming language arts/social studies unit. He knows his students need daily reading and writing activities. He wants his students to write for real audiences and to stretch their ability to think critically about what they read. The materials and projects he usually incorporates in this second semester unit include reading two survival novels, Jean Craighead George's *Julie of the Wolves* and Gary Paulsen's *Hatchet*. In addition to the language arts focus on comprehension of the novels, Mr. Xavier has designed a geography unit that includes climate and map studies so that students can evaluate the accuracy of the portrayal of the setting in the two novels. The unit culminates in a written and oral presentation of findings.

Over the last several years, Mr. Xavier has begun to incorporate technology into this teaching unit. Last year, he used the software *Reading Galaxy* as a way of introducing the novels *Hatchet* and *Julie of the Wolves*. The software program is designed to stimulate interest in reading, using a game-show format to present character, setting, initial conflicts, and author backgrounds for each of 30 popular middle school novels. He assigns the two parts of the program that relate to his novel unit as independent work in the learning center at the back of the classroom. He knows that it takes each student about 15 minutes to rotate through the game segments during the week before he is ready to pass out the novels. Last year he discovered that students' game play would provide a common background for his own introduction of the survival unit and increase students' readiness and motivation as they began to read the books themselves.

This year, Mr. Xavier has added the use of maps, both on the Internet and on CD-ROM. They are renewable resources that supplement his classroom supply of maps. He can print the electronic maps with various levels of detail. His school has a live Internet connection available in the resource center, and he sends different students to check daily weather conditions in Alaska and to evaluate the accuracy of the novels' depictions. He has discovered that his students read intently when they are involved in this kind of detective work, taking accurate notes and comparing information. He points out to his students that successful writers, even fiction writers, need to understand and include accurate information in their work.

Last year, Mr. Xavier used the Internet to locate a school in Alaska that was willing to become keypals (e-mail penpals) and correspond with his fifth graders. This year he and the Alaska teacher agreed to continue the project with their new classes of students. The Alaska students have read Wilson Rawls' *Where the Red Fern Grows*, and are as eager to learn about the Ozark Mountains in Mr. Xavier's state of Oklahoma as his students are to learn about Alaska.

This year, Mr. Xavier plans to use the Internet for additional author research by using the Web sites of the two authors (http://www.jeancraigheadgeorge. com and http://www.garypaulsen.com), and by gathering and downloading photographs of Alaska that will be used in students' printed or electronic culminating projects, oral reports, and papers.

Both Mrs. Kinsey and Mr. Xavier have been developing their comfort with technology for several years. The technology components of their teaching plans were added one piece at a time as each teacher became aware of resources that matched curricular goals and became comfortable with managing the technology use in the classroom.

Rationale for Using Technology to Enhance Literacy

These two classrooms provide detailed snapshots of teachers enhancing literacy development with technology. Mr. Xavier has noticed that his students are reading more thoroughly and analytically as they compare a novel's setting with daily weather patterns over the Internet. They also are writing more each day because their journal-writing time is now spent e-mailing messages to their keypals about what they are reading and learning. Some students are asking for additional time to explore information about the ecology and wildlife of the regions and to improve and edit their final projects because they want to send them to their keypals.

When Mrs. Kinsey reflects on her students' use of the technology in her classroom, she finds a high degree of involvement in, and support for, their emerging literacy skills and reading pleasure. She observes them selecting the print copies of the electronic books and reading them independently, away from the computer. She also sees lively interactions with the electronic versions, noting students spontaneously reading aloud, along with the computer, and conferring with reading partners about story events and characters.

A growing body of research findings indicate that technology serves as an effective means of engaging and motivating students to want to succeed (Fogarty, 1998; Hay, 1996; Kirkpatrick & Cuban, 1998; Strong, 1982). Hay (1996) found that fourth graders who usually were tense and worried when faced with the printed page were relaxed and smiling when using the computer. She also found that those typically unexcited about reading were motivated to succeed with a technology-based reading curriculum.

Technology also serves as a means for improving student performance. A study from the state of New York shows that in classrooms with more computers, student academic performance improves ("Study Shows Technology-Achievement Link," 1997). Student achievement outcomes consistently favor computer-using classrooms (Hyland, 1998; Kirkpatrick & Cuban, 1998). Reading software systems, in particular, improve students' performance on standardized test scores (Clariana, 1994; Hasselbring, Goin, Taylor, Bottge, & Daley, 1997; Wilson, 1993). Students with learning disabilities appear to improve in reading comprehension and vocabulary acquisition from computer-assisted instruction (Shiah, Mastropieri, & Scruggs, 1995). Moreover, access to online resources, activities, and communication helps elementary students perform better on student projects (Follansbee, Hughes, Pisha, & Stahl, 1997).

As Bracey (1992) contends, emerging technologies actually challenge the traditional view of literacy as interacting with printed text in a linear fashion. Students now have many technologies available to them on their desktops and through the Internet that enable them to navigate through information and ideas in a recursive fashion. Immediate access to icons, images, animations, voice, and sound supports students' comprehension of text by developing

Using Technology for Reading Development

schemata about the content on the screen. Written and spoken prompts built into the programs guide students as they interact with text.

Mrs. Kinsey and Mr. Xavier's informal observations corroborate with the research findings that the motivational, multisensory, and interactive features of technology help students comprehend the text they encounter.

Types of Technology for Reading Development

In the following section we focus on three categories of technology for reading development: electronic books, learning adventures, and reading comprehension and assessment software. We describe each category for its contribution to students' literacy development with a general focus on comprehension. We define comprehension simply as an active process of constructing meaning by using prior knowledge, previous experience, and information from the text to interact with the text (see Ruddell, 1994; Tierney & Pearson, 1994).

Electronic Books

Electronic books use popular children's trade titles in a multimedia format with original illustrations. Sometimes referred to as a variation of lap reading, electronic books are a powerful tool for introducing students to a rich array of literature and to the imaginative pleasure embedded in the reading process. Students can have the book read aloud, have the text and graphics animated with sound and voices, and receive help to enhance comprehension and recall. Because of the computer's infinite patience, electronic books allow students to revisit the text without teacher assistance. Electronic books usually focus on narrative text for emerging and developing readers, and expository text for developing and independent readers in grades 3 and beyond. As animated versions of narrative texts, electronic books heighten attention to the plot, the setting, and the characters. As narrated examples of expository text, electronic books broaden students' exposure to content with layers of information offered on every screen.

The use of electronic books has shown benefits to reading skills and reading development (Matthew, 1995; McKenna, Reinking, Labbo, & Watkins, 1996; Miller, Blackstock, & Miller, 1994; Stine, 1993). Students who use elec-

Wepner and Ray

tronic books and spend time interacting with the animated features demonstrate an ability to recount the story events (Underwood & Underwood, 1996).

Electronic books can be used for recreational reading, thematic units, author studies, and topical studies with instructional frameworks such as K-W-L, Directed Reading Activity, and Directed Reading–Thinking Activity.

Examples of electronic books: CD-ROMs and Internet sites

There are many versions and interpretations of electronic books ranging from those that simply put the book on the screen with minimal animation to those that expand the book with an extensive array of additional features. An example of the latter is Marc Brown's *Arthur's Teacher Trouble* with its 24 screen pages of the storybook. This storybook follows the main character, Arthur, through a school spelling competition. Underwood and Underwood (1996) describe this program as follows: Each screen page has part of the text of the story displayed and read aloud. A rich illustration from the text also is displayed. The user may then interact with both words and illustrations by a mouse click. Clicking a word results in its pronunciation. Clicking on a feature of the illustration results in some type of animation. Characters may provide additional dialogue or perform actions, and objects such as toys and cookies come alive, adding songs or actions.

Another example of an electronic book with nearly every screen feature programmed for some type of animation is *Just Grandma and Me Deluxe*. In addition to animated characters and objects throughout the story, *Just Grandma and Me Deluxe* reads the book in four languages (English, French, Spanish, and German) and offers a sticker activity for each page to teach vocabulary related to the picture. (A "sticker activity" is an interactive picture and pronouncing dictionary that allows students to paste each picture onto the screen.) Students play in the sand with animated beach tools to further explore elements of the beach, the setting of the story (see Figure 1 on the next page for sample screen).

Other examples of electronic books include Mercer Mayer's *Little Monster at School*; Marc Brown's *Arthur's Reading Race*, *Arthur's Birthday Deluxe*, and *Arthur's Computer Adventure*; Dr. Seuss's *The Cat in the Hat* and *Dr. Seuss's ABC*; Janell Cannon's *Stellaluna*; and Kevin Henkes's *Sheila Rae, the Brave*.

A series of CD-ROM electronic books that includes biographies for young children is reproduced by Troll Associates. Each package contains a CD-ROM version of the book and six printed books. Even with its minimal animation, this line of software defines highlighted words, asks questions about each page, creates a photo album for a sequencing activity, offers a time line of

Figure 1
Screen From *Just Grandma and Me Deluxe*

fence

chimney

door

leaves

nest

knothole

flower

stickers

English   French   Spanish   German

1

print

We went to the beach, just Grandma and me.

events, and enables students to write their own version of each page. Some of the titles of the 10 biographies include *Young Helen Keller: Woman of Courage*, *Young Harriet Tubman: Freedom Fighter*, *Young Orville & Wilbur Wright: First to Fly*, *Young Abraham Lincoln: Log-Cabin President*, and *Young Jackie Robinson: Baseball Hero*.

Another series of CD-ROMs that offers expository text is Scholastic's Smart Books, designed for students in the middle elementary grades. These electronic books provide tools for students to use as they interact with the text and offer the kind of background and context materials traditionally posted on bulletin boards and placed in learning centers to extend the reading experience. Two features characterize the Smart Books series: Smart Spots include multimedia annotations of primary source materials, time lines, speech excerpts, and actual news footage; Smart Tools include the ability to look up

Wepner and Ray

words, mark pages, highlight passages, post sticky notes with ideas, and write and publish one's own stories. Titles include *Titanic, Malcolm X: By Any Means Necessary, If Your Name Was Changed at Ellis Island*, and *Favorite Greek Myths*.

Electronic books are available on the Web, but they do not yet offer students the high level of interactivity that most CD-ROM versions do. Most of the stories are told in a linear fashion with little opportunity for the interactive play that CD-ROM electronic books afford. One site with electronic books (http://www.candlelightstories.com) offers stories such as *Thumbelina* and *Rumpelstiltskin*. This site links to additional storybooks with titles such as *The Lion King* (http://disney.go.com/Kids/lkstory), *Pochahontas* (http://disney.go.com/Kids/pocastory), and *The Hunchback of Notre Dame* (http://disney.go.com/DisneyBooks/new/hunch/story/hb_1.html).

A Web site that offers children's stories from books, some by well-known authors and others by new authors, is The Children's Literature Web Guide (http://www.acs.ucalgary.ca/~dkbrown/storcont.html). A site that sends students to storybook listings of nursery rhymes, fairytales, adventures, fables, and spooky tales is called The Realm of Books & Dreams (http://www.bconnex.net/~mbuchana/realms/page1/index.html). Berit's Best Sites for Children (http://www.cochran.com/theodore/beritsbest) is a directory of sites for kids up to age 12 that includes some stories already published. The aforementioned sites need to be assessed for their reading level in order to use them most appropriately. A site for more sophisticated readers, American Literary Classics (http://www.americanliterature.com), offers a chapter a day of classics such as Louise May Alcott's *Little Women*, Stephen Crane's *The Red Badge of Courage*, and Mark Twain's *The Adventures of Tom Sawyer*. Because there is such enormous variation in the quality of material posted on the Web as electronic books, we recommend that you use sites with stories that already have been published, are current, and are created and maintained by recognizable publishers, authors, or academic institutions.

Learning Adventures

Learning adventures offer students opportunities to build their vocabulary and comprehension as they work their way through a set of challenges. Learning adventures are designed to challenge students to explore and think about different environments and events. Students' higher level thinking skills frequently are used to solve a puzzle, find a clue, or get to the next level of the adventure.

Learning adventures for emerging and developing readers often use a main character who talks to students throughout the entire adventure. An example at this level is the software *The New Katie's Farm*. The main character, Katie, gives oral directions to students as they explore the sounds and eating habits of animals in a barn and play dress up with the same animals in a farmhouse. Students learn how to play with and care for real animals without having to read. Yet, for those inclined to read, a minibook about each of the animals is read aloud to supplement the farm adventure.

Learning adventures are particularly useful for independent readers because they engage students in active, fun-filled reading. Students are not focused specifically on the reading process, yet they need to use their knowledge and strategies to succeed. As we have noted, electronic books provide significant support for emergent and developing readers. However, for older students, the extended text of nonpicture books has been more difficult for CD-ROM publishers to adapt to the electronic environment. Learning adventures for middle and upper elementary students do require, support, and encourage students' developing reading proficiency.

The popular Carmen Sandiego series (for example, *Where in the World Is Carmen Sandiego?*, *Where in the USA Is Carmen Sandiego?*, and *Where in Time Is Carmen Sandiego?*) involves third- through eighth-grade students in detective adventures. Players must gather clues and draw conclusions about a thief's identity and about the geographic or historical destination to which the thief has just escaped. Because clues are spoken and appear as text on the computer screen, students are able to build both reading and listening skills, are exposed to language that stretches their receptive vocabulary (vocabulary used in silent reading and listening), and are rewarded for reading and listening carefully as they draw conclusions. In addition, the Carmen series is well known for its clever use of puns, plays on words, and other literary devices that provide humor while drawing students' attention to the multiple meanings of words.

In another learning adventure, *Oregon Trail* (see Figure 2 for a sample screen) and others in the Trail series (*Amazon*, *Yukon*, *Africa*, and *MayaQuest*) engage students in an extended simulation activity. Students are involved in reading, strategic thinking, planning, and decision making as they move along the chosen trail. Progress and gameplay rely on the active engagement of students.

In both of these learning adventures, thoughtful and careful reading is simply part of successful gameplay. Even though comprehension questions—the

Figure 2
Screen From *Oregon Trail*

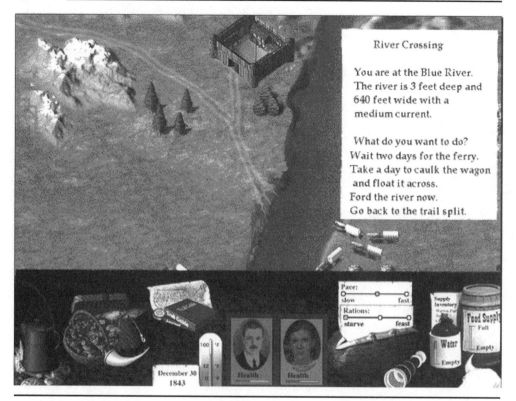

River Crossing

You are at the Blue River.
The river is 3 feet deep and
640 feet wide with a
medium current.

What do you want to do?
Wait two days for the ferry.
Take a day to caulk the wagon
and float it across.
Ford the river now.
Go back to the trail split.

bane of many a middle school reader's existence—are not part of the design of these programs, comprehension skills are the key to success with the activities.

Another benefit of multimedia learning adventures is the opportunity they offer for collaborative activities. When pairs or small teams of students work together at a computer workstation, lively discussions often take place about the meaning of clues. The visual and auditory environment of the computer screen enables teams to work together. Groups debate and agree on conclusions or strategies. Opportunities for active reading, discussion, and interpretation are inherent in collaborative involvement in these learning adventures.

Reading Comprehension and Assessment Software

A balanced reading program includes focused skill development along with immersion in whole works. Reading software in this category, used with existing reading programs, helps students develop their comprehension skills. These products typically have students read material, answer questions, and engage in activities related to the passages. Management systems often accompany these packages to monitor students' progress.

Some examples of this software genre were so popular in classrooms in the 1980s and early 1990s that their instructional frameworks were upgraded technologically for CD-ROM versions. An example at the primary level is *Tiger's Tales*, originally published in 1986 and then revised in 1995. This program is a collection of seven stories about the adventures of a cat named Tiger and his animal friends. Students make decisions throughout the stories, which change according to students' choices. Students actively participate in the story development while focusing on reading as a problem-solving activity.

An example of a classic reading comprehension software package at the elementary level is *M-ss-ng L-nks*, originally published in 1983 and revised in 1998. Designed by Carol Chomsky, Harry Chomsky, and Judah L. Schwartz, this software package challenges students to use structural cues to decipher passages. Its purpose is to help students increase their comprehension, make better use of context when reading, appreciate author style, build vocabulary, and improve spelling. Seven different puzzle formats are included that range from having all vowels hidden to having all letters hidden. The current CD-ROM version includes passages from 13 award-winning children's books (for example, E.B. White's *Charlotte's Web* and E.L. Konigsburg's *The Mixed-Up Files of Mrs. Basil E. Frankweiler*). The CD-ROM also includes passages about science on topics such as the planets and humans, and passages from an encyclopedia on topics of general interest such as ice cream, bicycles, and baseball. There also is a section that enables the teacher or students to write their own passages.

Another software package that contains reading passages is *Reading Galaxy*. This program provides motivating activities that introduce third- through eighth-grade students to 30 favorite books among middle school readers, including S.E. Hinton's *The Outsiders*, Mildred Taylor's *Roll of Thunder Hear My Cry*, Betsy Byars's *Summer of the Swans*, and Gary Paulsen's *Hatchet*. Some of the same titles in this program appear in *M-ss-ng L-nks*. *Reading Galaxy* provides just enough about each book's setting, initial conflicts, and characters to motivate students to read the entire book on their own. A game-show format quizzes students on their recall of details and main ideas in reading passages selected from the books, and of biographies of the books' authors. Students also improve their skimming and scanning techniques because they have opportunities to verify their answers by consulting the text. Text passages can be read aloud, providing support for less able readers (see Figure 3 for a sample screen).

Accelerated Reader is an extremely popular program, used widely in elementary and middle schools and libraries to track students' reading and comprehension of 22,000 trade books. Schools use this program to provide incentives for, and records of, students' free reading. Quizzes for each of the

Figure 3
Screen From *Reading Galaxy*

titles include recall of information about literary elements such as plot, setting, and characters.

Software developers also have designed comprehensive reading systems. Two examples are *WiggleWorks Plus* and *The Ribbit Collection*. These programs go beyond enrichment or supplementary activities; they move toward a central place in a teacher's reading curriculum. *WiggleWorks Plus* is designed as a complete early literacy system for grades K–2. Two types of reading material are used: (1) electronic storybooks, called WiggleWorks books, which are written specifically for the program; and (2) printed trade books available in electronic form from the publisher's anthology. Students hear the story text read aloud, record themselves reading the same text, enter their own text, hear their own text read aloud, develop word lists from the reading, and color and print their own versions of the stories. Complete lesson plans and an assessment module for the teacher are also part of the system.

The Ribbit Collection, part of the Little Planet Literacy series, offers a more multimedia-intensive approach to a comprehensive literacy system for grades K–2. This research-based program, developed in cooperation with Vanderbilt University, presents a series of video-style stories. Students are asked to sequence story segments and then retell the stories in their own words, both orally and in writing. The "anchored instruction" approach on which the program is based provides a series of language arts instructional activities derived from an "anchor story." Children hear and see the story, sequence visual segments of the story, retell the story orally, and then write about the story based on their retelling. Students' own retellings of the stories are added to the electronic library within the program, where they can be shared electronically and printed in book format. A Web site enables students to post letters about characters and stories. (This program is designed to build on young children's strengths because their oral language skills are more fully developed than their reading and writing skills.)

One advantage of a software program is its ability to provide diagnostic tools and individualized practice as well as assessment and record-keeping tools. These features are particularly important in a reading system that offers hundreds of activities and specific skill practice. *CornerStone Reading Comprehension*, for example, includes an extensive management system that lets teachers assess students, prescribe appropriate lessons from within the software, and track student progress. Diagnostic tests allow teachers to customize assignments to each student's specific strengths and weaknesses. Adaptive lessons monitor student understanding and supply needed guidance and practice. The software also is aligned to state curricula and correlated to major standardized tests. Numerous styles of printable reports are included in the management component, so teachers can track and report student progress. *CornerStone Reading Comprehension*, available for grades 3–8, focuses on strengthening basic reading skills and is particularly valuable for students with special needs.

Evaluating Reading Software for Your Instructional Needs

Software and the Internet are tools and resources, just like other media such as trade books, basal readers, Big Books, worksheets, cassette tapes, or daily newspapers. Before you select any software, you first should consider your curriculum and specific goals for your students. As Mrs. Kinsey and Mr. Xavier learned, a resource on a CD-ROM or on the Internet is only valuable when it fits within the larger context of the curriculum and provides an experience or a way of learning or interacting that is not already available in other media.

To Use or Not to Use Software

As you would for any resource, you first should define teaching and learning goals that might be accomplished with a piece of software. These goals might include

- introducing a concept or skill
- reinforcing a concept or skill
- practicing a concept or skill
- assessing a concept or skill
- providing enrichment activities
- providing resources to coordinate with an existing thematic unit
- providing resources to include as a learning center activity that can be carried out independently
- providing support for at-risk students

With your goals clearly in mind, an important second step is to consider your personal philosophy of teaching and the needs of the students who will be interacting with the software, as mentioned earlier in this book. Any software you select should reflect a philosophy in its design with which you feel comfortable. You may have students who need minimal distractions and a highly structured learning environment. You may want students to respond to their reading activities by writing. You may wish to have children read together. Or you may be looking for a way to increase students' motivation during sustained silent reading time. It is unlikely that the same software program will accomplish all of these goals, and the criteria you use to evaluate a particular software program will certainly vary, depending on which goals are most important to you.

Passing the Software Test

Figure 4 provides a checklist of software design features to consider. This checklist, representing what we have observed and learned from others about software design features (Bliss, 1998; Matthew, 1995, 1996), offers guideposts for determining whether selected software fits with your goals. There are certain assumptions that accompany this checklist:

- The software offers something special that you cannot offer with traditional instruction.

- The software accomplishes what it purports to accomplish.

- The concepts and content are accurate, developmentally appropriate, and considerate of race, age, gender, ethnicity, and disabilities.

Because the integration of technology can demand such a significant investment in time, money, and effort, we advocate no use rather than poor use of available software. Many Web sites are available for selecting software and other technology resource materials for literacy instruction. (See the textbox titled "Web Sites for Software Programs" on page 92.)

Although you have a checklist and a list of reviews, evaluating software still involves the specific needs of your students and your personal taste. Recently, at a teachers' workshop about software, we heard a wide variety of positive and negative responses to the same piece of software: "Great for kids who live in the city" "Useless to have them dress up the animals. What do they learn?" "Don't like the content of the information shared about each animal" "Think that it is a great way to explore different animal sounds" "Who is it for anyway, 4-year-olds or 8-year-olds?" These comments occurred after every demonstration. The teachers' judgments reflected their philosophies

Figure 4
Software Design Features to Consider

✔ The activities and tasks within the program are compelling enough to hold students' interest.

✔ The instructions to students are clear, concise, and easy to follow without significant adult help.

✔ The graphics and sound are high quality, are an integral part of the concepts and content taught, and are appropriate for the age level intended.

✔ The content fits into or expands beyond what students are supposed to be learning.

✔ The program stretches students' imagination and creativity beyond ordinary means.

✔ The program provides enough practice on important concepts, especially if you are looking for a program that builds skills.

✔ The program fosters interaction and cooperative activities, especially if you are looking for these kinds of activities within your classroom.

✔ The text is narrated so that students can read the book or passage independently, and the text is highlighted as it is read so that students can follow along.

✔ The program will develop with the students over the course of the year, or accommodate differing ability or age levels.

✔ Record-keeping or assessment features are built into the program, especially if this is an important issue in providing accountability for your use of technology.

✔ The publisher provides a teacher's guide, with lessons, ways to introduce the program to your students, and supplementary handout materials to assist you.

✔ A printed copy of a book on screen is available for students to use independently.

about teaching and their experiences with children, and they realized that the quality of software truly is in the eyes of the user. Even the most brilliant productions may not be useful for the needs or abilities of specific students. Only you can make that determination.

Certain thought processes need to go into evaluating a software package's value for your unique teaching environment. Look at both the content load and the skills required for using the software. If your students can read the content, it still may be difficult for them to process the concepts or perform the tasks. Alternatively, even if your students cannot read the content, there may be enough reading assistance in the program (text that is read aloud, characters that give prompts, or intuitive interface design) that they can process the content. Software programs also may serve one type of population (urban students learning about the farm), and not another. Parts of the product may be useful for all students, or different parts may be useful for different types of students. The best way to determine a product's usefulness, in whole or in part, is to watch your own students' responses to and involvement with the product. See Figure 5 for a list of ways to plan for and manage your software use.

Web Sites for Software Programs

1. The ReviewZone site (http://www.thereviewzone.com/reading-writing-index.html) features reviews of software, hardware, computer books, and cutting-edge technology for parents and teachers. Reviewer Tina Velgos, an experienced freelance technology writer and parent of two school-aged children, offers independent product reviews of each content area, including reading and writing, that are child tested and parent approved. She includes with each review the grade level, available platforms, price with lab pack options (opportunities to purchase multiple copies of a disk for multiple computers in a classroom or computer lab), and publisher information. Also included is a list of the best software packages published for each year and an alphabetized listing of CD-ROM publishers.

2. The California Instructional Technology Clearinghouse site (http://www.clearinghouse.k12.ca.us) offers instructional technology resources that support California's curriculum frameworks and standards. More than 3,000 recommendations are available using seven strands of criteria: keyword, subject, technology type (for example, CD-ROM or computer-interactive video disc), platform, language, grade level, and other criteria (for example, exemplary rating only or closed caption available). Each listing includes the necessary purchasing information, a description, support materials available, system requirements, curriculum applications, and strategies for use.

3. The BrainPlay site (http://www.brainplay.com) reviews and sells software, videos, toys, and video games. Products are organized by category (for example, reading) and by age level. Each product is reviewed and rated for its usefulness to learning, its appeal, and its ease of use. Free product demonstrations are available for downloading. This site encourages teachers and parents to write their own reviews about any of the software reviewed or sold.

4. The SuperKids Educational Software Review site (http://www.superkids.com) provides reviews of educational software by content area, news about important issues, and views of visionaries and policy makers. Each review rates the software according to its educational value, its appeal to children, and its ease of use. Reasons for each rating are given in narrative format. System requirements also are provided.

Figure 5
Considerations for Software Use

Planning Considerations

✔ Develop your own skills and confidence in using the software so that you can answer students' questions confidently.

✔ Read the manual to familiarize yourself with the software's features and to get practical ideas.

✔ Consult the teacher's guide that accompanies the school edition of the software for specific lesson plans and ideas for integrating the program.

✔ Check the publisher's Web site for assistance and ideas.

✔ Ask others who are using the software for ideas.

✔ Identify what the software can do that other instructional strategies cannot do.

✔ Stretch your own imagination for unanticipated uses of the software (for example, having students read aloud words on the screen to promote phonemic awareness).

Management Considerations

✔ Use the program with students to see how those of varying abilities interact with it.

✔ Model ways in which students could use different types of programs to get maximum use from each one's features.

✔ Create rules and a computer schedule to assist with equitable and appropriate use.

✔ Pair students appropriately so that at least one of the students is computer literate.

✔ Provide time for discussion of the software so that students have opportunities to verbalize what they are experiencing.

Web Sites as Teacher Resources

As we shared in previous sections, the Internet provides new resource opportunities for teachers of literacy, both for their own preparation and for direct use by students. Publishers' sites and distribution sites, such as the online bookstore Amazon.com (http://www.amazon.com), offer opportunities for visitors to review the books sold. Students can read reviews submitted by other readers, and they can upload and post their own reviews. Naturally, you will want to protect students' anonymity by posting reviews under the school name.

Several authors have their own Web sites; for example, Dr. Seuss (www.randomhouse.com/seussville), Marc Brown (http://www.pbs.org/wgbh/arthur), and Jean Craighead George (http://www.jeancraigheadgeorge.com). These sites provide author information, book summaries, photos, and regular updates about book-related activities or authors' speaking engagements. Students engaged in an author study may find these sites to be helpful sources of information. (See the following section for an example of an author study.)

Teachers from around the United States are using the Internet to locate resources for planning units and specific lesson plans in language arts and other content areas. Connecting Students (http://www.connectingstudents.com) provides resources and lesson plans. EDSITEment (http://edsitement.neh.gov), sponsored by the National Endowment for the Humanities and others, reviews and carefully selects top Web sites for literature. Sites such as the Scholastic Network (www.ScholasticNetwork.com) provide a wealth of language arts lessons, activities, and resources. For example, there are regular guest appearances by authors who answer student-submitted questions. In addition, some sites act as matchmaking areas for teachers who wish to set up keypals or class exchanges for their students. Classroom Connect (http://www.classroomconnect.com) hosts a popular site that many educators use to exchange lessons and contact one another to set up collaborative projects and classroom exchanges. Web66 (http://web66.coled.umn.edu) is a site open to any school in the United States that wishes to post a school Web site. Visiting this Web site will help you to locate a school and classroom with which you could set up an e-mail relationship for your students or an exchange of lessons and projects with a teacher.

Many communities, cities, and states host Web sites that are rich with local photographs, maps, and historical information. All of these resources can be accessed, printed, or downloaded to enrich the context for a particular reading activity or to support students' projects and presentations.

Instructional Plans

In this section we offer six instructional plans: one for emerging readers, three for developing readers, and two for independent readers. The software packages mentioned in this section can be used as a whole-class activity, but are best used independently or in student pairs. Additional unit and lesson ideas also are available in the software products' teacher's guides and manuals.

For Emerging Readers

Learning adventure with animals

This instructional plan helps students acquire beginning reading skills as they learn about farm life and farm animals with *The New Katie's Farm* (see

Figure 6
Instructional Plan for Learning Adventure

Objectives: To follow oral directions; acquire a sight vocabulary; use listening skills and self-discovery to experience cause-effect relationships; and learn about the habits and characteristics of farm animals.

Materials: Software package *The New Katie's Farm*; K-W-L chart; books about animals; and response journals.

Activities: 1. Discuss animals using K-W-L chart.
2. Demonstrate and use *The New Katie's Farm*.
3. Discuss what was learned with K-W-L.
4. Read books about animals.
5. Write in response journals.

Assessment: Determine students' learning by their responses to the "L" part of K-W-L and response journal entries.

Figure 6 for plan). Use the K-W-L (Ogle, 1986) instructional framework to prompt students to share what they know and want to learn, and what they learned and still want to learn. Begin by asking students what they know about a farm and farm animals. Have students listen to one another's ideas, and record students' ideas on a K-W-L chart. Ask them what they want to learn about animals. Have students use *The New Katie's Farm*, a software program described earlier, to explore Katie in the barn and Katie in her house. After finishing the adventure, have students speak about what they learned and what they still want to learn with the K-W-L chart. If possible, show Web sites about farm animals. Yahooligans! Directory (http://www.yahooligans. com/Science_and_Oddities/Living_Things/Animals/Farm_Animals) offers five sites about the farm and farm animals. Children's Television Workshop (http://www.ctw.org) offers a Web site with online stories in which students choose what happens next at various points in each tale. One story is *Elmo Minds the Farm* at http://www.ctw.org/preschool/stories/readme/0,1162, 2220,00.html.

Encourage students to look at books from the classroom library or school library about a farm animal by setting up an inviting display. A list of books about the farm is available on the Web (http://www.meddybemps.com/9.2g. html). Have students record what they learned in a response journal.

For Developing Readers

Thematic plan on differences

This unit uses the theme of differences as it helps students acquire basic literacy skills (see Figure 7 for plan). Unit concepts about differences are used as a framework for working with the unit activities and materials. These concepts include "We can learn a great deal from people and places that are different from us or different from our experiences" and "New situations are often frightening at first, but they also offer new experiences and friends."

Use the following motivational request to begin the unit: "Think about someone you know who is very different from you." Introduce the software package *Stellaluna* by explaining that Stellaluna, a young fruit bat, is being raised by a family of birds because she was accidentally separated from her mother. Stellaluna finds herself in a new environment where she must adjust to many different routines and behaviors. When she finally finds her mother again, she has a new appreciation of both bats and birds, in spite of the differences between the two species. This electronic book, a replica of the Janell Cannon book, includes an additional "Bat Quiz" activity to help students practice their reading skills as they learn more about bats.

Ask the following follow-up questions: "What was Stellaluna able to do that was different from the family of birds who adopted her?" "What could the little birds do that was hard for Stellaluna?" "How did the mother bird help Stellaluna?" and "What qualities did Stellaluna have that helped her learn to live with the birds?" Create an activity sheet to further develop students'

Figure 7
Instructional Plan for Differences Unit

Objectives: To acquire sight vocabulary; create simple sentences with objects in the environment; learn about the differences between characters; and write about differences using a writing program.

Materials: Software packages: *Stellaluna* and *Storybook Weaver*; and activity sheet and books on differences.

Activities: 1. Use *Stellaluna* and discuss differences as they relate to the character Stellaluna.
2. Read books on differences.
3. Demonstrate and use *Storybook Weaver*.

Assessment: Determine students' learning by their responses to questions and activity sheet and by their writing assignment with *Storybook Weaver*.

Figure 8
Instructional Plan for Fables Unit

Objective: To understand the elements of a fable as a literary genre through reading and writing fables.

Materials: K-W-L chart; software package *The Tortoise and the Hare*; and additional resources for studying fables, including selected Web sites.

Activities: 1. Discuss fables using the K-W-L chart.
2. Have students use classroom and library resources to seek information and examples of fables.
3. Use *The Tortoise and the Hare*.
4. Have students write their own fables with electronic writing tools.

Assessment: Check students' responses to the "L" part of K-W-L and students' fables.

thoughts about adapting to new environments and appreciating differences with questions such as, "What qualities did Stellaluna have that enabled her to adapt to a strange environment?" and "Think of something that you can do well that would help you in a new environment."

Introduce other books that address differences or adapting to new situations in their storyline such as Jean Craighead George's *There's an Owl in the Shower*, Barbara Cohen's *Make a Wish, Molly*, Lynn Reiser's *Margaret and Margarita*, Mary Hoffman's *Amazing Grace*, and Florence Heide and Roxanne Pierce's *Timothy Twinge*. Have students discuss the differences among characters, and the situations to which characters must adapt in each of the books.

Have students create a story of their own about someone who learns from encountering a different environment or situation, using the software program *Storybook Weaver*. This open-ended writing and drawing tool helps students write and illustrate stories using a simple word processor and a variety of graphic features. It includes thousands of graphic images from folklore and the modern-day world, a spell check and thesaurus options, text-to-speech capabilities, and a paint program.

Study of literary genre: Fables

Matthew (1996) offers a way to study fables with the K-W-L technique (see Figure 8 for plan). Ask students "What is a fable?" and have them write their responses in the first column in a K-W-L chart. After students share what they know, ask them what they want to know. Have students use CD-ROM versions of encyclopedias, selected Web sites, and other classroom and library resources to find answers to their questions and examples of fables.

Have students listen to one another's answers as they complete the last column of their K-W-L chart. After you establish an understanding that fables are stories with animals as characters and have a moral, have students read *The Tortoise and the Hare*. As a follow-up activity, have students write and illustrate their own fables to demonstrate their understanding of this genre. Publish the fables as a class anthology that can be shared with another class in the building. Refer to the teacher's guide that accompanies the program for additional activities with fables. See Chapter 5 for examples of word-processing, multimedia, and hypermedia programs available for electronic writing and publishing of students' fables.

Author study: Marc Brown

The first step in any author study is to select a fine author who has a large, varied body of work, and then collect as many of that author's books as possible for classroom use. Marc Brown is an ideal choice because he has written and illustrated fiction, nonfiction, and poetry. Collect as many books by him as you can. Introduce the author and examples of his writing, using both print and electronic versions (see Figure 9 for plan). Four of Brown's Arthur Adventure series are available in electronic form: *Arthur's Teacher Trouble*, *Arthur's Birthday Deluxe*, *Arthur's Reading Race*, and *Arthur's Computer Adventure*. The teacher's guides for these four titles provide more than 60 lessons from which you can se-

Figure 9
Instructional Plan for Author Study on Marc Brown

Objectives:	To develop an appreciation of an author's work and typical style; read a number of books by the same author; and identify ways to recognize the work of a particular author.
Materials:	Software packages: *Arthur's Teacher Trouble*, *Arthur's Birthday*, *Arthur's Reading Race*, and *Arthur's Computer Adventure*; a variety of books written by Marc Brown; and writing materials.
Activities:	1. Collect and create a classroom display of books by Marc Brown and read aloud from this collection for several days. 2. Provide time for children to use the electronic versions of the Arthur stories. 3. Discuss identifying features of Brown's work. 4. Review letter format and and have students write letters to the author.
Assessment:	Assess students' responses to questions and discussion and their letter writing assignment.

Figure 10
Instructional Plan for Slavery Unit

Objectives: To engage in a variety of reading and writing activities about a content topic; use software and Web sites to learn about a famous slave; and use a cooperative group writing activity to share knowledge and ideas about a famous slave's experiences.

Materials: Books and Web sites about slavery and a famous slave; software package *Young Harriet Tubman: Freedom Fighter*; and journals.

Activities: 1. Introduce slavery with a semantic map.
2. Use printed and Web-based resources and software products for reading and research.
3. Use reading, discussion, and journal writing to discuss biography.

Assessment: Evaluate students' expanded semantic map about slavery and students' journals.

lect follow-up activities for your reading. The author's Web site (http://www.pbs.org/wgbh/arthur) provides additional ideas and resources.

After reading any Marc Brown book, ask students how they can tell that he is the author or illustrator. Possible identifying characteristics include the main characters, the way the illustrations are drawn, the setting of the story, the minor characters, or the way the story ends. Help students notice that these characteristics help them become acquainted with an author. Review what your students already know about writing friendly letters. Then have them compose letters to Marc Brown in which they comment on their reading and ask the author questions. Young readers will come away from this study with new insights about the craft of writing and of developing interesting characters.

For Independent Readers

Theme unit on slavery

An instructional plan that includes technology can evolve either from identifying software that fits with a plan or by creating plans that capitalize on specific software. The route taken depends on the curriculum, the availability of resources, and the time for making such connections. The following is an instructional plan that was developed before software and Web sites were identified.

While learning about slavery, students are introduced to biographies, retellings, and concepts such as freedom, the Underground Railroad, and the U.S. Civil War (see Figure 10 for plan). Begin with a semantic map created by the entire class that enables students to share their knowledge of slavery. (See Chapter 7 for a description of the software product *Inspiration* that creates semantic maps.) Use their ideas to introduce them to the famous slave Harriet Tubman. Have students read and conduct research about Harriet Tubman and slavery using the software *Young Harriet Tubman: Freedom Fighter*, as well as books and Web sites (see Figure 11 for a sample listing). A few books include Rae Bains's *Harriet Tubman: The Road to Freedom* and Ann McGovern's *Runaway Slave: The Story of Harriet Tubman* and *Wanted Dead or Alive: The True Story of Harriet Tubman*.

Instructional strategies to use include teacher read-alouds, guided and reflective discussion, students' journal writing, and students' paired reading. Return to the class's semantic map to include the information learned.

Theme unit on survival

This unit for independent readers weaves together two books with a variety of reading and multimedia presentation software to promote students'

Figure 11
Web Sites About Harriet Tubman and Slavery

Essays About Harriet Tubman
    Harriet Tubman: Moses of the Civil War
        (http://www.camalott.com/~rssmith/Moses.html)
    Harriet Tubman
        (http://160.79.207.23/blackhistory/nhtubman.html)
    Harriet Tubman & The Underground Railroad
        (http://www2.lhric.org/pocantico/tubman/tubman.html)

Resources on Harriet Tubman
    Harriet Tubman Resources on the World Wide Web
        (http://www.nyhistory.com/harriettubman/website.htm)

Resources on Slavery
    Chronology on the History of Slavery 1619 to 1789
        (http://innercity.org/holt/slavechron.html)
    The Emancipation Proclamation
        (http://www.nps.gov/ncro/anti/emancipation.html)
    Africans in America
        (http://www.pbs.org/wgbh/aia)
    The Dred Scott Decision
        (http://www.historyplace.com/lincoln/dred)

Figure 12
Instructional Plan for Survival Unit

Objectives: To explore the concept of survival through reading, discussion and writing; compare how characters in two novels survive; and write character analyses using a writing or multimedia presentation program.

Materials: Software packages: *Reading Galaxy*, *Oregon Trail*, *Titanic*, and *M-ss-ng L-nks*; multimedia authoring tools *Kid Pix Studio Deluxe* and *HyperStudio*; and activity sheets and books on survival such as *Hatchet* and *Julie of the Wolves*.

Activities: 1. Introduce survival unit concepts, and explore concepts with various software related to the survival themes.
2. Have students read *Hatchet* and *Julie of the Wolves*.
3. Have small-group and class discussion of survival in the novels.
4. Demonstrate and use *Kid Pix Studio Deluxe* or *HyperStudio* to create character analyses and to present conclusions about survival based on reading.

Assessment: Determine students' learning by their responses to questions and contribution to discussion and by their writing assignment or presentation with *Kid Pix Studio Deluxe* or *HyperStudio*.

thinking about the concept of survival (see Figure 12 for plan). The books are Gary Paulsen's *Hatchet* and Jean Craighead George's *Julie of the Wolves*. The software programs include *Oregon Trail*, *Titanic*, *M-ss-ng L-nks*, *Reading Galaxy*, *Kid Pix Studio Deluxe*, and *HyperStudio*.

Unit concepts about survival should be introduced as the context for the various activities. These concepts include (1) "People mature and grow through facing hardships," and (2) "Determination and the ability to learn from one's mistakes play an important role in one's ability to survive."

Introduce the unit and the concepts through brainstorming. Select a recent natural disaster (such as a storm or earthquake) or challenging adventure (for example, a mountain climb or solo voyage) and invite students to define the physical and emotional challenges that face the participants, as individuals and groups. Discuss possible solutions and resources needed for individuals and groups to survive these challenges. Then introduce the two books with characters who face survival challenges. Have students analyze the main characters and discuss how the survival concepts relate to each book.

Introduce *Oregon Trail*, *Titanic*, or the portions of *M-ss-ng L-nks* or *Reading Galaxy* that relate to *Hatchet* and *Julie of the Wolves*. Give students an opportunity to see how these same survival concepts are presented in the narratives of these programs. Finally, using *Kid Pix Studio Deluxe* or *HyperStudio*, or any of the programs described in Chapter 5, have students create a journal from the viewpoint of the character in one of the books, describing the ways that character developed strategies that enabled him or her to survive. Both of these programs enable students to make electronic presentations as well as print versions of the journals. Additional books dealing with survival include Jean Craighead George's *My Side of the Mountain* and *Julie of the Wolves* and Gary Paulsen's *DogSong*.

Concluding Remarks

With our more than 30 collective years of working with technology in classrooms, we believe more than ever that technology improves one's ability to teach. Unlike any other tool or methodology, technology offers versatility, accessibility, individualization, and opportunity. Multiple options are available with the way in which reading material is presented, the way in which students can read, and the way in which students' reading is assessed. We have witnessed students' excitement when they are working with technology, and we have observed teachers' delight in working with technology for literacy development. We encourage you to experiment and explore with the information, ideas, and instructional plans in this chapter to take yourself to yet another level in your own professional development.

References

Accelerated Reader [Computer software]. (1999). Wisconsin Rapids, WI: Advantage Learning Systems.

Africa Trail [Computer software]. (1997). Cambridge, MA: The Learning Company.

Amazon Trail [Computer software]. (1998). Cambridge, MA: The Learning Company.

The Art Lesson [Computer software]. (1996). Cambridge, MA: The Learning Company.

Arthur's Birthday Deluxe [Computer software]. (1997). Cambridge, MA: Brøderbund/The Learning Company.

Arthur's Computer Adventure [Computer software]. (1998). Cambridge, MA: Brøderbund/The Learning Company.

Arthur's Reading Race [Computer software]. (1996). Cambridge, MA: Brøderbund/The Learning Company.

Arthur's Teacher Trouble [Computer software]. (1993). Cambridge, MA: Brøderbund/The Learning Company.

Bains, R. (1990). *Harriet Tubman: The road to freedom.* New York: Troll.

Bliss, J. (1998, August). Getting the most from software. *Technology & Learning,* p. 16.

Bracey, G.W. (1992, Fall). Technology, falling SAT scores, and the transformation of consciousness. *Technos Quarterly for Education and Technology* [Online], *1*(3), 1–5. Available: http://www.technos.net/journal/volume1/3bracey.htm

The Cat in the Hat [Computer software]. (1997). Cambridge, MA: Brøderbund/The Learning Company.

Clariana, R.B. (1994). *The effects of an integrated learning system on third graders' mathematics and reading achievement.* (ERIC Document Reproduction Service No. ED 409 181)

Cohen, B. (1995). *Make a wish, Molly.* New York: Doubleday.

CornerStone Reading Comprehension [Computer software]. (1999). Cambridge, MA: Skills Bank/The Learning Company.

Dr. Seuss's ABC [Computer software]. (1995). Cambridge, MA: Brøderbund/The Learning Company.

Favorite Greek Myths [Computer software]. (1994). New York: Scholastic.

Fogarty, R. (1998). The intelligence-friendly classroom: It just makes sense. *Phi Delta Kappan, 79*(9), 655–657.

Follansbee, S., Hughes, B., Pisha, B., & Stahl, S. (1997, Winter). Can online communications improve student performance? Results of a controlled study. *ERS Spectrum,* pp. 15–26.

George, J.C. (1974). *Julie of the wolves.* New York: Harper Trophy.

George, J.C. (1991). *My side of the mountain.* New York: Viking.

George, J.C. (1995). *There's an owl in the shower.* New York: HarperCollins.

Green Eggs and Ham [Computer software]. (1996). Cambridge, MA: Brøderbund/The Learning Company.

Hasselbring, T.S., Goin, L., Taylor, R., Bottge, B., & Daley, D. (1997). The computer doesn't embarrass me. *Educational Leadership, 55*(3), 30–33.

Hay, L. (1996, March). Implementation and integration of a technology-based reading curriculum. In B. Robin, J.D. Price, J. Willis, & D.A. Willis (Eds.), *Technology and Teacher Education Annual, 1996: Proceedings of 7th International Conference of the Society for Information Technology and Teacher Education* [Online], Phoenix, AZ. Available: http://www.coe.uh.edu/insite/elec_pub/html1996/03readin.htm

Heide, F.P., & Pierce, R.H. (1993). *Timothy Twinge.* New York: Lothrop.

Hoffman, M. (1991). *Amazing Grace.* New York: Dial.

Hyland, T. (1998, Spring). Readers play catch up—and win. *Technos Quarterly for Education and Technology* [Online], *7*(1), 1–6. Available: http://www.technos.net/journal/volume7/1hyland.htm

HyperStudio [Computer software]. (1995). El Cajon, CA: Roger Wagner Publishing.

If Your Name Was Changed at Ellis Island [Computer software]. (1994). New York: Scholastic.

Inspiration [Computer software]. (1988–1999). Portland, OR: Inspiration Software.

Just Grandma and Me Deluxe [Computer software]. (1997). Cambridge, MA: Brøderbund/The Learning Company.

Kid Pix Studio Deluxe [Computer software]. (1998). Cambridge, MA: Brøderbund/The Learning Company.

Kirkpatrick, H., & Cuban, L. (1998, Summer). Computers make kids smarter—right? *Technos Quarterly for Education and Technology* [Online], *7*(2), 1–10. Available: http://www.technos.net/journal/volume7/2cuban.htm

Little Monster at School [Computer software]. (1995). Cambridge, MA: Brøderbund/The Learning Company.

Malcolm X: By Any Means Necessary [Computer software]. (1994). New York: Scholastic.

Matthew, K.I. (1995). *A comparison of the influence of CD-ROM interactive storybooks and traditional print storybooks on reading comprehension and attitude.* Unpublished doctoral dissertation, University of Houston, TX.

Matthew, K.I. (1996, March). The promise and potential of CD-ROM books. In B. Robin, J.D. Price, J. Willis, & D.A. Willis (Eds.), *Technology and Teacher Education Annual, 1996: Proceedings of 7th International Conference of the Society for Information Technology and Teacher Education* [Online], Phoenix, AZ. Available: http://www/coe.uh.edu/insite/elec_pub/html1996/03readin.htm

MayaQuest Trail [Computer software]. (1997). Cambridge, MA: The Learning Company.

McGovern, A. (1965). *Runaway slave: The story of Harriet Tubman.* New York: Scholastic.

McGovern, A. (1991). *Wanted dead or alive: The true story of Harriet Tubman.* New York: Scholastic.

McKenna, M.C., Reinking, D., Labbo, L.D., & Watkins, J.H. (1996). *Using electronic storybooks and beginning readers* (Instructional Resource No. 39). Athens, GA: University of Georgia, National Reading Research Center. (ERIC Document Reproduction Service No. ED 400 521)

Miller, L., Blackstock, J., & Miller, R. (1994). An exploratory study into the use of CD-ROM storybooks. *Computers in Education, 22,* 187–204.

M-ss-ng L-nks [Computer software]. (1998). Pleasantville, NY: Sunburst Communications.

The New Katie's Farm [Computer software]. (1996). Galesburg, MI: Lawrence Productions.

Ogle, D. (1986). K-W-L: A teaching model that develops active reading and expository text. *The Reading Teacher, 39,* 564–570.

Oregon Trail [Computer software]. (1999). Cambridge, MA: The Learning Company.

Paulsen, G. (1996). *Hatchet.* New York: Alladin.

Paulsen, G. (1998). *DogSong.* New York: Alladin.

Rawls, W. (1984). *Where the red fern grows.* New York: Bantam Starfire.

Reading Galaxy [Computer software]. (1996). Cambridge, MA: Brøderbund/The Learning Company.

Reiser, L. (1996). *Margaret and Margarita.* New York: Greenwillow.

The Ribbit Collection [Computer software]. (1996). Somerville, MA: Houghton Mifflin.

Ruddell, M.R. (1994). Vocabulary knowledge and comprehension: A comprehension-process view of complex literacy relationships. In R.B. Ruddell, M.R. Ruddell, & H. Singer (Eds.), *Theoretical models and processes of reading* (4th ed., pp. 414–447). Newark, DE: International Reading Association.

Shiah, R.L., Mastropieri, M.A., & Scruggs, T. (1995). Computer-assisted instruction and students with learning disabilities: Does research support the rhetoric? *Advances in Learning and Behavioral Disabilities, 9,* 161–192.

Sheila Rae, the Brave [Computer software]. (1996). Cambridge, MA: Brøderbund/The Learning Company.

Stellaluna [Computer software]. (1996). Cambridge, MA: Brøderbund/The Learning Company.

Stine, H.A. (1993). *The effects of CD-ROM interactive software in reading skills instruction with second-grade Chapter 1 students.* Doctoral dissertation, The George Washington University, Washington, DC.

Storybook Weaver [Computer software]. (1996). Cambridge, MA: The Learning Company.

Strong, M.W. (1982). Student self-tracking using a microcomputer. *Proceedings of the Association for Educational Data Systems* (pp. 333–335). Orlando, FL: Association for Educational Data Systems.

Study shows technology-achievement link. (1997, June). *Electronic School*, p. A.

Tierney, R.J., & Pearson, P.D. (1994). Learning to learn from text: A framework for improving classroom practice. In R.B. Ruddell, M.R. Ruddell, & H. Singer (Eds.), *Theoretical models and processes of reading* (4th ed., pp. 414–447). Newark, DE: International Reading Association.

Tiger's Tales [Computer software]. (1995). Pleasantville, NY: Sunburst Communications.

Titanic [Computer software]. (1994). New York: Scholastic.

The Tortoise and the Hare [Computer software]. (1993). Cambridge, MA: Brøderbund/The Learning Company.

Underwood, G., & Underwood, J. (1996, March). Gender differences in children's learning from interactive books. In B. Robin, J.D. Price, J. Willis, & D.A. Willis (Eds.), *Technology and Teacher Education Annual, 1996: Proceedings of 7th International Conference of the Society for Information Technology and Teacher Education* [Online], Phoenix, AZ. Available: http://www.coe.uh.edu/insite/elec_pub/html1996/03readin.htm

Where in the USA Is Carmen Sandiego? [Computer software]. (1998). Cambridge, MA: Brøderbund/The Learning Company.

Where in the World Is Carmen Sandiego? [Computer software]. (1998). Cambridge, MA: Brøderbund/The Learning Company.

Where in Time Is Carmen Sandiego? [Computer software]. (1996). Cambridge, MA: Brøderbund/The Learning Company.

WiggleWorks Plus [Computer software]. (1999). New York: Scholastic.

Wilson, L. (1993). *Enhancing the academic skills of adolescent students with learning disabilities through computer assisted instruction.* (ERIC Document Reproduction Service No. 377 898)

Young Abraham Lincoln: Log-Cabin President [Computer software]. (1996). Mahwah, NJ: Troll.

Young Harriet Tubman: Freedom Fighter [Computer software]. (1996). Mahwah, NJ: Troll.

Young Helen Keller: Woman of Courage [Computer software]. (1996). Mahwah, NJ: Troll.

Young Jackie Robinson: Baseball Hero [Computer software]. (1996). Mahwah, NJ: Troll.

Young Orville and Wilbur Wright: First to Fly [Computer software]. (1996). Mahwah, NJ: Troll.

Yukon Trail [Computer software]. (1997). Cambridge, MA: The Learning Company.

CHAPTER 5

Using Technology
for Writing Development

JANE E. SULLIVAN AND JEAN SHARP

Michele, a sixth grader, props her outline against the computer monitor and, clicking on the *ClarisWorks* software program icon, settles back to work. Her report is due in three days. She already has bookmarked five Web sites on the Internet for this project. She will use tables from three sites to illustrate her report. The other sites, too, have pictures that she will cut and paste into her finished assignment.

She spreads her fingers across the keyboard, resting each one on the correct position—*a-s-d-f* for the left hand and *j-k-l;* for the right one. Michele composes at the keyboard, glancing at notes she has taken in preparation for her draft. She modifies her brainstorming outline as new ideas occur to her. Here and there she corrects an error, but she knows the serious editing will come after she is satisfied with her revised draft.

For Michele, and learners like her, reading, writing, and technology come together in a symbiotic relationship. The reading she does informs her writing. Studying the craft of authors as she reads helps her improve her own writing skills, and the technology she employs—a computer with access to the Internet and a CD-ROM encyclopedia—invites her to question, explore, gather, and synthesize information and to communicate that information to her audience.

Michele's understanding of writing is that it is a process that demands thoughtful planning, careful revision, and critical editing. She knows that her purpose for writing should be clear to her. She writes now for an audience of her classmates and her teacher because she will give an oral report on her research. Earlier, she sent an e-mail message to her older brother who is away at college. She wrote it quickly without paying too much attention to her writing.

Within the last two decades a revolution has taken place in writing instruction in the elementary grades. With the research of such notable figures as Nancie Atwell, Lucy Calkins, Peter Elbow, Donald Graves, and Donald Murray, teachers have learned much about the writing process. They have incorporated techniques such as "Writers Workshop" into their teaching to assist young learners in applying writing strategies themselves. With the availability of computers connected to the Internet and loaded with CD-ROM reference programs, writing has been further enhanced. Technology allows students in our classrooms to move forward in their writing development by providing them with access to a wide range of resources. Other technology such as presentation software makes writing tools available that allow them to shape their writings for a variety of purposes and audiences.

For two decades researchers have asked, "What impact does technology have on the quality of writing?" and have found conflicting results. Bruce (1999) cites evidence from research that a writer, whether working at a computer or with pen and paper, uses essentially the same methods. Fluency, logical sequencing, attention to detail, word choice, and other patterns of writing do not change. Writers appear to make fewer mechanical errors when working on a computer. It also appears that writing while working in a computer lab encourages greater social interaction and learning (Hawisher & Selfe, 1999). There is much evidence that, despite the potential that technology has to enhance classroom instruction, change occurs only if teachers reshape the strategies they have used in the past (Reinking, Labbo, & McKenna, 1997). In their study of QUILL, a comprehensive project that integrated process writing with computer applications, Michaels and Bruce (1989) concluded that an innovation, no matter how well conceived or how well executed, cannot ensure positive changes in instruction. What is needed for success is a combination of technology with its potential for positive change and a teacher who adjusts instruction to take advantage of that potential. Nevertheless, despite the need to better coordinate traditional instruction and technology, computers continue to grow in popularity as tools for writing—both in the classroom and at home.

This chapter shares examples of practical applications of the computer and other forms of technology in teaching writing. We begin with the premise that the teacher uses the model of process writing, with its recursive components—prewriting or brainstorming, drafting, revising, editing, and publishing. In today's Writing Workshop classrooms, students write daily in notebooks, brainstorming ideas that will later develop into a piece of writing. In share sessions and "Author's Chair" celebrations, students share their polished pieces with classmates and study the work of published writers. Their teachers read aloud to them, then pause and encourage them to reflect on the craft of the writer. They learn about strong leads, the importance of word choice, and staying on topic. They return to their desks and apply those strategies they watched their teachers use. Within such a framework, the creative teacher incorporates technological tools such as creative writing programs and the Internet to enhance instruction.

The range of available technology is broad. Some examples such as overhead projectors and television sets are commonplace, whereas others such as DVD (digital video disc) players and individual computers for every student are not. The technology we have chosen to include in this chapter meets several practical criteria suggested by Burns, Roe, and Ross (1999):

1. It addresses the content of the writing program.
2. It is motivating to students.
3. It clarifies the particular strategy the teacher stresses.
4. It lends itself to use within the classroom structure.
5. It is easy to implement, instructionally sound, cost effective, and more efficient than other possible approaches.

Why Use Technology for Writing?

The advantage of using technology is to capitalize on the positive features it makes available to the learner, features such as a colorful display that intrigues students and a large screen that provides opportunities for collaboration and reinforces the social nature of learning. Anyone observing Sherri Brecker monitoring her students as they work at the computer could see these points verified. (See the accompanying textbox "Collaboration at Work in the Computer Lab.") Teachers who innovate, who find themselves individualizing to a greater extent, and who model the tasks they teach report positive results when technology is used. Changes occur when teachers introduce challenging problems, work to build a community of learners, and provide instructional feedback that is timely and meaningful. Incorporating a variety of software into their teaching strategies fosters authentic writing experiences, aids students in organizing and retrieving content area information, and assists them in generating reports, stories, and newsletters.

Technology, implemented as a suitable tool in the writing classroom, holds forth a promise of excellence. In the following sections we will provide illustrations of some of the ways technology has been integrated with writing instruction, the software that teachers have found useful, and details of these applications.

Collaboration at Work in the Computer Lab

Sherri Brecker watched her fifth graders working in the computer lab one morning. On the previous day, Mrs. Brecker had presented a minilesson on word choice in Writing Workshop. Now her students would begin the first step in applying that learning. The students had located 20 words in the selection they were reading in their classroom book club. Under Mrs. Brecker's direction, they accessed the Web site they would use (http://www.puzzlemaker.com) and the specific application, Word Search. Then they entered those 20 words and waited for the computer to make a word search puzzle.

Students comfortable with using a computer had located the site easily, which put them ahead of their peers. Without prompting from Mrs. Brecker, they assumed the role of "trouble shooter" with neighboring students who had not been successful. Excitement filled the room. It was hard to miss the social interaction that took place.

Walking down the rows of computers, stopping now and again to point out a misspelled word or suggest a more challenging word choice, Mrs. Brecker could easily monitor the students' work. The ease with which she could observe student writing and the quick turn-around time needed to respond to it was evident. It happens, just as the research says it does.

Mrs. Brecker's follow-up plan took place several days later. Students listed their 20 words in *Microsoft Word*, then they accessed an online thesaurus (Visual Thesaurus at http://www.plumbdesign.com/thesaurus) to locate synonyms for the words. They returned to the online Puzzlemaker. This time they selected Crossword and entered the words along with their synonyms. Then they waited while the program created a crossword puzzle using the synonyms as clues. Once again, the animated voices of students who were sharing their puzzles with their neighbors filled the room. They had discovered that word study does not have to be tedious.

On the Ground With Writing Tools

Keyboarding: Rationale, Programs, and Uses

As computers grew in popularity among elementary-age students, teachers in business education became concerned that little or no attention was being given to instruction on techniques for entering text. From experience, they knew that once learned, poor techniques such as looking at keys, using only two fingers, or wrong finger placements are hard habits to overcome. Thus, questions about the "when" and "what" of teaching keyboarding were raised.

If we acknowledge that computers and accompanying software have a place in the writing curriculum, then we must also acknowledge that keyboarding instruction belongs there as well. Studies demonstrate that the dictated compositions of primary-age students who have not yet mastered the mechanics of writing are better in quality than those written themselves (King & Rentel, 1981). It also has been pointed out that handwritten and dictated compositions of fifth and sixth graders reflect little qualitative difference (Scardamalia, Bereiter, & Goelman, 1982). Such evidence supports the conclusion that when skills needed for writing become automatic the writer begins to focus more on the content than on the mechanics.

Students unfamiliar with keyboard letter placement are similar to those students who are unskilled in handwriting. They cannot give full attention to the content of their text. The ability to locate letters on the keyboard automatically allows students to focus on the higher level thinking skills that result in better quality and more prolific writing.

The question concerning the age of students at which correct keyboarding techniques should be introduced is controversial. Teachers familiar with elementary school students claim success with first and second graders. Business education specialists refute that view, pointing out that the finger span and flexibility of young students prevent them from using home keys so early. However, business education specialists differ about when formal keyboarding instruction should be introduced, although they do agree that correct technique should be introduced as early as possible. In an online course on using computers called Computer Science and Business Education (http://www.crews.org/media_tech/compsci), a college instructor arranged for students to question keyboarding experts on various topics connected with teaching that skill (see http://www.crews.org/media_tech/compsci/teachers/papers/keyquestions.htm). One of the questions asked of the experts was, "At what grade should keyboarding instruction be introduced?" One expert advised seventh grade; another believed it should not occur before fourth or fifth grade. One expert, who had taught keyboarding to second graders, responded that most of the students could not stretch their fingers nor remember the letters under them. Third graders she taught, however, began to develop the needed dexterity. The majority of experts surveyed recommended that formal keyboard instruction should occur at the fifth-grade level. Officials in the state of Virginia appear to agree; the Standards of Learning for that state (http://www.

pen.k12.va.us/go/Sols/science.html#TheRole) place the mastery of basic keyboarding skills at fifth grade.

A feature article titled "Keyboarding and Your Classroom" on the Ingenuity Works Web site (April 1999) listed a suggested keyboard curriculum. The author pointed out that in the primary grades, the focus should be on overall familiarity with letter keys, the return key, the space bar, and the home row. Actual "touch" typing should not begin until fourth grade.

One school district uses the *Herzog Keyboarding* program and Alpha Smart keyboards to introduce formal keyboarding techniques in third grade. The Herzog system uses HUB KEY sensors, which adhere to the keys on a standard keyboard and, according to the distributor, give the fingers a wider range of motion (http://www.herzogkeyboarding.com).

Although there are many recommendations, the underlying theme is that letter position should be the emphasis in primary grades, with the introduction and focus changing to the techniques of "touch typing" as students develop the dexterity and finger span required for that technique.

In tandem with the question, When to teach? is the equally important one, What do you teach? Keyboarding instruction focuses on three major categories—technique, accuracy, and speed—with technique usually emphasized first. Current information on the stress that keyboarding places on the muscles, tendons, and bone structure accentuates the importance of ergonomically correct environments for students. Keyboarding techniques, then, embrace more than correct placement of fingers on the home keys. Instructors are advised to take into consideration factors such as the angle that students' wrists and arms form when placing their fingers on the keyboards as well as the contour of chairs and the posture and leg placement that such contours promote. Keyboarding techniques include good habits such as keeping backs straight, placing fingers on the home keys, positioning wrists above the keyboard, and looking at the text being entered rather than the computer monitor or the keys themselves.

Although software packages offer opportunities to introduce students to the keyboard and the location of keys, they merely provide an environment that allows students to practice. An adult knowledgeable in keyboarding instruction must monitor students so they learn all the elements of keyboarding technique. Once technique has been established, the teacher can shift emphasis to speed and accuracy. In these areas, keyboarding software can play a motivating role, and there are several software packages available that are designed to reinforce typing technique, speed, and accuracy. *Type to Learn* is one such package. In this software, students learn the technique of "reaching for keys" by watching on-screen fingers demonstrate the movement. Then, they are given a chance to imitate it. The program moves at a slow pace, introducing two keys per lesson, followed by extensive practice provided through entertaining games. One component of the program, Notepad, allows students to learn word-processing basics while experimenting with skills they have learned. In another component, Warpspeed, students copy paragraphs while the computer records their speed and accuracy. For practice using the shift and number keys and improving accuracy, students can choose from the different skill games that are available. There are also features that allow the teacher to control items such as vocabulary level, size of text, and speed and accuracy goals. Computer instructors have found this program particularly effective with younger students.

JumpStart Typing is another software package emphasizing keyboarding skills. This program provides a motivating practice environment that centers on simulated athletic activities such as snowboarding, cliff hanging, and skateboarding. Initially, students view video clips that teach correct keyboarding hand placement and posture. A built-in diagnostic function evaluates their progress and adjusts the difficulty appropriately. Once they have learned correct finger placement and typing posture, students move to the activities that stress speed and accuracy. In one exercise, Keyboard Kicks, students move their soccer players and kick the ball with every accurate letter entry. As players respond correctly, the pace accelerates, providing practice in speed as well.

Another popular keyboarding package is *Mavis Beacon Teaches Typing*. In this program, students can practice beginning, intermediate, or advanced level typing. This program's strength lies in the practice it provides because it responds to keyboard patterns used by learners and then customizes the lessons to fit their specific needs. Although illustrations are available that demonstrate correct finger reaches, the small size of the illustrations makes them difficult to see. The program best serves students who simply need practice in keyboarding.

PAWS in Typing Town, designed for primary and middle school students, emphasizes technique over speed and accuracy. After each of the 16 lessons included, students may choose one of three options for practice. The first, Journal, allows them to apply the skills they learned by using a simple word processor. Should they need to reinforce what they have learned, they can choose Technique. Here they can view video clips that demonstrate correct posture and key reach. The third option, Arcade, allows students to review and practice skills by playing one of eight games available. The accompanying manual contains useful guidelines and teaching suggestions.

Slam Dunk Typing uses a series of fast-paced basketball games. There are seven different drills with ten levels in each drill. The drills cover a range of skills from beginner to advanced level. Statistics are kept on speed, accuracy, and errors. An online coach monitors progress and offers advice.

Mastering keyboarding enables students to focus on software designed to enhance their writing skills. In the next section, we discuss various computer environments for entering text and the potential for enhancing students' writing skills that software within these categories offers.

Computer Environments for Text Entry

Among software programs that provide a space to write, some act simply as a blank page on which users can enter text, revise it, and print it. This was the function of early versions of the word processor. As word-processing programs grew in popularity, however, enhancements such as a spellchecker and thesaurus were added to augment the programs and optimize their utility. In today's market, minimally enhanced word processors have been replaced by versions with capabilities that extend to graphics, clip art, bibliography formatting, and links to database and spreadsheet programs.

There is no definitive line that separates the myriad programs that are dedicated to text entry as opposed to data entry. To guide teachers through the forest of software designed for writers, we have chosen to separate them into three categories. Those programs whose major emphasis is text entry are referred to as "word-processing" packages. Although many of the packages available today offer enhancements such as graphics or clip art, students use them primarily to enter and format text. Some software packages extend their focus beyond text entry. These packages are designed to foster creativity in students by integrating text and visuals. We have chosen to group these packages under the label "creativity." Finally, we discuss software packages that allow students to produce a finished product that requires text entry and creativity, but whose capabilities take students beyond such writing. These programs, with their multiple enhancements, challenge students' problem-solving ability and, thus, we group them under the label "productivity."

In these three types of software, speech capabilities have become an expected program feature. Publishers address this need by integrating text-to-speech and voice recording capabilities into their programs. The text-to-speech feature uses computer voices to read text that students have entered via the keyboard. Voices installed in the user's system folder are sometimes described as robotic, although this feature has improved over time. In programs that use text-to-speech, students often will find a selection of voices from which to choose—male and female as well as adult and child. There are sometimes silly voices, too; "Bubbles," for example, sounds as if someone is talking underwater. Programs occasionally provide options that alter the pitch and tempo of the computer voice as well. In text-to-speech the computer reads the text students have misspelled, which sometimes results in mispronunciation of words.

Voice recording, a growing feature of these kinds of programs, allows students to read stories in their own voice, using the computer's microphone and simple record buttons. This feature overcomes the two disadvantages of text-to-speech: The voice is natural speech, and mispronunciation is not a barrier. However, recording voices requires more harddrive space to store sound files on computers, and this becomes a significant limitation when many users share a computer. Therefore, some programs impose a time limit for voice recording, often indicated by a progress bar. In either type of program just discussed, speech capabilities provide an option for students to hear their stories read aloud, which is something that greatly appeals to them.

Word processing

Word processing is probably the most familiar computer application that people use and is most likely to be found on computers in the classroom as well as computers in the home. Today's word-processing programs provide an array of features that allow students to enter text and customize it by selecting features such as font, style, and size. The more comprehensive packages popular with adults and older students, for example *ClarisWorks* or *WordPerfect*, contain sophisticated formatting options that adjust text to meet any user's needs. These word-processing programs often provide users with an easy entry point that allows them to use the program with just the basic formatting procedures. Once they have mastered the fundamentals, students can explore a palette of choices that invites them to manipulate their text. Most current word processors support a variety of page formats, allow for the insertion of pictures and tables, include tools that grow with students, and provide expanding features that students can access when they discover the need.

Word-processing packages designed for young students are usually fairly easy to use. Most of these combine simple word processors with a paint program that allows students to create illustrations using a file of available icons. For beginning writers, *Sunbuddy Writer* is a simple word-processing and writing program. Each tool is labeled by the narrator as the cursor passes over it. The number of tools available can be limited to writing with the keyboard, finding a word, saving, and printing. As students master these tools, the number of tools can be expanded to include copy, cut, paste, and even record for sound effects. A word finder helps students find and spell just the right words, and a rebus option lets them replace words with pictures.

Creativity

Word-processing programs primarily emphasize students' interaction with text, whereas creativity programs provide a setting that engages them in a visual environment as they create their stories. Creativity programs, like word-processing programs, are open-ended writing tools that invite students to bring their own ideas to the computer. However, one of the distinguishing characteristics of creativity programs is their emphasis on picture creation as an integral part of the story-writing process; they often offer various graphic features, including clip art and drawing and painting tools. Students are encouraged to illustrate as well as compose their story. Thus, students can frame their written text in different formats. They can create original art, focus on adding captions to their art, print out the text in the form of a book or a newsletter, or even write play scripts.

Students in early elementary and middle grades develop stories that are illustrated with pictures they create from features built into programs such as *Storybook Weaver Deluxe*. This program combines a child-friendly word processor with an extensive library of graphics and sounds that make it easy for young authors to bring stories to life. Students can hear their stories read by either the computer's text-to-speech feature or their own recorded narration. With features such as a spellchecker, thesaurus, story starters, and dual-language option, *Storybook Weaver Deluxe* offers a range of support for writers. Figure 1 on page 116 gives an example of a lesson plan one teacher developed to have third graders do retellings of their favorite fable using this program. This plan illustrates the creativity such a program promotes.

First and second graders also can become adept at creating their own stories and printing them in book form in a program such as *EasyBook Deluxe*. With this software, students can design their own books by writing and illustrating each page. *EasyBook Deluxe* includes backgrounds, stamps, and other basic drawing tools. Young students also can easily access the writing tools, along with a spellchecker and thesaurus. A variety of print options allow stu-

Figure 1
Instructional Plan for Responding to Literature Through Story Retellings

Objective: To have students write and illustrate retellings of familiar tales using a story-writing software package.

Materials: Fables and folk tales including *Aesop's Fables* and *Grimms Fairy Tales*; and software program *Storybook Weaver Deluxe*.

Activities: 1. Have students read a variety of fables and fairy tales and, with a partner or individually, choose one tale to retell.
2. Have students plan their retelling within three pages—a beginning, middle, and end—and write their retelling on paper.
3. Have them read their draft to several classmates and revise the retelling as necessary.
4. Have students create their final retelling using *Storybook Weaver Deluxe*. They should create a title page, story illustration, and text for each page of their retellings. They should print their story retelling to share with classmates.

Assessment: Base assessment on the evaluation of the final story retellings, including a title page and three story pages, that together make up a class book.

dents to print their own stories in sizes ranging from a mini- to a poster-sized book. Stories also can be read aloud using the program's text-to-speech feature.

Kid Works Deluxe is an engaging word-processing/creative-writing program that is somewhat difficult to use at first. Once students sign in, they are free to start writing or illustrating their own picture books. There are standard choices for fonts and a set of drawing tools. Students can change the words of their story into pictures and can hear their writing read by one of six different "bug" voices. Pictures can include their choice of sound effects as well as backgrounds and stickers, some of which are animated. The program includes a "transparency option" for teachers, a removable overlay that can be placed on top of a student's work so the teacher can note errors and suggest corrections. This program's wide array of tools and options does make it difficult for some students to master, however.

Students also enjoy using *Imagination Express* for creative writing. This product is a storybook construction kit. It invites students to combine background scenes, resizable stickers (clip art that can be resized), and background music as they create their own electronic books. For each sticker, students can record speech or sounds, and some of the stickers are animated. Each product in the *Imagination Express* series has a thematic focus called a "destination." Destinations include Neighborhood, Castles, Ocean, Pyramids, Rainforest, and Time Trip USA.

Productivity

In the productivity category, we have listed those software packages whose primary function is to produce an end result that goes beyond text enhanced by illustrations and/or audio. Among these programs, we include packages that are frequently labeled "desktop publishing" tools. These packages are more versatile than those in the previous two categories. Using such tools, students can print signs, banners, letterheads, and greeting cards, and they can produce newsletters, create original drawings, and import photographs or scanned images.

In this section we also discuss packages that add sound and motion to the extended capabilities. Similar in function to desktop publishing software, some packages allow users to create multimedia environments by including commands that will animate images or activate audio and video clips accompanying the text or visuals. In fact, such packages are referred to as "multimedia" software. The label "hypermedia" is sometimes used when such packages allow users to create hypertext-type links.

Among productivity software packages is *The Print Shop Deluxe*, designed for students from kindergarten through grade 12. This is a full-featured printing program that students can use to create greeting cards, banners, newsletters, Web pages, and more. With thousands of graphics and photos, layouts and templates, photo-editing capabilities, and a graphic reference book, this is a very complete tool that is fairly easy to use. Writing for authentic purposes becomes more than an empty phrase in a language arts classroom that has access to this kind of program.

Student Writing Center is a package designed for grades 4 and up. Students can use this program for projects such as reports or newsletters or for writing in a journal or making a sign. The program includes such functions as creating headers and footers, numbering pages, resizing, and flipping or cropping images. There are online writing and grammar tips as well as a built-in thesaurus and spellchecker. A nice feature of this program is a command that formats, alphabetizes, and correctly punctuates source information, thus creating a table of bibliographical references.

Another example of desktop software is *FrameMaker*, a complete publishing package that includes a word processor, page designer, and graphics editor.

Templates provide students with preset page layouts, text formats, and other features. Book-building features help prepare documents for publication. Teachers can use a program such as *FrameMaker* to have students create memoir books as one teacher did (see Figure 2).

When teachers integrate the more complex technology of the programs described with various class projects, they need to plan carefully to help students feel comfortable working with the software. In the beginning, teachers may sometimes need to focus on techniques for using productivity software. This is a necessary, but sometimes time-consuming, first step. Fortunately, software publishers make every effort to make their programs easy to learn and use. The growing standardization of function commands and the similarity in program features and screen layouts in software packages of the same genre lend themselves to transfer learning. New software packages that reflect this user-friendly attribute require less teaching time, which means that teachers can more quickly shift the role of the technology from an entity to be learned to a tool that can assist learning. As young writers become acclimated to the technological environment, they move comfortably into more complex writing packages that support and motivate their learning.

There are some software packages in this productivity category that function as tutorials, nudging writers to organize ideas logically and to include pertinent

Figure 2
Instructional Plan for Responding to Literature Through Memoir

---

Objective: To explore memoir as a genre and use a desktop publishing program to create a memory book for the class.

Materials: A copy of Byrd Baylor's *I'm in Charge of Celebrations*; and the software package *Framemaker* or another desktop publishing program.

Activities: 1. Read *I'm in Charge of Celebrations*.
2. Have each student complete a personal profile of their likes and dislikes.
3. Survey the class and compile a top 10 list of favorite movies, musical groups, school lunches, etc. This will be a "snapshot" of the class.
4. Have students from each class in the grade level write reflections for a "Remember When" page in the memoir book.
5. Have students use *Framemaker* to compile the personal, class, and grade-level information for a Class Memory book.

Assessment: Assess students' learning by the personal, class, and grade-level information included in the publication of the Class Memory book.

---

details in their writing. *PostCards*, designed for grades 5 through 8, stimulates writing with prompts and guides to help users organize their thoughts. The program allows students to take virtual journeys to Japan, Ghana, Mexico, or Turkey. Students read short paragraphs about the country and examine photos, illustrations, charts, and maps. From the information, they compile a journal about the country. The students send postcards, which are rectangles made up of story frames with partial sentences that serve as prompts. Students complete the sentences by inserting the information they learned about the country they visited. The accompanying teacher's manual contains suggestions for research as well as short stories in the settings of the countries. Although every student may not need such a program, it is motivating to reluctant writers who need the structure and prompts the program provides.

Other packages are designed to take users through the complete writing process. For example, *Writers Studio* guides students in grades 3 through 8 step by step through the prewriting, drafting, revising, editing, and publishing stages. Some students, but probably not all, can benefit from such scaffolding. The package includes such features as graphic organizers, lists of topics, and a planner to keep students focused. The package also contains 100 writing ideas, student-generated spelling lists, managed reports, and online checklists for evaluation of student work.

A similar program, *Expression*, helps students organize their ideas visually. Graphic planning helps students generate and explore ideas as well as organize materials. Students can switch between the graphic planning, an outline, and a word processor as they refine their writing.

A program such as *PowerPoint*, designed to create visual presentations in a multimedia environment, allows students in Grade 5 and higher to add interest and structure to oral presentations. Students enter the major points of their presentation on slides. They can then project these slides and refer to them as they speak, keeping themselves on track and allowing the audience to follow the presentation. Used extensively in professional presentations, this program has become a popular tool in classrooms. Students can learn the basic commands rather easily and realize instant success. Once adept at creating simple slides that contain their major points, clever students learn to animate their presentations, bringing each point into view at a click of the mouse. It is an easy step from that stage to the next when sounds can be introduced to accompany the slides. Clip art or photos also can be inserted into slides. The final enhancement is a set of sound effects that can accompany slides as they appear on the screen. Students in Sherri Brecker's class presenting the results of an "I-Search" (Macrorie, 1997) dazzle their classmates with the animation and color available in the program while elaborating on the points in their visual outline (see Figure 3).

Presentation programs have the added advantage of combining writing with speaking, linking two important language arts skills in a meaningful way. One teacher formed a collaboration between fifth graders and kindergarten

Figure 3
Instructional Plan for Using the I-Search as a Device to Teach Informational-Text Writing

Objectives: To have students use the I-Search strategy to identify and research a topic; write a narrative of the journey they took to gather the information for their reports; use *PowerPoint* to outline their research findings; and, using *PowerPoint*, explain their findings to the class in a prepared speech.

Materials: Informational books and reference works on their topics; sources on the Internet; and software programs *PowerPoint, ClarisWorks* (or another word-processing program), and *Grolier Multimedia Encyclopedia*.

Activities: 1. Have students identify a topic they would like to research, record all they already know about the topic, and list 25 questions about the topic for which they will attempt to find answers.
2. Distribute a worksheet, with "Date" and "Progress" as headings that will serve as a log for recording progress on research. These are to be filled in every day.
3. Discuss methods students can use to locate the answers to their questions (for example, interviews, surveys, Internet searches, or an encyclopedia).
4. Assist students in selecting appropriate methods for their research and show them how they can use a word processor to prepare necessary forms for gathering information.
5. When all necessary data are collected, have students use the word processor to draft written narratives describing the journeys they took to gather information. If applicable, have students use a spreadsheet (*ClarisWorks* or *Excel*) to tally the results of any survey data collected.
6. Have students prepare *PowerPoint* slides and practice the speech they will present to the class about the findings of their research.
7. Have students give their speech and follow it with a question-and-answer period in which fellow students may ask questions after listening to the presentation.

Assessment: Evaluate students' learning with a portfolio that will include a list of questions, a daily log of activities, a written narrative of their I-Search journey, and a copy of the *PowerPoint* presentation.

Figure 4
Instructional Plan for Responding to Literature Through Bookmaking

Objectives: To have kindergarten students work with fifth- or sixth-grade buddies to learn about animals found at the local zoo; explore research using a variety of print and electronic media; learn facts about a particular animal; and share their facts in a class book and an electronic book.

Materials: A variety of animal books and alphabet books; and software packages *Grolier Multimedia Encyclopedia* and *PowerPoint*.

Activities: 1. Ask each team to choose a zoo animal to research.
2. Have the older student in each team read at least two different sources to the kindergarten student to find answers to questions about this zoo animal. Questions should include what the animal looks like, where it lives, what it eats, and so on.
3. Have students plan a small-group presentation to share their research results.
4. Have each team complete a page about the zoo animal for a class book. The page should include a hand-drawn picture and several written facts about the animal.
5. Have each team use *PowerPoint* to create a slide for their zoo animal that includes a photograph of the animal and two of the facts the students researched.
6. Have each team show the slides as they give a short speech before the rest of the class.

Assessment: Assessment may include the speech explaining results of students' research and the publication of the research electronically in a *PowerPoint* slideshow.

students that resulted in the production of an electronic book. Pairs of students, consisting of one fifth grader and one kindergartner, created the book using *PowerPoint* (see Figure 4) and presented the book to several audiences.

Kid Pix Studio Deluxe also offers young computer users opportunities to create in a multimedia environment. This program allows students to build a series of animated pictures with creative backgrounds and combine them with text of varied fonts and sizes. More than 800 different picture stamps, drawing tools, realistic sound effects, music clips, and photos are available. Lisa Vitosky, working in collaboration with the classroom teacher, showed third graders how to use this program to create slideshows as part of a research project on animals (see Figure 5 on page 122). Another class used *Kid Pix Studio Deluxe* to create their personal response to Faith Ringgold's *Tar Beach* (see Figures 6 and 7 on page 123).

Figure 5
Instructional Plan for Creating an Electronic Animal Alphabet Book

Objective: To have students locate information on a specific animal and compile an illustrated book that presents the results of the research.

Materials: Informational books on animals; the Internet; and the software package *Kid Pix Studio Deluxe*.

Activities:
1. Assign each student a letter of the alphabet and an animal whose name begins with that letter.
2. Give each student a worksheet with the following headings: Habitat, Appearance, Food, Enemies, and Behavior. The worksheet also should include suggestions for possible resources students might use (Internet sites, an encyclopedia, or specific book references).
3. When the research is completed, have students create a storyboard made up of five squares, corresponding to the five categories of information they were to locate.
4. Have students write the information they found for each category and draw rough sketches that illustrate the slides they will construct.
5. Have them add rough drafts of a title page and end page for their book.
6. Show students how to transfer the information to *Kid Pix* slides, have them add sound effects and transitions for each slide, and record their voices as they read their text aloud and rerun their electronic book to check for needed revisions.
7. Have students present their slideshow to an audience of parents and classmates.

Assessment: To assess students, use a portfolio that will include worksheets, a list of references used, the storyboard draft, and the final *Kid Pix* slides.

On a different dimension are those software packages that allow students to create plays enacted on the screen by animated characters. *Opening Night* is a creativity program for third through eighth graders that turns a computer into a theater stage on which students can place realistic-looking actors and props from Victorian England. Students can select from sets, props, and actors. Each actor can walk and perform a variety of actions. The program also includes lighting effects, sound effects, and music. Students can make their scene come to life by recording the actors' movements, entering dialogue, and playing back the scene. The text-to-speech feature allows them to hear the actors' lines. One teacher taught students how to use *Opening Night* to act out the mystery stories they wrote using a matrix logic puzzle (Mysteries in the Logic Lounge, 1999) to create the plot (see Figure 8 on page 124).

Figure 6
Instructional Plan for Responding to Literature Through Illustration

Objective: To have students create a personal response to literature through illustration and use a drawing/painting tool to create their illustration.

Materials: Faith Ringgold's *Tar Beach* and *Kid Pix Studio Deluxe*.

Activities: 1. Read the story *Tar Beach* to students.
2. Have students brainstorm their responses to the question, What would you own if you "flew" over it?
3. Teach students to use *Kid Pix Studio Deluxe* and guidelines for illustrating.
4. Have students create individual slides with their illustrated answer to the question.
5. Have them present their *Kid Pix Studio Deluxe* slideshow to an audience of classmates and/or parents, giving a brief speech as they show their slide.

Assessment: Determine students' learning by a slideshow that contains final illustrations in response to the literature question.

Figure 7
Example of Student's Personal Response to *Tar Beach* With *Kid Pix Studio Deluxe*

Figure 8
Instructional Plan for Responding to Literature Through Plays

Objectives: To have students work in teams to explore deductive reasoning and matrix logic; explore mystery as a genre; and create a mystery play.

Materials: Marjorie Weinman Sharmat and Marc Simont's *Nate the Great* and other mystery stories; and the software package *Opening Night*.

Activities:
1. Share a variety of mystery stories with students.
2. Introduce deductive reasoning skills using Mind Benders series and matrix logic puzzles.
3. Have students, working in small groups of three or four, create a matrix logic puzzle for a mystery play. Each scene in the play should eliminate a suspect.
4. Have students plan their mystery by completing a description of the mystery, the setting, props, a list of characters, and the dialogue for each character.
5. Have students create the mystery play using *Opening Night*.

Assessment: Base assessment on the matrix designed to illustrate the logic of the mystery, and copies of the electronic plays the students created.

HyperStudio is another popular multimedia package. Using pages called "cards" and files referred to as "stacks," this program allows users to branch to different cards through a system of links called "buttons." Thus, *HyperStudio*'s hypertext format enables users to create and navigate through multiple cards. The capability of including sounds, video clips, photos, original graphics, and clip art makes this program particularly motivating to students.

HyperStudio projects have been used at many grade levels. For example, students worked with a kindergarten teacher to create their own stories with accompanying pictures, and the teacher scanned her students' pictures into a *HyperStudio* stack. The parents were delighted when their children's works were shown at a parents' night assembly. Graduate students in a university reading clinic had their young students write story summaries of books they were reading in the tutoring sessions. The finished products, including the tutored students' photos, artwork, and recorded voices reading the text they had written for each *HyperStudio* card, were demonstrated at the final session of the clinic. Pairs of students gave oral presentations to their parents describing their work. Students in a primary class used the program to demonstrate their creative solution to a problem presented in a piece of literature (see Figures 9 and 10).

Figure 9
Instructional Plan for Responding to Literature
Through Creative Problem Solving

Objectives: To have students explore the creative problem-solving process; use the creative problem-solving process to solve a problem presented in literature; and illustrate their creative solutions using a multimedia program.

Materials: Don and Audrey Wood's *King Bidgood's in the Bathtub*; and the software program *HyperStudio*.

Activities: 1. Discuss strategies for solving problems creatively.
2. Have students, as a group, identify a problem within the school that needs a creative solution, then have them brainstorm potential solutions for the problem.
3. Read *King Bidgood's in the Bathtub* to the class.
4. Have students explore a creative solution for getting King Bidgood out of the bathtub.
5. Have students, working in pairs or small groups, decide on a solution and illustrate that solution on paper.
6. Have students create the solution in *HyperStudio*, using the drawing tools.

Assessment: Determine students' learning by their creative solutions in a *HyperStudio* stack.

Figure 10
Example of Student's Creative Solution to *King Bidgood's in the Bathtub* With *HyperStudio*

I would make a button that would make the water cold. Then it would overflow and he would have to get out and clean it up.

Back

These are only a few examples of projects teachers have carried out using multimedia software. *HyperStudio* maintains a Web site (http://www.hyperstudio.com) on which many more student projects are displayed. From the Web site, teachers also can request copies of a *HyperStudio* tutorial booklet created by the publisher, which has proven helpful to students learning the basics of the program.

When teachers take advantage of packages that invite students to create and produce products such as those described and include these products in integrated units in their curriculum, writing becomes an authentic process. Students have audiences and valid purposes that prove far more motivating than a typical class composition written only for the teacher. Students take more pride in their work when they know that what they write will be read by classmates, parents, school administrators, and other readers around the world via the Internet.

Innovative Teachers' Applications of Technology

Teachers frequently use technology in the writing classroom to enhance their teaching. One of the most common applications is the use of the overhead projector to model writing. Lucy Calkins (1994) writes, "I cannot overemphasize how important it is that we be authentic, real, vulnerable people in our classrooms, influencing the community by our demonstrations" (p. 144). Nancie Atwell (1998) tells us, "I use the overhead almost every day—to demonstrate my writing in minilessons, show how a student solved a writing problem, present a poem to the group for discussion, or record information I want kids to copy into their writing-reading handbooks" (p. 102). Allowing students to write in front of their peers is another particularly effective use of this piece of equipment.

Using technology, a computer can be connected to an LCD (liquid crystal display) projector, which projects the image onto a screen, permitting teachers to demonstrate a particular computer application to a small group of students or to the entire class. This is an effective beginning step when introducing projects that involve technology. Teachers can give additional guidance later as students work on their projects individually or in pairs. Teachers also can use a program such as *PowerPoint*, described earlier, to enhance their teaching or a program such as *Inspiration* to create an idea web or concept map. *Inspiration* is an easy-to-use tool designed to map out ideas in a visual fashion. The program starts with a blank grid, then provides a set of drawing tools and more than 500 icons to create an idea web. This tool is ideal for helping students understand the steps of a class project.

In another lesson, a teacher used *Inspiration* with an LCD projector to introduce a lesson about prefixes and how they change meanings of words. This lesson was one step in teaching students the importance of word choice in writing. The teacher used the program to create a web of words, all of which began with the same prefix. Students analyzed the words, some common and others uncommon, to compare the prefix and root words and arrive at the definitions of the unknown words. The display, prepared before the lesson and managed by one of the teacher's students, captured the students' attention. (See Chapter 7 for additional information about this software product.)

Teacher applications of technology can be used for a variety of purposes. One teacher (Dickenson, 1992) found that preparing comments on a word processor with a template that she had created proved far more effective for her students than placing written comments in the margins of their drafts. Her students reported that they appreciated the suggestions and incorporated them into their writing. It also gave the teacher a permanent record of her remarks that she used for evaluating later drafts.

Students work at their own pace in a Writing Workshop classroom. Some are still in the first draft stage, others are busy revising, and still others are ready to share their work with their classmates. Database programs such as *ClarisWorks* or *Excel* help immensely when teachers keep track of their students' progress. Atwell (1998) writes, "I note each student's plans for writing workshop: what they tell me each day when I call the role [sic] and take the status-of-the-class. I record topic, genre, and what the writer intends to do" (p. 107). Some teachers allow students or an appointed captain to enter data in a database that contains categories such as starting, editing, conferring, work in progress, and so forth.

Teachers who use book clubs in their language arts program find databases helpful in tracking the progress and interaction within various discussion groups. If teachers require their students to write and discuss various responses to reading (for example, comparing and contrasting plots and characters across books and determining the importance of setting to the particular story), they can have students record the various techniques they have analyzed into a database. Teachers can check the variety and appropriateness of students' responses from time to time. Teachers also can keep a record of books students have read on a database. Using databases allows teachers to display updated hard copies of the records as a reminder to students of what they have accomplished.

Into Cyberspace With Writing

The Internet and e-mail have introduced a dimension in writing instruction that continues to grow. Creative projects take place daily that were unheard of a few years ago. Through the World Wide Web (WWW), learners have access to the most remote corners of the world. MayaQuest, a project that was active on the Internet for several years, allowed students to interact with archeologists in the Guatemalan jungles who were excavating ancient ruins. A summary of the project is now available on *MayaQuest Trail* CD-ROM or disk. Classes can track the progress of the annual dogsled race in Alaska, the Iditarod (http://www.Iditarod.com), making Gary Paulsen's own account of his experience in that race, *Woodsong*, more than a fictional story. (See Chapter 7 for a library/media specialist's project with this Web site.) Web sites abound where students can gather data for research papers, learn about projects that other classes have created, interact with adult authors or students their own age, and even publish their own writing.

Many school administrators have taken precautions to prevent students from stumbling by chance or by design on sites that could contain inappropriate language. Filters such as *SurfWatch* are available that block such language. Ask Jeeves for Kids (http://www.ajkids.com), one Internet browser available, has a built-in filter. Ask Jeeves has many features that make this browser easy for younger Internet users to search for their topics. Directions for using the search feature are given in language students can understand. They enter topics in a familiar language structure, such as, Where can I find information about frogs?, and "Jeeves" prompts until the point at which the question is automatically converted to the logic that search engines require. Ask Jeeves links to many sites that publish students' writing or that set up keypal (e-mail penpal) partners with other students around the world.

E-mail as a communication tool offers incredible potential for the writing program. E-mail allows creative teachers to enhance the curriculum with innovative projects that involve individual keypals or interactive group conversations. Writing in the classroom, then, takes on new meaning for students when their words are sent to and read by others.

E-mail projects between or among classes promote writing skills and provide opportunities for students to learn firsthand about other cultures. Leu, Karchmer, and Leu (1999) describe the Hobart-Malang Electronic Mail Project. In 1997, girls of school years four, five, and six at Fahan school in Hobart, Tasmania, and SDNP Elementary in Malang, Java, Indonesia, won first prize in the International Cyberfair competition for the development of the first school-based electronic-mail link between Australia and Indonesia. The project, created by Mary Fearnley Sanders of the University of Tasmania Faculty of Education, linked both teachers and students in the two schools through e-mail. Global Schoolhouse Projects and Programs (http://www.gsn.org/project/index.html) is one of many Web sites where teachers can link their students with others in collaborative projects.

Undergraduate students at a university in New Jersey carried out an e-mail project with students at a local school district (Sullivan, 1998). In this project, the university students shared ideas about selections from children's literature with fifth-grade, special-needs students. Groups of students were assigned a book to read and discuss once a week through e-mail. In their messages, the university students applied strategies to prompt higher level thinking skills such as problem solving or drawing inferences. As part of the approach used, the university students modeled thinking behaviors in messages to the fifth graders. They reflected on the literary elements found in the books they shared (for example, character development, foreshadowing, and tension). They also prompted the younger students to make comparisons with events in the story and their own life's experiences. In the fifth-grade classroom, the teacher helped students prepare their responses through oral discussion groups. Students took notes and decided what would be the focus of their next response. They composed their responses on a word processor, then cut and pasted them to the e-mail message space.

McKeon and Burkey (1998) carried out an e-mail project between preservice teachers and fourth and fifth graders in which literature was used as a vehicle for language and reading enhancement. The goal of their project differed slightly from the one just described: Sullivan's students held informal discussions about the literature selections, whereas McKeon and Burkey's students actually taught their correspondents specific lessons through e-mail. In both projects, results pointed to positive experiences for the university-age students and for their younger partners.

Teachers can find other opportunities to encourage student writing on the Internet. KidPub (http://www.kidpub.org) is a well-organized Web site that provides students opportunities to see their writing published on the Internet. Students can submit their poems and stories, using a form provided at the site. Directions for submissions are explained clearly, and the stories are posted within 3 days of being received. A particularly useful feature at this site is the KidPub Publisher's Picks link. The publisher provides reasons for choosing particular stories or poems. Thus, students not only read their own work or work written by peers, but also get some pointers in what makes a piece of writing good. For example, about one submission, the poem "moonlight woods" (sic) by Tally, age 12 (http://www.kidpub.org/kidpub/moonlight _woods-Tally.html), the publisher wrote, "Tally paints a beautiful word picture with a neat twist. Using short, evocative phrases like this is a powerful way to help the reader feel like he or she is experiencing what the words describe." Some of the writing examples have been submitted individually. Others are collections of students' writings that have been submitted by their teachers. At the KidPub site, students also can search for keypals.

For teachers who use international projects, Planet Friendship (http://www2.arnes.si/~sskkssb6s) is an interesting site. Coordinated by 12 students from a high school in Brezice, Slovenia, the project consists of a global map of the Planet Friendship, a love and friendship declaration in a variety of languages, a penpal database, words of wisdom, essays, and an activities site. The project offers opportunities to link writing with other curricular areas.

The emergence of Web site packages has made creating one's own Web site a popular pastime for many students. *Web Workshop* is one example of a software package that does not require knowledge of Hypertext Markup Language (HTML), the language of the World Wide Web. The program includes an easy-to-use interface along with backgrounds, clip art, and paint tools that students can use to create their own Web pages. A strength of this program is the inclusion of the filter *Surfwatch* which, similar to those filters mentioned, blocks material on the Internet that may not be appropriate for children. This program enables teachers to set up a Web site for their class and then link individual student Web pages to it. Creating their own Web sites is motivating for most students, more of whom are creating such sites each year.

Concluding Remarks

The potential for technology's use in writing grows exponentially. Multimedia presentations accent the strong link between the language and visual arts. Teachers' admonitions for clarity, details, and logic become meaningful in light of the instant audience that the Internet creates. Classrooms of the future will hold endless writing opportunities for teachers and students, providing them with virtual passports to places that today's students do not even know exist. The creativity of teachers and students will soar to new limits. But, all this will be possible only if today's teachers make it so. Technology itself is inanimate, and it will remain so unless innovative users breathe life into it.

References

Atwell, N. (1998). *In the middle: New understandings about writing, reading, and learning* (2nd ed.). Portsmouth, NH: Heinemann.

Baylor, B. (1995). *I'm in charge of celebrations.* New York: Aladin.

Bruce, B. (1999). Challenges for the evaluation of new informational communication technologies. *Journal of Adolescent & Adult Literacy, 42,* 450–455.

Burns, P.C., Roe, B.D., & Ross, E.P. (1999). *Technology for literacy learning: A primer.* Boston: Houghton Mifflin.

Calkins, L. (1994). *The art of teaching writing.* Portsmouth, NH: Heinemann.

ClarisWorks [Computer software]. (1997). Santa Clara, CA: Claris.

Dickenson, P. (1992). *Feedback that works: Using the computer to respond.* Paper presented at the Annual National Basic Writing Conference, College Park, MD.

EasyBook Deluxe [Computer software]. (1998). Pleasantville, NY: Sunburst Communications.

Excel [Computer software]. (1996). Redmond, WA: Microsoft.

Expression [Computer software]. (1996). Pleasantville, NY: Sunburst Communications.

FrameMaker [Computer software]. (1995). San Jose, CA: Adobe Systems.

Grolier Multimedia Encyclopedia [Computer software]. (1999). Danbury, CT: Grolier Interactive.

Hawisher, G., & Selfe, C. (1999). Reflections on research in computers and composition studies at the century's end. In J. Hancock (Ed.), *Teaching literacy using information technology* (pp. 31–47). Newark, DE: International Reading Association.

Herzog Keyboarding [Computer software]. (1999). Tucson, AZ: Herzog Keyboarding.

HyperStudio [Computer software]. (1996). El Cajon, CA: Roger Wagner Publishing.

Imagination Express [Computer software]. (1994). Redmond, WA: Edmark.

Inspiration [Computer software]. (1997). Portland, OR: Inspiration Software.

JumpStart Typing [Computer software]. (1998). Torrance, CA: Knowledge Adventure.

Kid Pix Studio Deluxe [Computer software]. (1998). Cambridge, MA: Brøderbund/The Learning Company.

Kid Works Deluxe [Computer software]. (1997). Torrance, CA: Knowledge Adventure.

King, M.L., & Rentel, V.M. (1981). Research update: Conveying meaning in written texts. *Language Arts, 58,* 721–728.

Leu, D.J., Karchmer, R.A., & Leu, D.D. (1999). Exploring literacy on the Internet. *The Reading Teacher, 52,* 636–643. Available: http://www.readingonline.org/electronic/RT/rumphius.html

Macrorie, K. (1997). The Reawakening of curiosity: Research papers as hunting stories. In C.B. Olson (Ed.), *Practical ideas for teaching writing as a process at the high school and college levels* (pp. 152–155). Sacramento, CA: California Department of Education.

Mavis Beacon Teaches Typing [Computer software]. (1996). Cambridge, MA: Brøderbund/The Learning Company.

MayaQuest Trail [Computer software]. (1998). Cambridge, MA: The Learning Company.

McKeon, C., & Burkey, L. (1998). A literature-based email collaborative. In E. Sturtevant, J. Dugan, P. Linder, & W. Linek (Eds.), *Literacy and community, the twentieth yearbook* (pp. 84–93). Commerce, TX: College Reading Association.

Michaels, S., & Bruce, B. (1989). *Classroom context in literacy development: How writing systems shape the teaching and learning of composition* (Technical Report No. 476). Urbana-Champaign, IL: Center for the Study of Reading.

Microsoft Word [Computer sofware]. (1999). Redmond, WA: Microsoft.

Mind Bender series (1998). Pacific Grove, CA: Critical Thinking Books & Software.

Mysteries in the logic lounge. (1999). In P. Murphy, E. Klages, P. Tesler, L. Shore, & The Exploratorium, *The brain explorer.* New York: Henry Holt.

Opening Night [Computer software]. (1995). Cambridge, MA: MECC/The Learning Company.

Paulsen, G. (1991). *Woodsong.* New York: Puffin.

PAWS in Typing Town [Computer software]. (1996). New York: SRA/McGraw-Hill.

PostCards [Computer software]. (1996). North Billerica, MA: Curriculum Associates.

PowerPoint [Computer software]. (1996). Redmond, WA: Microsoft.

The Print Shop Deluxe [Computer software]. (1996). Cambridge, MA: Brøderbund/The Learning Company.

Reinking, D. (1997). Me and my hypertext:) A multiple digression analysis of technology and literacy (sic), *The Reading Teacher, 50,* 620–643.

Reinking, D., Labbo, L., & McKenna, M. (1997). Navigating the changing landscape of literacy: Current research in computer-based reading and writing. In J. Flood, S.B. Heath, & D. Lapp (Eds.), *Handbook of research on teaching literacy through the communicative and visual arts* (pp. 77–92). New York: Macmillan.

Ringgold, F. (1996). *Tar beach.* New York: Dragonfly.

Scardamalia, M., Bereiter, C., & Goelman, H. (1982). The role of production factors in writing ability. In M. Nystrand (Ed.), *What writers know: The language, process and structure of written discourse* (pp. 173–210). New York: Academic Press.

Sharmat, M.W., & Simont, M. (1977). *Nate the great.* New York: Young Yearling.

Slam Dunk Typing [Computer software]. (1997). Cambridge, MA: Creative Wonders/The Learning Company.

Storybook Weaver Deluxe [Computer software]. (1996). Cambridge, MA: The Learning Company.

Student Writing Center [Computer software]. (1993). Cambridge, MA: The Learning Company.

Sullivan, J. (1998). The electronic journal: Combining literacy and technology. *The Reading Teacher, 52,* 90–93.

Sunbuddy Writer [Computer software]. (1996). Pleasantville, NY: Sunburst Communications.

Surfwatch [Computer software]. (1996). Los Gatos, CA: Spyglass.

Type to Learn [Computer software]. (1996). Pleasantville, NY: Sunburst Communications.

Web Workshop [Computer software]. (1996). Pleasantville, NY: Sunburst Communications.

WordPerfect [Computer software]. (1995). Ottawa, ON: Corel.

Writers Studio [Computer software]. (1998). Sunnyvale, CA: Computer Curriculum Corporation.

CHAPTER 6

Using Technology
for Content Area Literacy

BETTY D. ROE

Mrs. Groce's third-grade class is studying flight. She introduces the day by reading from such books as *The Wright Brothers* by Russell Freedman, *The Glorious Flight* by Alice and Martin Provensen, and *Lost Star* by Patricia Lauber. Then students view an *mPower* presentation that she has prepared, using scans of photographs taken from the literature books, and text, pictures, and video clips of Amelia Earhart and the Wright Brothers from *Grolier Multimedia Encyclopedia*.

Mrs. Groce offers students unit-related activities in every subject from a thematic unit by Vaden (1991). She uses a table for students to re-create a time sequence of events relating to flight, a diagram on which students can label plane parts, a table and bar graph that students use for mathematical calculations, a time line of milestones in history for students to study, a world map to locate the world's busiest airports, and an activity in which students write job descriptions (using *The Student Writing Center*) after studying flight careers. Some activities for the children involve accessing Web sites, such as http://quest.arc.nasa.gov/aero/wright/kids, the Wright Flyer Online site. One of the links at this site is to Student Stumpers, where students connect with other students who are also learning about flight. Students make up challenging questions about flight for other students to solve. Other sites that are used in this unit are as follows:

http://hawaii.psychology.msstate.edu/invent/air_main.shtml
http://www.youngeagles.com/games/index.html
http://www.phxskyharbor.com/skyharbr/kids/index.html
http://www.fi.edu/flights
http://www.aero-web.org/history/wright/wright.html

http://www.firstflight.org/shrine/wright_brothers.html
http://www.catskill.net/evolution/flight/home.html

Students use these sites to do activities such as word searches, student stumpers, dot-to-dot aviation puzzles, paper airplane construction, scavenger hunts, and science projects. Mrs. Groce lets the students choose online activities that interest them most.

Later students will create their own slide presentations using *KidPix* as a culminating activity.

In content area classrooms, teachers are concerned with transmitting content in the most effective way possible. Because reading and writing are common tools for learning content, content area literacy becomes critical to this learning. Many types of technology, from audiotapes to computer applications, can be used to increase both content literacy and the learning of specific content.

Definition of Content Area Literacy

Content area literacy is "the ability to use reading and writing for the acquisition of new content in a given discipline" (McKenna & Robinson, 1990, p. 184). Content area literacy applies to all grade levels. It goes beyond general reading ability because it involves the reading and writing of material that contains different expository text patterns, a higher concept density than is generally found in narrative texts, and specialized and technical as well as general vocabulary.

Influences on Content Area Literacy

A student's content area literacy depends on several factors: prior knowledge about the subject, attitude toward the subject, interest in the subject, purpose for reading and writing, readability level of the material, and the style of writing used in the particular material. Prior knowledge about the topic helps students read the material with comprehension because the vocabulary is familiar, at least in oral communication, which makes the written material more predictable and provides more basis for making inferences. It helps students write about the topic more effectively because existing schemata (clusters of related concepts) help students organize their knowledge for presentation.

Content area literacy depends on a student's attitude toward the subject and interest in the specific topic of study because they both affect the effort and the degree of concentration that the student is likely to attain. Students who are interested in and have positive attitudes toward a subject will put more effort into reading and writing about it and will be more likely to persist in literacy activities over time. Students need effort and concentration to activate prior knowledge, make inferences, analyze content area material critically, and write about it accurately, critically, and creatively.

The student's purpose for reading or writing about content material also affects content area literacy. Purposeful reading results in better comprehension because it focuses the reader's attention. The purpose for writing also focuses the writer on pertinent facts and theories in the subject area and encourages organization of the material for a meaningful presentation.

The readability level and style of writing of material being read may affect content literacy adversely if the material is written at a high level of difficulty or if the author's style is not familiar to the reader. However, a comfortable level of difficulty and a familiar style can enhance content literacy.

Benefits of Using Technology to Support Content Literacy

Central to content area literacy is familiarity with vocabulary that is specific to particular content areas. Because vocabulary terms are labels for schemata, concept development becomes an important part of content instruction.

Involvement of sensory input of different types enhances concept development. Technology allows you to use still and moving images, sound, and print to help students develop more complete understandings of concepts being presented. In presenting print, you can use a variety of technological tools, ranging from transparency projectors to computers. Taped sounds and commentaries, videotaped live action, or animations also can enhance concept development. You can present these sounds and images on videotape recorders, video disc players, DVD (digital video disc) players, or computers. For example, to develop the concept "mammals," you could use printed lists of the characteristics of mammals, labeled diagrams of these characteristics, still pictures of various mammals, and video clips of the mammals in their native habitats (accompanied by their actual sounds and voiceovers pointing out the characteristics).

Electronic reference works used to improve understanding of a concept may provide both visual and auditory inputs that students can access as needed. This multimodal stimulation and provision for repetition in a variety of ways enhances learning. The interactivity is particularly helpful. Students also have more control over their learning paces and modes when using many of these applications.

Technological Tools for Instruction

Today there are many technological tools to enhance content area instruction. Students need general literacy skills for using most of the applications, but specialized literacy skills also are needed for many. These skills are discussed in the following sections about particular technology applications.

Transparencies

Most classrooms are equipped with overhead projectors, but they are often underused. Instructional transparencies are useful for presenting an outline or web of the material to be included in a lesson, providing visual referents for new vocabulary, presenting labeled diagrams of parts of items under study (for example, parts of a leaf), or showing, through use of overlays, the relative positions of components of a complex organism (such as systems in the human body) or machine (systems in an automobile). Artistic teachers are often the ones who use transparencies most, but these visual aids are helpful for other teachers, as well. Outlines and webs require no artistic talent, and many prepared transparencies are available for almost any content topic. Students also can make transparencies that result from small-group discussions and use them to share with the rest of the class. You can invite students to write their own contributions on blank transparencies when the class is brainstorming about a topic in order to activate schemata before reading takes place. These student uses of transparencies require organizational skills.

Audiotapes

Audiotape recorders and tapes are inexpensive and readily available in most classrooms. Prerecorded audiotaped materials about many content area subjects also may be purchased. Some materials have accompanying printed transcripts that allow students to hear the information as they read it, reinforcing the new vocabulary and providing support for students who do not read on a level necessary to read the materials independently. You may wish to create your own audiotapes of reading assignments and make them available for use with students who cannot read the material with comprehension without such help. You can ask students who are good readers to make the tapes, but you should check tapes made by students before they are used for instructional purposes. This activity often will help the student who makes the tape as much as the one who listens to it.

As a part of a unit study, you can designate specific students to listen to different audiotapes. In this case the students can take notes about the information found on the tapes and share the information they have gleaned with other class members.

Students also can audiotape class discussions for later notetaking or checking of notetaking that was done when the discussion was ongoing. They may audiotape interviews with resource people who provide class-related information. Later they may transcribe these interviews and use them for references for research papers or oral presentations. They also can audiotape class skits and oral presentations for evaluation purposes. Such tapes are often kept in portfolios as evidence of learning.

Videotapes

Videotape recorders and camcorders are generally available in schools, if not in individual classrooms. Videotapes are used in most of the same ways that audiotapes are used, except for making tapes for read-alongs. They add a visual dimension to the presentation of and recording of events that makes them more effective in concept development activities and sometimes in evaluation procedures, because more information is available about the presentations. A book available for creating videotapes is *Creating Videos for School Use* (Valmont, 1995).

Educational Television

Classrooms often have their own televisions, and many teachers plan certain classes around educational television programs, such as "The Charlie Horse Music Pizza," a music education program on the Public Broadcasting System for the primary grades. Educational programs may offer actual instruction in the content area or they may provide background or elaborative information about a unit of study. General broadcast television programs often offer good content material for some classes also. You may videotape programs that do not occur at convenient times in the school day and play them for the class later. If this is done, you must follow copyright laws carefully. There are limitations on the number of times a tape can be viewed and the time frame within which the viewing may occur. Sometimes you simply may ask students to watch the programs for homework and hold a class discussion later. In either case, you can have students take notes on the material and write reports or reviews on some of it.

Video Discs (Laser Discs)

Video discs require special players that are fairly expensive and therefore are not available in all classrooms. Nevertheless, when they are available, they offer good instructional opportunities. They allow you and your students to access the data on them randomly, making them more flexible and interactive than television programs or videotapes. Locations on the discs are accessed through the use of a barcode reader or through a computer connection. Video discs also provide sharper images and clearer sound than videotapes do. Many excellent prerecorded video discs are available. Bonnie Ashburn, a third-grade teacher in Crossville, Tennessee, uses the *U.S. States and Regions* video disc program as the focus of social studies lessons. A sample lesson is shown in Figure 1.

Digital Video Discs (DVDs)

Many functions of videocassette recorders (VCRs), video discs, and compact discs (CDs) soon may be taken over by DVDs. A DVD, a disc that is the same size as a CD, delivers outstanding video and audio and holds much more data than a videotape, video disc, or CD ("A DVD Primer," 1999). Set-top DVD players connect directly to televisions, but there are also DVD-ROM drives

Figure 1
Transportation Lesson (Third Grade)

Objectives: To compare characteristics of rural and urban areas; compare forms of transportation in rural and urban areas; and compare different forms of transportation found in a city.

Materials: *U.S. States and Regions* video disc; pictures and postcards showing New York City transportation; and a U.S. map or computer atlas program or computer connected to the Internet.

Activities: 1. Have students take an imaginary plane ride to New York.
2. Locate your town and New York on an in-class U.S. map, a computer atlas program, or an Internet site that has maps.
3. Introduce and show the video disc, in the section called "People Movers," pausing at points suggested in the program guide.
4. Share and discuss pictures and postcards that include New York sights and types of transportation.

Assessment: Base assessment on students' ability to name the different forms of transportation shown in the video and pictures.

---

that are available for computers. CDs also can be played in DVD-ROM drives. A slight drawback for DVDs is that some computer processors are not currently fast enough to manage the higher quality content (Stabenau, 1999).

Movies and reference works are both appearing in DVD-ROM format. Two examples that could be useful in classrooms are *Birds of the World* and *The Complete National Geographic: 109 Years of National Geographic Magazine*. *Birds of the World* allows students to "learn about anatomy, courtship and mating rituals, and nesting and migration cycles" of 786 birds from around the world (http://www.multicom.com/catalog/page/dvd_birds.html). The *National Geographic* DVD-ROM offers much pertinent material for social studies and science classes.

Computer Applications

Many of the technological tools in use today are computer based. The following computer-based applications are useful in teaching content subjects and depend on the use of literacy skills and strategies.

Electronic databases

Electronic databases allow the categorization and storage of data, as well as electronic searches for retrieving the data. Students can develop databases of information related to the topics under study and later search these databases as reference sources for related class activities (for example, to confirm or reject viewpoints offered in class discussion or as input for writing research papers on the content). Using databases requires students to make judgments about relevant data and ways of data presentation and allows them to analyze and synthesize large amounts of related data (Heide & Henderson, 1994).

Electronic encyclopedias are elaborate electronic databases (on CD-ROMs, DVD-ROMs, or the Internet) that provide information on almost any content topic. Some provide text only, but most of the current ones are multimedia encyclopedias that offer hypermedia connections, allowing students who are reading about a class topic to click on a word or icon that will link them to related information in the form of an article, a still picture, an animation, a video clip, or an audio clip. Such reading is nonlinear and can result in navigational problems if a student follows links from one article to the next and gets further and further from the initial article. However, a "Back" button on the navigation bar of the program will back students out of the sequences they have followed, one step at a time, even if the program does not have a special function to help students return to the original entry.

Developing an Electronic Database

In a social studies class, you might want your students to make a database on the Presidents of the United States. You could assign individual students or small groups of students to be responsible for collecting data on one or more presidents and for entering the data into the class database. Students might collect the following categories of data: age when elected, home state, political party, time in office, and most outstanding accomplishment as president. After all the presidents' information has been entered into the database, the students may sort the database in different ways to find out likenesses and differences among the chief executives. For example, they could sort on home state and discover how many presidents came from each state, which states have never produced a president, and so on. Older students might have discussions about reasons for some of the results.

Similar databases could be formed on heads of state of different countries. Databases on primary industries in or primary exports of different countries also could be constructed.

Literacy skills involved: reading resources for details, categorizing information, making comparisons and contrasts, and drawing conclusions based on the data.

Many electronic encyclopedias allow material to be copied to notepads, edited, and printed. This material may form the basis for class reports, but you have to show students how to put the information into their own words and to integrate the material from the encyclopedia with material from other references. When material from the encyclopedia simply has to be chosen and printed, instead of having to be rewritten, the temptation for students to copy it directly, without attribution, may increase. You need to prevent this temptation by giving imaginative assignments that require the reporting of information in unique formats or from different perspectives. For example, students might have to incorporate the information into a friendly letter or an advertisement or write the material from the viewpoint of a historical figure. (See Chapter 8 for additional thoughts about avoiding plagiarism.) *Grolier Multimedia Encyclopedia Online* (http://gme.grolier.com) and *Encyclopaedia Britannica Online* (http://www.eb.com) are two examples of online encyclopedias. Several others are available.

Electronic atlases are also types of electronic databases (on CD-ROMs, DVD-ROMs, or the Internet) that are useful reference tools in content classrooms. They provide students with maps of areas under study. Students may choose distant views to see the location of a place in relation to the entire hemisphere or zoom in to views that are closer to discover features of the immediate surroundings. An example of one electronic atlas is found in Figure 2.

There are several Web sites that have links to online atlases (http://www.kidinfo.com/References/Atlases.html and http://www.lib.utulsa.edu/netref/maps.htm). Some individual atlases that may be used are Atlapedia Online (http://www.atlapedia.com), MapQuest (http://www.mapquest.com), and National Geographic's Map Machine (http://www.nationalgeographic.com/resources/ngo/maps).

There are many other database programs (available on disk, CD-ROM, or DVD-ROM) that contain material useful in content area instruction. Some of these are discussed in later sections related to specific content areas.

Figure 2
Example of an Electronic Atlas

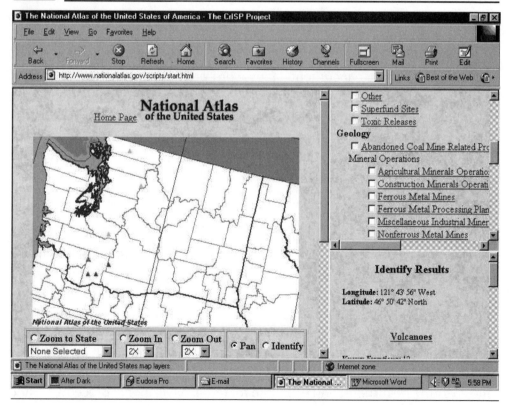

Simulations

Simulations mimic actual situations. Electronic simulations make possible experimentation in the classroom with past or current real-world situations that are too expensive or potentially dangerous to actually perform in a classroom. The computer provides a model of the situation, and students are allowed to manipulate actions and events in order to reach specific goals: for example, successful completion of a trip in a wagon train or profitable operation of a business. These simulations can be content specific, but all of them require substantial literacy skills. Program users must think critically and draw conclusions about written and visual information. Students make choices about the events involved in the simulations, and the computer's responses vary according to the individual choices. Students may use reference books to help them make decisions. Content-specific simulations are discussed in the sections of this chapter focusing on various content areas.

Word-processing and desktop publishing software

Word-processing software allows students to write reports and revise them with a minimum of frustration because they can insert material, delete material, and move material with a few mouse clicks or keystrokes. This makes them more receptive to revision of material to clarify its focus, add needed detail, or delete irrelevant material. Desktop publishing software allows the integration of text and graphics in a document. Many word-processing programs also incorporate elements of desktop publishing, allowing students to produce attractive illustrated reports, newspapers, magazines, and Web pages related to areas of study. There are even multimedia word-processing programs that blur the distinction between word-processing software and presentation software (described following). (See Chapter 5 for additional information.)

Presentation software

Multimedia presentation software, such as *mPower*, *HyperStudio*, and *PowerPoint*, makes possible informative, eye-catching presentations by teachers and students alike. As explained in Chapter 5, these types of programs allow the user to combine print, graphics, still and moving images, sound effects, and speech to present information on topics being studied in class. Such projects require much planning before implementation, and they work well for students in cooperative groups. Users must make decisions about organization of the presentation, design elements to include (color schemes, backgrounds, and so forth), documentation of source material, navigational procedures, and media to include. Students may construct storyboards as a part of the planning process. Brunner (1996) suggests that teachers base evaluations of the projects on these elements.

Barbara Vaughn, a seventh-grade literacy teacher, works with Nickey Franklin, a seventh-grade social studies teacher, to integrate the learning of literacy and social studies content through technology use. She uses the instructional plan in Figure 3, incorporating presentation software, for the sequence of lessons in the unit on states in the United States.

Figure 3
Instructional Unit on U.S. States (Seventh Grade)

Objectives:	To integrate the learning of literacy skills and strategies with the learning of social studies content; provide students with experience using traditional print sources and the World Wide Web as information sources; provide students with experience using the *mPower* program to construct a class presentation; and expose students to information about all 50 states while they become experts on their own states.
Materials:	Software package *mPower*; reference sources in print format; and a list of required information.
Activities:	1. Familiarize students with the workings of the *mPower* software.
	2. Review with students some available print resources in the library and library search procedures, and familiarize students with search strategies for use of the World Wide Web (use of the browser and search engines).
	3. Provide a list of required information for inclusion in the projects (for example, state motto, state tree, state flower, state bird, picture of state flag drawn freehand or used from clip art file, map of state drawn freehand or used from clip art file, state song, number of counties, length, width, number of square miles, and a superlative about the state).
	4. Give students time to work on their projects in the classroom, library, or computer lab.
	5. Let all of the students view all of the presentations when they are completed.
Assessment:	This presentation will receive grades in both social studies and English classes. The social studies grade will be based on how much information the presentation contains (10 points are assigned to each required item). The English grade will be based on the amount of information and the effectiveness of the presentation: Is it logically organized? Does it flow smoothly? Were pictures used to supplement the information? Did the presentation contain music? Were the grammar and mechanics (spelling, capital letters, and punctuation) correct?

The Internet

As explained earlier in this volume, the Internet is an international network of computer networks that can communicate with one another through the use of computer addresses (Uniform Resource Locators, or URLs). There are more than 30 million of these connected computers (Bruce, 1998), and each computer has its own address. The World Wide Web (WWW, or the Web) is a part of the Internet that allows users to access multimedia materials (video, sound, graphics, and animations) through the use of a Web browser (for example, *Internet Explorer* or *Netscape Navigator*). As described in Chapter 2, the browser makes it possible for users to click on links found on one Web site to material on other sites on the Web and go there immediately, without having to type in the URL for the specific computer. There are sites on the Web that are useful resources for teachers and students in any content area discipline. Examples of sites for different disciplines are found in Figure 4.

Navigating the Web. Because of the nature of the Web, navigation problems may arise. Students may wander far afield from their original topic as they follow hyperlinks to related sites. By clicking the "Back" button on the navigation bar of the browser, users can usually retrace their steps in the movement through sites and return to the original locations. If at any time users find sites that they may want to visit again, they can add the sites to the bookmarks that the browser allows users to save and organize into folders. Visiting the sites at a later date will require only clicking on the bookmarks, instead of keying in the URLs for the sites.

Search engines on the Web, such as AltaVista and WebCrawler, allow users to do keyword searches for particular topics. Users must then examine the search results for appropriate material. Some will be useful, but others will not be on target for students' needs.

Using the Internet for study and research. To use the Internet for study and research, students need to realize the differences in the organizational patterns of Internet sites from those of books. Instead of a table of contents, the Internet site provides a main menu, which is a list of the major topics available on the site. This menu often is on the home page of the site. Sometimes this menu is in words that are hyperlinks to other pages in the site, sometimes it has icons that provide the links, and sometimes it has both. Clicking on a topic from the main menu may take the user to actual information or to another menu page that further refines the focus of the search. Many submenus may be embedded in a site. Rather than offering informational footnotes or endnotes, an Internet site generally provides hyperlinks to such materials, which may reside

Figure 4
Examples of Sites for Different Disciplines

Mathematics
Houghton Mifflin's Brain Teasers (http://www.eduplace.com/math/brain)
The Good News Bears Stock Market Project
(http://www.ncsa.uiuc.edu/edu/RSE/RSEyellow/gnb.html)
Eisenhower National Clearinghouse for Mathematics and Science Education
(http://www.enc.org/index.htm)

Science
NASA Human Spaceflight (http://shuttle.nasa.gov/index.html)
The MAD Scientist Network (http://www.madsci.org)
Science Learning Network (http://www.sln.org)
Eisenhower National Clearinghouse for Mathematics and Science Education
(http://www.enc.org/index.htm)
Space Telescope Science Institute (http://www.stsci.edu)

Social Studies
The American Civil War Home Page
(http://sunsite.utk.edu/civil-war/warweb.html)
Library of Congress—Selected Civil War Photographs
(http://rs6.loc.gov/ammem/cwphome.html)
Kid Info...Atlases (http://www.kidinfo.com/References/Atlases.html)
The University of Tulsa McFarlin Library Reference Center
(http://www.lib.utulsa.edu/netref/maps.htm)
Atlapedia Online (http://www.atlapedia.com)
MapQuest (http://www.mapquest.com)
National Geographic's Map Machine
(http://www.nationalgeographic.com/maps/index.html)
The White House for Kids
(http://www.whitehouse.gov/WH/kids/html/kidshome.html)
The Good News Bears Stock Market Project
(http://www.ncsa.uiuc.edu/edu/RSE/RSEyellow/gnb.html)

The Arts
The Art Teacher Connection (http://www.inficad.com/~arted)
The Charlie Horse Music Pizza Web Site
(http://www.pbs.org/charliehorse)

Cross-Curricular
Grolier Multimedia Encyclopedia Online (http://gme.grolier.com)
Encyclopaedia Britannica Online (http://www.eb.com)
Library of Congress (http://www.loc.gov)
Teachers@Work (http://teachers.work.co.nz)

on separate Web pages. Appendixes, glossaries, footnotes, and bibliographies may be separate Web pages at a given site and can generally be located from the main menu.

Electronic mail (E-mail). If classroom computers are connected to the Internet, in addition to the capability to search sites on other computers for information, students have access to worldwide electronic mail. You may set up keypal (e-mail penpal) partnerships for your class with classrooms in schools in other states or countries for the purpose of discussing information related to a unit of study, as mentioned in Chapter 4. Literacy teachers may pair students to share general information in order to have focused writing practice, but teachers in other content areas may match students to discuss information about common areas of study. Some even perform environmental experiments in their own locations and share the information obtained in order to compare the two locations.

E-mail exchanges also may take place between an expert in an area of study and the class. For example, a well-known archeologist might correspond with the class about archeological digs. Sometimes professors may pair teacher education classes in content area methods courses with elementary students for discussion of content issues. For example, my literacy methods students at Tennessee Technological University are paired with classes of seventh graders from Livingston Middle School in an adjoining county to discuss literature selections that both groups are reading. The partners communicate about the selections through regularly scheduled e-mail exchanges. The university students try to model literary analysis and reading strategies, while conversing with the seventh graders about a book that they are both reading. Students and teachers at both levels have evaluated the exchanges positively over the 3 years of their use (Burns, Roe, & Ross, 1999; Roe & Smith, 1997; Roe, Stoodt, & Burns, 1998).

An exchange between a university student and a seventh grader is shown in Figure 5. They are beginning to read a second book together, one that has been chosen by the seventh grader. The university student took the lead on the discussion of the previous book, Jerry Spinelli's *Maniac Magee*; the seventh grader is taking the lead on this book, Kevin Henkes's *Words of Stone*. She has become accustomed to analyzing the story and providing her reasoning. The exchanges have become true discussions between interested readers.

Electronic mailing lists (listservs) on a topic of study may be subscribed to for a period of time. With such lists, all subscribers receive the messages sent to the list. Often many messages per day arrive and may clog up the mail sys-

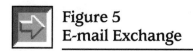

Figure 5
E-mail Exchange

Subject: Segment 1 Words of Stone
Date: Mon, 15 Mar 1999 11:30:56+0000
From: Barbara Vaughn<vaughnb01@ten-nash.ten.k12.tn.us>
To: Kristen Pennycuff<pennycuffk@ten-nash.ten.k12.tn.us>

Dear Kristen,
      Sorry I haven't written in so long. It took me a long time to start the book. Do you like it so far? I think it's sad, mean and cool altogether. It think it's sad because both Blaze an Joselle have lost their moms. Joselle hasn't lost her mom physically, but mentally her mother is gone. The reason I think it's mean is because of what Joselle did to Blaze. Writing those cruel messages on the stones was really mean. Cool, well I really can't explain what I mean by that, but when I read further into the book, I'll be able to explain what I mean. Would you do that to someone if they had lost their mother? I sure wouldn't and would hope that they wouldn't do it to me.
      Well, I'll talk to you soon. Hope you enjoy the book.

Your friend,
Tamyra

Subject: Tamyra Albanese: Book Two, Segment One
Date: Wed, 17 Mar 1999 08:43:32-0500
From: Kristen Pennycuff<pennycuffk@ten-nash.ten.k12.tn.us>
To: Barbara Vaughn<vaughnb01@ten-nash.ten.k12.tn.us>

Dear Tamyra,
      I am having a very hard time with this book. It is so realistic, and I can't seem to get the characters out of my mind. My heart breaks for Blaze and Joselle. I agree with your statement that Joselle hasn't lost her mother physically, but mentally instead. I think it is so cruel for "The Beautiful Vicky" to make Joselle feel that she is in the way. Joselle's memories of her mother's actions seem to be conflicting, varying from a person who spends quality time with her child to a cruel, self-centered woman. I can see that Joselle models her behavior after the undesirable traits her mother has, and I wonder how this will affect her future actions. To answer your question, I certainly could not deliberately use another's pain against him or her.
      Blaze has dealt with an unfair amount of tragedy in his short life. He seems to yearn for the serenity of letting go, but I'm not sure he knows how. It is reassuring that he wants to sleep in the dark and ride the Ferris wheel alone. I wonder what role this Claire will play in helping overcome the pain.
      Have a wonderful day! Kristen

tem if they are not read, analyzed, and deleted fairly quickly. You may wish to scan the messages in order to filter out any comments that are inappropriate for classroom consideration and then let students read and evaluate the others. This evaluation is an authentic critical reading activity. The class may subscribe to a list only long enough to ask some specific questions and record the answers; they can unsubscribe when they have obtained desired information.

You may wish to subscribe to RTEACHER (http://www.reading.org/publications/journals/RT/rt_listserv.htm), an electronic mailing list for teachers who wish to discuss literacy and technology issues with educators around the world. Other options exist for teachers and students, depending on their interest areas.

Discussion groups, newsgroups, or forums are electronic bulletin boards on the Web that allow users to go to a network location and read messages posted on the group's topic or post comments themselves. Unless the discussion group has been set up for a particular group (perhaps a school system) and can be entered only by use of a password, you may not want to use it as a class assignment because there may be inappropriate comments posted.

Web page publication is a way that you can give your students an audience for the results of their research papers and other projects. If students know that people throughout the world, not just you, will read their work, they have an incentive to organize it carefully and work on presenting it in a written form that is coherent, free of grammatical and mechanical errors, and visually appealing. Many current word-processing programs, for example *Microsoft Word*, offer output options for Web publishing. In addition there are special programs such as *FrontPage* dedicated to this function.

Technological Applications Across the Curriculum

Technology in Mathematics Instruction

The most pervasive application of technology in mathematics instruction is use of the calculator. It can be used to do rapid computations that would take much time for a student to do by hand. Speeding up the process of computation leaves the student free to spend more time on the problem-solving aspects of the discipline. Statement problems are generally the biggest concern of mathematics students. They involve all levels of comprehension, from reading for details, to making inferences about operations needed to solve the problems, to evaluating the reasonableness of the results. When students use the calculator for the mechanical computation process, their mental energy is available for these comprehension tasks.

Students can do rapid computation on computers, as well, and spreadsheet software is often a part of math lessons. Spreadsheets allow users to enter data and calculation formulas to work on problems involving large collections of data. When data are changed, added to, or deleted from the spreadsheet, the results are recalculated automatically. In her seventh-grade literacy class, Barbara Vaughn promotes math literacy through teaching the use of math tools, such as spreadsheets. She gives students a detailed study guide for a hands-on introduction to the spreadsheet in *ClarisWorks*. Then she follows up with use of the application in other lessons. Figure 6 on the next page presents one of her lessons.

Some teachers use Internet sites for mathematics instruction. The Good News Bears site (http://www.ncsa.uiuc.edu/edu/RSE/RSEyellow/gnb.html) is a stock market game for middle school students in which students use online stock market data, do research on stocks, and buy and sell them to produce the best possible portfolio, as they compete with others (Leu & Leu, 1999). It is a great way to use authentic math applications to motivate student involvement. Students must use research skills, think critically, and draw conclusions. (This site has English and social studies applications also.) You also may wish to have your students visit an Internet site that has math puzzles for the students to work. Houghton Mifflin's educational Web site has a Brain Teasers section (http://www.eduplace.com/math/brain) that provides students with a new problem each week for each grade level. The site offers students Hint and Solution buttons, in case they have difficulty.

Video disc programs, such as *Windows on Math*, are useful for math instruction as well. Bonnie Ashburn, a third-grade teacher, uses this program as shown in Figure 7 on page 151.

Television and VCR technology can be helpful in the math classroom also. For example, the videotape series called Numbers Alive shows students in grades 5 through 7 how mathematics relates to everyday living (Willis, 1998). This is a needed approach to mathematics instruction.

Much computer-assisted instructional software designed for mathematics instruction is available. Some is merely drill and practice, such as *Math Magic*. Nevertheless, students often will practice mathematical computations in a gamelike situation more willingly than they will with paper and pencil. Some software is tutorial, leading students through the steps of a mathematical process, as they

Figure 6
Lesson on Using Spreadsheets (Seventh Grade)

Objectives: To use a spreadsheet to solve a mathematical problem that has a real-life application; and provide practice in previously taught skills of categorization and drawing conclusions.

Materials: *ClarisWorks* spreadsheet software; and handout with problem assignment.

Activities: 1. Provide students with the following problem assignment:

Problem 1: Judy gets $6 per week for her allowance. This week she spent $2 for a notebook. The rest she put in her savings bank. Create a spreadsheet for Judy so she can keep track of her expenses. Put her expenses into the categories Food, School Supplies, and Savings.

What type of graph will best display the data so Judy can see what fraction or percent of her allowance she has spent in each category? Use the spreadsheet to create a graph of the data. What percent of her allowance did she spend in each category? Make up some numbers for additional weeks of allowance and spending and put them in your spreadsheet. Create a graph to show how she has spent her money at the end of 10 weeks. Print your graph and turn it in to the teacher for evaluation.

2. Then give the students the following instructions:

Problem 2: Keep an accounting of your expenses for a week. If you have an allowance, include only the things that you spend from your allowance in this accounting. If you do not have an allowance, but someone else pays your expenses, list all of the items that required an outlay of money for you.

Take your own allowance, or an amount that you believe would be a reasonable allowance for you, if you do not have an allowance, and make a spreadsheet for yourself. You may use the categories that were used in the problem above, or you may devise your own categories. Make a graph to show what percent of your allowance (or imaginary allowance) you spent in each category.

Print out the results and turn in to the teacher.

Assessment: Evaluate students on their ability to set up the spreadsheet for Problem 1 (30 points); the graph for Problem 1 (30 points); the spreadsheet for Problem 2 (20 points); and the graph for Problem 2 (20 points).

Figure 7
Video Disc Instruction on Fractions (Third Grade)

Objectives: To identify fractional parts of a whole; and compare fractions to determine whether they are equal to, greater than, or less than a given amount.

Materials: "Fraction Action" and "Comparing Quantities" sections of the *Windows on Math* video disc; Bruce MacMillan's book *Eating Fractions*; link-blocks, geo-boards, and worksheets; and fruit juices.

Activities: 1. Read the book *Eating Fractions* and discuss the content.
2. Introduce the video disc, which includes movie segments and still images.
3. Have the students use link-blocks and geo-boards to help them complete worksheets on fractions in small groups.

Assessment: Have each student complete a worksheet individually to check understanding; and have students work in small groups to make their own magic potions (from amounts of fruit juice), similar to the concoctions made in an episode on the video disc, and write out the recipes, using fractions.

---

are required to respond to questions and receive feedback on their performance. Some of the best mathematical experiences available with computer programs may be those gained with simulation programs such as *The Math Shop Series*, in which students solve problems related to customer services in stores. Other simulations in content areas such as social studies ask students to calculate distances, determine money needed for an enterprise, and so forth. These simulations allow students experience with real-life uses of mathematics.

Technology in Science Instruction

Science instruction offers a multitude of opportunities to use technology. Transparencies, television programs, videotapes, video discs, and computer programs are commonly used. Instructional transparencies are helpful for teaching science topics because transparencies with overlays can show relationships of different systems within the same body or machine in a very effective manner. In addition, steps in a scientific process are easily depicted with such overlays to show progressive changes. Of course, transparencies do not need overlays to be effective; they may just make a verbal description of a complex situation more concrete by providing a visual organizer or representation.

Educational television programs and videotapes are available on many scientific topics—for example, animals in their habitats, volcanoes and their effects on the surrounding areas, planets in our solar system, and the effects of air and water pollution on animal life. Bill Nye "the Science Guy" has a science show on television, and a videotape collection of 10 episodes is available as "Disney Presents Bill Nye the Science Guy Sampler III" (Willis, 1998). These television programs or videotapes make good introductions for specific science units to build and activate schemata about the topics, and they are helpful follow-up presentations when used to summarize learning about a topic and spark discussion.

Interactive video discs, such as those in the *Windows on Science* program, provide photographs, animations, video clips, and diagrams on various science topics. You can present information, stop for discussion, and access the video discs randomly, as the topics surface in oral presentation of material or discussion. Figure 8 describes a video disc activity that Julia Elmore, a sixth-grade teacher in Crossville, Tennessee, uses for science instruction.

Computer-assisted instruction in science has some exciting applications. In simulations of science labs, students can handle hazardous materials and see the reactions when various chemicals are mixed, without the danger of poisoning or explosions. Other simulations allow students to participate in dissecting animals (for example, frogs) without problems such as protests from animal rights activists or concerns with the use of formaldehyde.

Internet projects that are pertinent to science study are widely available. Students in schools around the world participate in scientific studies of temper-

Figure 8
Learning About the Formation of the Solar System
(Sixth Grade)

Objective: To acquire information about the solar system.
Materials: Handout called the "Travel Guide to the Solar System" (containing a description of the features of each planet); "Earth Science, Volume 2" section of *Windows on Science* video disc; and drawing program or *MSKids* computer software.
Activities: 1. Introduce the topic of study by showing the video disc, using the barcode reader and the barcodes in the manual to allow stops for discussion.
              2. Have each student select a planet and design a postcard for that planet (drawing is freehand or done on the computer, using a drawing program or *MSKids*).
              3. Display the postcards on the bulletin board.
Assessment: Have students fill out a planet summary chart.

ature patterns, air and water pollution, ecosystems, and many other topics. Students collect information about the group's topic at their location and share it with the other participants through e-mail or a Web site (see the textbox in Chapter 1, "The GLOBE Project"). Students also follow ongoing scientific activity by real scientists as they complete archeological digs or fly space missions. Some sites allow students just to view the results of a day's work or to see video of the work in progress. Others allow students to communicate with scientists through e-mail. For example, the NASA (U.S. National Aeronautic and Space Administration) Shuttle Web (http://shuttle.nasa.gov/index.html) has information about shuttle missions that are ongoing, and the Mad Scientist Network (http://www.madsci.org) allows students to ask scientists questions. Leu and Leu (1999) suggest visiting the Eisenhower National Clearinghouse for Mathematics and Science Education (http://www.enc.org/index.htm) for a central source of information on mathematics and science education, which contains a variety of information about useful sites, teaching techniques, and instructional resources. They also recommend using the Science Learning Network (http://www.sln.org), which has an inquiry resources page (http://www.sln.org/resources/index.html) with links to interactive science activities connected to science museums. In addition to connections to science activities that are categorized by topic and grade level, the site has a projects area and an online chat area that allows communication with science teachers from other locations. Students can learn about scientific topics and view pictures from the Hubble Space Telescope at the Space Telescope Science Institute site (http://www.stsci.edu).

When students use the Internet for science instruction, literacy and content learning are intertwined. Students who participate in interactive Internet projects must do all types of reading—from literal to critical or creative—must write to convey information to a real audience, and often must devise visual means of displaying and sharing results. These students read reference materials, integrate information from different sources, do hands-on activities, and produce verbal or visual reports of the results.

Technology in Social Studies Instruction

In social studies instruction, transparencies have many uses. One excellent use is to show with map overlays the changes in an area over time. These changes may involve such features as vegetation, temperature, or political boundaries.

There are television programs, videotapes, and video discs available for many curricular topics, from current election debates, to historical reenactments, to travelogues. An example is a set of six videotapes containing the Public Broadcasting System's "Liberty! The American Revolution" (Willis, 1998). These programs can be used to introduce, elaborate, or culminate a unit study.

For social studies there are some drill-and-practice computer programs that focus on information such as states and capitals, but the programs that are most impressive and useful are simulations. The *Oregon Trail* is a simulation that allows students to experience vicariously a trip in a wagon train. Decisions must be made about supplies to be bought, when to hunt for food, and other concerns of the travelers. Students must think critically about the material that is presented, draw conclusions, and take action based on these conclusions; then they see the consequences of their actions.

Internet sites such as the American Civil War Home Page (http://sunsite.utk. edu/civil-war/warweb.html), which has links to other sites with pictures, maps, and diaries, are available for most social studies topics. The Time Line of the Civil War, 1861, Web site (http://rs6.loc.gov/ammem/tl1861.html) also would enrich a Civil War unit. Other good social studies sites are listed in Figure 4 (on page 145).

Another good use of the Internet for social studies is to locate keypals for your students in other parts of the world. The students can discuss their local environments with their partners and learn about geographic, cultural, or political aspects of a different area.

Technology in Instruction in the Arts

Art instruction has some obvious technological possibilities. For example, paint and draw programs are available for use by instructors. Lake (1999) starts instruction with paint programs, which are more suited to freehand drawing than are draw programs. She uses *Kid Pix* for children in kindergarten through Grade 2 and *SuperPaint* and *Art Dabbler* for older students. Students can upgrade to a more advanced program called *Painter* after they master the easier program. *ClarisWorks* also has a good paint feature. Use of these programs can prepare students to use more advanced packages such as *PhotoShop*. Ideas for lessons are found on the Web site called The Art Teacher Connection (http://www.inficad.com/~arted).

The computer can facilitate art history reports, using word-processing or desktop publishing programs. Students can use presentation software such as *mPower* or *PowerPoint* to create multimedia presentations about painters, sculptors, or architects. They can also post reports to Web sites.

Use of a computer program on CD-ROM, such as *The Art Lesson* that tells about illustrator Tomie dePaola and his work, is also useful for art instruction. Many programs that focus on particular artists are available.

Technology can greatly enhance music instruction. Public television programming such as "The Charlie Horse Music Pizza" show can help primary-grade children learn about music. Each episode includes an element of music education as a part of the storyline. There are games, activities, and crafts that are related to music production. "The Charlie Horse Music Pizza" Web site (http://www.pbs.org/charliehorse) has pages for children and parents. The page for children (http://www.pbs.org/charliehorse/kids/index.htm) offers opportunities to meet the characters, do projects and crafts, and play games. The page for parents (http://www.pbs.org/charliehorse/parents/index.htm) contains episode descriptions, press releases, and more. The episodes include

Evaluating Web Sites

When you are evaluating Web sites, you must consider the reliability of the sources of the material, accuracy of the content, clarity of the material presented, and purposes of the sites. Ask yourself the following questions when judging a Web site:

1. Can you determine who has developed the site? (If not, you may not want to place undue confidence in its contents.) If so, is the developer a reliable source for the information you are seeking? (A noted authority on the topic or an agency of the government would be considered reliable. Someone you have not heard of before may need to be investigated.)

2. Is there enough information given on the site developer that qualifications can be checked? (If not, be cautious.)

3. Are sources provided for information displayed on the site, so the user can cross-check information? (If they are, this is a definite plus.)

4. Does any of the information conflict with reliable sources that you have consulted? (If some of the information is in question, all of it is suspect.)

5. Is the layout of the site busy and confusing, making information difficult to locate and evaluate? (Disorganization, particularly, is a bad sign.)

6. Is site navigation easy? (Sloppy navigational methods sometimes indicate a lack of attention to detail.)

7. Is the presented material grammatically correct, and is it free from errors in spelling and mechanics? (If it is not, the clarity is badly affected.)

8. Is the site free of advertising? (If not, look for possible bias of information presented, based on the advertising present.)

9. If currency of information is important, can you tell when the page was developed and last updated? (If not, be careful in accepting the information. If currency is not a factor—for example, for a Civil War site on which the material is not likely to become dated—this will not be a major concern.)

such topics as how to tune ukuleles, singing techniques and breath control, and types of music, harmony, and lyrics. A teachers' guide can be located at http://www.menc.org/guides/charguid/charopen.html.

Students also can write reports on composers and musicians in the same ways that they can prepare reports on art topics. In addition, they can include actual music clips in multimedia presentations.

Using technology for research in any content area

Technology can make research reports in any content area easier to complete. Consulting one or more electronic encyclopedias about the topic being studied may provide students with ideas for organizing information and for keywords to use in Internet searches for more information. Some commercial software packages, videotapes, or video discs may have pertinent information for the topic of study, as well. Students will need appropriate skills for using the media center to locate such resources, and an ability to generate keywords and conduct Internet searches as described earlier. They must evaluate material from the Internet as to accuracy and reliability of information, and perhaps verify it in other reference materials, so lessons in these skills are appropriate. The textbox on evaluating Web sites contains questions to ask about the sites.

After information has been located from various sources, students will have to use their notetaking and organizational skills to shape the reports. Word-processing software can make it easier to move chunks of material to

Figure 9
Using Technology to Develop Science Fair Projects
(Sixth Grade)

Objective: To develop science fair projects.
Materials: Computer with Internet connection; and spreadsheet software and word-processing software.
Activities: 1. Have students choose topics to investigate, then use the Internet to collect information for their literature reviews.
              2. Have students form their hypotheses, perform their experiments, and observe results.
              3. Have students enter their data on spreadsheets, then make graphs of the results.
              4. Have students write their reports on the computer, using word-processing software.
Assessment: Check final reports for accuracy, completeness, clarity, and mechanics of writing.

fit into the chosen organizational patterns. Julia Elmore, a sixth-grade teacher, has her students use technology to research and produce science fair projects, following the lesson plan in Figure 9.

Final Remarks

You as a content area teacher have a remarkable array of technological tools available to enhance your teaching. There are many concepts that can be communicated effectively through visual, auditory, and multimedia presentations. In addition, Internet connections put the classroom in touch with resources throughout the world, and they make possible communication with experts in particular curricular areas and with other students.

You should not use technological tools indiscriminately, however. Matching the technology to the classroom needs can result in improved teaching and more motivated learners, but it requires careful evaluation of the materials used, in terms of accuracy of information presented, quality of presentation, appropriateness for the particular students, and appropriateness for the curricular connections. And any use of the Internet by students must be carefully planned and supervised.

Learning to use new technologies can require some initial effort, but the benefits to students are great. Available materials and equipment can promote student learning through technology in all content areas.

References

A DVD primer. (1999). *T.H.E. Journal*, *26*(6), 23.

Art Dabbler [Computer software]. (1997). Carpinteria, CA: MetaCreations.

The Art Lesson [Computer software]. (1996). Cambridge, MA: The Learning Company.

Birds of the World [DVD-ROM]. (1999). Brookvale, NSW: Webster.

Bruce, B. (1998). New literacies. *Journal of Adolescent & Adult Literacy*, *42*, 46–49.

Brunner, C. (1996). Judging student multimedia. *Electronic Learning*, *15*(6), 14–15.

Burns, P.C., Roe, B.D., & Ross, E.P. (1999). *Teaching reading in today's elementary schools*. Boston: Houghton Mifflin.

ClarisWorks [Computer software]. (1997). Santa Clara, CA: Claris.

The Complete National Geographic: 109 Years of National Geographic Magazine [Video disc]. (1998). Washington, DC: National Geographic Society.

Freedman, R. (1991). *The Wright brothers: How they invented the airplane*. New York: Holiday House.

FrontPage [Computer software]. (1999). Redmond, WA: Microsoft.

Grolier Multimedia Encyclopedia [Computer Software]. (1999). Danbury, CT: Grolier Interactive.

Heide, A., & Henderson, D. (1994). *The technological classroom: A blueprint for success.* Toronto: Trifolium Books.

Henkes, K. (1993). *Words of stone.* New York: Puffin.

HyperStudio [Computer software]. (1999). Torrance, CA: Roger Wagner Publishing.

Internet Explorer [Computer software]. (1999). Redmond, WA: Microsoft.

Kid Pix [Computer software]. (1993). Cambridge, MA: Brøderbund/The Learning Company.

Lake, B. (1999). The art teacher connection [Online]. Available: http://www.inficad. com/~arted

Lauber, P. (1990). *Lost star: The story of Amelia Earhart.* New York: Scholastic.

Leu, D.J., & Leu, D.D. (1999). *Teaching with the Internet: Lessons from the classroom.* Norwood, MA: Christopher Gordon.

MacMillan, B. (1992). *Eating fractions.* New York: Scholastic.

Math Magic [Computer software]. (1994). Tucson, AZ: Mindplay.

The Math Shop Series [Computer software]. (1999). New York: Scholastic.

McKenna, M., & Robinson, R. (1990). Content literacy: A definition and implications. *Journal of Reading, 34,* 184–186.

Microsoft Word [Computer software]. (1999). Redmond, WA: Microsoft.

mPower [Computer software]. (1999). Charlotte, NC: Multimedia Design Corporation.

MSKids [Computer software]. (1999). Redmond, WA: Microsoft.

Netscape Navigator [Computer software]. (1999). Mountain View, CA: Netscape Communications.

Oregon Trail [Computer software]. (1999). Cambridge, MA: MECC/The Learning Company.

Painter [Computer software]. (1999). Carpinteria, CA: MetaCreations.

PhotoShop [Computer software]. (1995). San Jose, CA: Adobe Systems.

PowerPoint [Computer software]. (1996). Redmond, WA: Microsoft.

Provensen, A., & Provensen, M. (1983). *The glorious flight: Across the channel with Louis Bleriot, July 25, 1909.* New York: Viking.

Roe, B.D., & Smith, S.H. (1997). University/public schools keypals project: A collaborative effort for electronic literature conversations. In *Rethinking teaching and learning through technology.* Proceedings of the Mid-South Instructional Technology Conference, Murfreesboro, TN.

Roe, B.D., Stoodt, B.D., & Burns, P.C. (1998). *Secondary school literacy instruction: The content areas.* Boston: Houghton Mifflin.

Spinelli, J. (1992). *Maniac Magee.* New York: HarperCollins.

Stabenau, J. (1999). DVD: "The multimedium." *Syllabus, 12*(5), 40–43.

SuperPaint [Computer software]. (1997). San Jose, CA: Adobe Systems.

U.S. States and Regions [Video disc]. (1997). Atlanta, GA: Optical Data School Media.

Vaden, J. (1991). *Flight.* Westminster, CA: Teacher Created Materials.

Valmont, W.J. (1995). *Creating videos for school use.* Boston: Allyn & Bacon.

Willis, W. (1998). Software: Focus on videotapes. *T.H.E. Journal, 25*(6), 24–26.

Windows on Math [Video disc]. (1996). Atlanta, GA: Optical Data School Media.

Windows on Science [Video disc]. (1994). Atlanta, GA: Optical Data School Media.

SECTION 3

A Marriage Made
in Cyberspace

■ This section contains two chapters to explore ways in which instructional technology can be integrated into the literacy curriculum and to identify strategies for meeting technology challenges in this decade and beyond. Chapter 7 looks at how teachers and students are actually integrating technology into today's classrooms, with the emphasis on learning assisted *by* technology, not the learning *of* technology. Chapter 8 reaffirms that you should spend time integrating technology with literacy development. With many current issues addressed, this chapter helps you commit to using technology as a way of life in your literacy curriculum.

CHAPTER 7

What Do Teachers Do
in Technology-Rich
Classrooms?

WILLIAM J. VALMONT

Until recently, there was so much emphasis on learning how to use computers, how to use electronic mail, how to make a CD-ROM (compact disc read only memory) work, and so forth that the *content* of learning was not emphasized. The focus in educational circles today, however, is on how learning is being *assisted* (enabled) by modern technology, not on the learning of technology itself. With computers and technicians in the schools, with public demand for teaching students to use computers effectively, and with the vast amount of information that students can now access on the Internet, the roles of both teachers and students have changed drastically. Some of those changes are discussed following. This chapter also describes how teachers and students are using and can use technology in today's classrooms.

Teachers' Roles in Technology-Infused Classrooms

As you read examples in this chapter of what many teachers are now doing in their classrooms to promote literacy, you will be struck by how creative these teachers have been in designing classroom activities that facilitate students' learning with the help of technology. Although technology-using teachers plan classroom instruction on a large scale, students initiate, think, and make decisions daily in the classroom. Teachers think of wide themes they want students to explore, find both print and electronic materials related to the themes, and prepare students to deal with gathering, organizing, and sharing their new-found knowledge with others. Most teachers who recognize the benefits of using technology across the curriculum are now spending time locating materials on the Internet that will support their thematic activities. Teachers are becoming better facilitators, helping students stay active in their pursuit of knowledge.

Teachers today are making more authentic assignments and engaging students in topics that have themes of high interest to them. They are motivating students through the use of computers and telecommunications in ways that ensure students will be eager to participate in various literacy projects. They also are helping students design presentations of their research findings to share with their classmates, their parents, and people around the world.

Out of necessity, teachers are helping students learn to filter information because of the unbridled nature of the Internet. They are using filtering systems that block certain sites, and are having students sign agreements (acceptable use policies) that promise that they will not purposely visit inappropriate Web sites. You can visit the following sites to learn about programs specifically designed to restrict access to certain Web sites: *Net Nanny* (http://www.netnanny.com), *CYBERsitter* (http://www.cybersitter.com), *Surf-Watch* (http://www1.surfwatch.com), and *Cyber Patrol* (http://www.cyber patrol.com). Teachers also are monitoring where on the Internet students are or have been on a specific computer. This can be done easily by looking at the browser's history or cache (see the accompanying textbox for an explanation).

Checking a Computer's History and Cache

Netscape: In the Web browser *Netscape Communicator*, click on the word "Tools" in the pulldown menu, then click on "History." You will see a record of Web sites that have been accessed from that computer, when they were first and last visited, and other information. This will let you know when and where students have been on the Internet. In the "Preferences" section of the "Edit" pulldown menu, you can decide how long you wish to keep the history in the computer's memory. The history also can be cleared from the Preferences page.

Cache: On the "Start" menu of the *Windows* program, click on the "Find" then the "Files or Folders" area. Type the word "cache," and a list of all files in the computer with that word in them will appear. Jot down the paths and inspect the files to determine what Internet sites were visited. Similar steps can be taken for Microsoft's *Explorer* browser, but the names of the buttons are different.

Today's teachers are taking greater responsibilities for the learning that occurs when students visit a school's computer laboratory. Previously, teachers could allow the lab assistant or computer teacher to instruct the class. With the advent of more inservice instruction for teachers and more in-classroom computers, behaviors have changed. Now, all teachers *must* know how to organize instruction in ways that take advantage of the computers that are being placed directly in classrooms. When entire classes attend computer labs, teachers are taking a more active role in what students do there because many students are now using the labs to use the Internet to find information relating to the thematic projects designed by their classroom teachers—not the lab assistants. Teachers also are now more active in scheduling lab time, integrating it with class work, and preparing students so they can efficiently and productively use their limited lab time. Unfortunately, in some schools where there are few or no computers in classrooms, students still spend a mere 45 to 50 minutes each week working in school computer labs, which is an inadequate amount of time for them to work on extended projects.

Helping students be productive on the Internet involves helping them deal with the millions of pages of information that can be found. Teachers are helping students learn how to do the following:

- Think carefully about what they want to find on the Internet and determine which key search words will be most helpful *before* going to a computer.

- Conduct efficient searches using the best search engines and strategies for limiting searches. Using Boolean keywords, Web sites are located efficiently; for instance, by typing in "International AND Reading AND Association" on the search screen, the first search results would report mostly sites related to the International Reading Association rather than sites that contain just one of those words. The ProFusion search engine (http://www.profusion.com/users/searchtips.html) has a clear explanation of how to use AND, OR, NOT, and NEAR or the symbols &, *, !, and ~ to limit searches so the most likely sites will be reported as a result of a search.

- Look for key words in the entries that are reported as the result of a search to determine which of the possible entries merit further scrutiny.

- Skim, once at a site identified by a search, to decide whether it would be worthwhile to spend more time at that site.

- Record the URL (Uniform Resource Locator) information as well as main points and pertinent information while at a site in case the site closes or cannot be accessed again.

Meta Searches: Searching Multiple Search Engines at Once

Searching for information on the Internet can be slow and inefficient using a single search engine at a time. Lycos, Excite, LookSmart, Snap, and Infoseek, for instance, are each individual search engines. Comparing results of searches of these engines reveals that each is likely to report somewhat different results. That is, they appear to return information from different portions of the Internet. Recently, however, engines that search more of the Internet (but still not all) and quickly obtain results have been created. Meta searches report results from a combination of less powerful search engines, and this can speed up your search. Apple Computer has incorporated "Sherlock" as a find feature on Apple computers that have the operating system 8.5 or higher. Sherlock searches multiple search engines at one time and ranks them by relevance.

Several pertinent Web site search engines and their Uniform Resource Locators (URLs) are listed here:

Profusion (http://www.profusion.com)

Dogpile (http://www.dogpile.com)

Metacrawler (http://www.go2net.com/search.html)

All4One Search Machine (http://all4one.com)—This site reveals, in frames, four separate search engines such as Lycos, Infoseek, and others.

For a useful and complete list of search engines, visit Beaucoup! at http://www.beaucoup.com/1metaeng.html, or visit the Best Meta Search Engines page at http://kresch.com/search/searchme.htm for a listing of more search engines.

[This draws from Valmont, W.J. (1999, July). Web watch: Reference sites. *Reading Online*. Available: http://www.readingonline.org/electronic/watch/valmont. See this URL for additional information about online reference materials.]

- Determine information about the author of a Web site. (What are the author's credentials? What is the author's purpose? Can the author be contacted personally? How can the information be corroborated? Who sponsors the site?)

- Attend to copyright laws and avoid plagiarism when using text, photos, graphics, video, animation, or sound from a Web site.

- Make correct citations and credits for materials used in written work or electronic presentations. Students encounter many sources on the Internet that they can reference in their own works. Citations that are based on American Psychological Association style can be found in *Electronic Sources: APA Style of Citation* (http://www.uvm.edu/~ncrane/estyles/apa.html), and the Modern Language Association's style formats can be found at http://www.uvm.edu/~ncrane/estyles/mla.html.

• Verify information, whenever possible, using other sources.

Although teaching with technology has not altered the need for whole-class instruction at given times, teachers appear to balance instructional configurations so there is less large-group instruction and more small-group and individualized instruction. Often groups of students, using a variety of software programs, pursue part of an overall theme while other groups work on different parts, perhaps on the Internet. Students also often work in groups to prepare presentations for their classmates and tend to work independently to prepare reports to share later.

The role of teachers in the technology classroom has changed dramatically. Many teachers have quickly discovered that there is now more to read, write about, talk about, and hear others report and discuss, and they are finding creative ways to engage students in literacy activities. Because of the presence of computers and telecommunications in classrooms, teachers now, more than ever, are master planners. They are seeking out other teachers on the Internet to exchange ideas. They are becoming instrumental in locating students, perhaps from other parts of the world, in other schools who can relate to their students. They are more alert to helping students act on information responsibly, and, best of all, they are helping students become more critical readers and thinkers because much of the information students might encounter on the Internet has not been filtered. Literacy educators are the ones who first help students learn to reason well. Many of the new roles teachers are playing are directed at teaching students to use good judgment in finding, using, and sharing information.

Students' Roles in Technology-Infused Classrooms

Computers, camcorders, and other pieces of equipment in classrooms are expensive. Also, because computers, printers, and scanners are electrical appliances, student safety must be a major consideration. Students are learning to be responsible for the careful use of available technologies when they are made a natural, important part of instruction. If students purposely mistreat equipment, they will face greater accountability by using sign-in sheets and recording the dates and times that they work with a piece of equipment. Responsible and congenial use of technology means, for instance, not using e-mail or photocopiers to create unwelcome messages to others. When computers are used by many students who share an e-mail account, misuse could be a problem that only careful monitoring can alleviate.

Students can monitor their own use of the computer in situations in which they outnumber the resources available. Sign-up sheets with, perhaps, 15- or 30-minute time slots have been used effectively in some schools to remind students that they must share with others. Equal access by all students needs to be a high priority.

Another student responsibility is to help others master both the technologies being used and the software programs that are available. Depending on prior classroom and home experiences, some students are more technologically perceptive than others. Often students are happy to help one another, but monitoring is recommended to ensure that peer instruction is being carried out properly. Students are pleased when they can teach their teachers, too, and many teachers are feeling more secure in knowing that their students can help.

Students play important roles in technologically infused literacy classrooms. They have responsibilities for using technology as an effective tool in their pursuit of learning, for using technology wisely and ethically, and for helping others gain expertise with technology. Students are becoming creators of knowledge, and they are feeling empowered by this opportunity. They sense that they have added value to knowledge when they put together a set of materials for a presentation in a way that no one else had done before.

School and Community Roles

Graduates of today's schools must know how to use computers and other high-tech devices for their personal and job-related well being. For years, governmental agencies at national, state, and provincial levels have used computers and the Internet extensively; so have the military, libraries, medical institutions, businesses, and industries. The schools appear to be the last major structure of society to obtain technology. Around the world, business and community leaders recognize that they have the responsibility to assist schools in obtaining and using technologies that will enable students to learn better. They want technologically capable workers to graduate from the schools to be competitive with others in the information age. Teachers, administrators, school boards, and others must seek partnerships with as many organizations as possible to strengthen the resolve of communities to infuse technology into all areas of the curriculum. Legislation should be encouraged to support school efforts to build a technology infrastructure and to pay for the adequate preparation of teachers to use technology.

Internet laws are in their infancy, particularly on the international scene. There are major disagreements about control of the Internet's content, access, and expense. Issues of freedom of speech, adult privileges, the protection of young people, economics, incorrect and/or malicious materials being foisted on unsuspecting people, and others are being debated. These issues and others will be decided at many levels of society, and they should be debated at the local level. For instance, some schools have policies that students' names, faces, or any other personal information will not be placed on the Internet. Others permit first names and photographs—but not last names. Still other schools permit distance photos of children, but not close-ups. Decisions need to be made at local, district, or state levels about what forms of parental permission should be sought before placing student information or likenesses on the Internet. Community members, for example, have an interest in ensuring that the local schools create and enforce acceptable use policies, and parents will want to be informed about schools' efforts to make contracts with students about such policies.

Because few adults grew up with access to the technologies students routinely learn with today, school-community partnerships can be formed to help parents gain enough expertise with technologies so they can help preschool and primary-grade students profit from their use. For instance, some schools provide evening computer classes in which parents are taught how to operate and use computers and peripherals such as scanners and digital cameras. If families are to support their own children's learning efforts and homework, they must have help from the schools. In turn, people with technological expertise who work outside the schools can contribute to the education of teachers.

Finally, schools need plans to help them prepare to move from where they are to where they want to be with technology in, perhaps, 5 years. Creating a school technology plan provides an excellent opportunity for schools to reach out to their communities for advice and support. Through this effort, it is likely that more support for a school's initiatives will be garnered when influential community members learn how much needs to be accomplished. On the North Central Regional Educational Laboratory's Web site is a page called "Critical Issue: Developing a School or District Technology Plan" (http://www. ncrel.org/sdrs/areas/issues/methods/technlgy/te300.htm) that contains an excellent discussion of the topic of school technology plans and gives state and district examples.

A profitable role of a school, then, is to engage the community in supporting its technology initiatives and its efforts to seek resources for, and advice about, its teaching and learning goals. A beneficial role of a community is to contribute whatever expertise and resources it can provide to help schools acquire and use technology wisely. Every area of the school's curriculum is being affected because technology is being better used as a teaching tool. No community can ignore its responsibilities without negative consequences.

Assessment

Technology is expensive, and taxpayers want evidence that the infusion of technology into schools is worth the cost. There are many attempts to quantify what students are learning, but the task is daunting. It may be years before convincing proof is found, mainly because it will take a thorough study of people growing up immersed in technology to examine how they differ in the ways they learn and what they have learned. Today's young technologically astute people will be compared with the present older generation, just as people growing up in the age of television were compared with the radio generation. Literacy teachers, however, can take steps to assess progress. While helping children develop literacy, teachers can observe how students interact with learning technologies (process) and record the concrete results of their efforts (product).

Observations of progress can be made of students' interactions with computers through asking questions such as, "Does the student rejoice or complain about working with (a certain piece of software)?" and "Is the student unhappy when it is time to leave the computer lab?" This is the kind of data that teachers can note easily. In addition, individual conferences to discuss what students are learning and checklists can be developed to keep track of such observations.

Products (for example, specific writing projects, ongoing performance portfolios, end-of-year product portfolios, electronic presentations, artwork, or music produced on an electronic musical keyboard) can be kept and analyzed to show growth. Records can indicate improvement over time by looking at the number of books (print or electronic) read and the quality of reports written. Records also can indicate growth in speaking in front of others, the ability to listen and understand others, and the ability to use graphic information for learning and sharing ideas.

In sum, many of the same ways teachers have been assessing growth in literacy skills can continue to be used in the technology-infused classroom, perhaps simply by adding technology items to such measures.

Components of a Technology-Rich Classroom

Classrooms range from those that have just one computer to those more ideal settings in which there may be one computer for every four or five students. According to the U.S. Office of Educational Technology in the U.S. Department of Education (http://www.ed.gov/Technology/pillar1.html), the national student-to-computer ratio was 11:1, but the ratio of students with access to multimedia computers was only 35:1.6 as of February 1999. This means that for many students, access to powerful computers that can produce audio, video, text, graphics, and animation is still problematic, which limits what some teachers can do in the classroom.

Computers, however, are not all that is needed to infuse technology into the curriculum. The following are the items that a group of educators on the Tucson Unified School District (TUSD) #1 Technology Futures Team believe they need to have in their elementary classrooms:

- A telephone line in each classroom for communicating with other teachers, parents, and administrators. It has been said that teachers are the last professionals in the United States to get telephones in their offices.

- Internet capabilities beyond only one computer. Having your own computer connected to the Internet is important, but having multiple Internet connections so groups of students can work together at the same time is important, too. Ideally, each student should have access to the Internet as needed throughout a school day.

- At least six multimedia workstations (one of which is the teacher's) that have multimedia computers with CD-ROMs and sound capabilities and are networked. Teachers who actively make, use, and demonstrate effective electronic presentations need a sophisticated workstation as much as a desk.

- A digital camera for capturing visual images for reports and presentations, and for developing materials for Internet pages.

- A scanner to digitize text and graphics.

- A color printer (that also prints in black and white) for a variety of projects that need more professional-looking design and color.

- An LCD (liquid crystal display) projector for casting computer images onto a screen if students are to share electronic presentations with other students, parents, or other groups.

- An e-book reader, a book-sized instrument that can be used to download books and other materials from the Internet to be read away from a desktop computer.

- CD Tower that holds numerous CD-ROMs to permit access to several at a time.

- A television and videocassette recorder (VCR) to show live or videotaped materials.

- Home-share computers (computers that students can take home) for students to use for learning outside of school.

- A home-share computer for teachers who have their own computers at home as well as those who do not. Often school and home computers do not have the same programs or versions of programs, causing difficulty for teachers who are trying to work in both places. At a minimum, software to use at home, paid for and supported by the school, is needed so teachers can do some work at home.

- Money to participate in online "quests" (GalapagosQuest at http://www.quest.classroom.com/galapagos1999/splash.asp, for instance) so students can communicate with and participate in real-time events with the experts and students in other schools. Often there are shared decision-making opportunities for students during online quests.

- *WebWhacker 2000* or similar software to place copies of Web sites on a computer's harddrive. (See the accompanying textbox for more information about this software.)

- Dictionaries, encyclopedias, and other references in CD-ROM form to use to write materials and edit them.

- A subscription to Classroom Connect (for information, see http://www.classroomconnect.com).

- Remote access to the school's server from home to access e-mail and the Internet.

The TUSD #1 Technology Futures Team suggests placing a teacher-trainer in each school to provide inservice education as beginning teachers are hired and as new hardware, software, and Internet capabilities are developed. They also believe that a full-time technician is needed in each school to solve problems with software, hardware, and the school's technology infrastructure.

Components of Classroom and Student Management

Until the late 1990s most schools sent students to computer laboratories by classroom or in small groups to learn how to use computers and basic computer programs. Because computers were mostly new to teachers and students alike, instruction in computer labs seemed like a necessary step in getting started. Many believed that computers had to be learned fairly thoroughly before they could be used for learning anything else. More recently, the trend has shifted to considering computers as teaching tools that students can learn *incidentally* as they engage in authentic learning tasks. More and more computers are being placed directly into classrooms where teachers and students are engaged in technology-assisted learning activities on a daily basis.

The presence of ample computers and Internet connections in your classroom ultimately will determine how effectively you will be able to influence learning. The next sections of this chapter look at grouping arrangements in classrooms, time management, computer management, and theme or unit management.

Types of Grouping Arrangements

The one-computer classroom presents the most difficult situation for attempting to integrate technology into the reading and language arts curriculum. With a class size of between 20 and 30 students, you can use the computer for presenting materials (if it is a multimedia computer), or you can allow students to work at the computer in a rotation that is painfully slow for those who have authentic reasons to use a computer frequently. Often, if there is only one computer in a classroom, it is an older model with few features, and it may not be capable of accessing the Internet. Software may be old and may not perform well. Old software may be simply drill and practice, nothing like the interactive software currently available. You can screen old software to determine if it is of any educational value today. Students can practice their keyboarding and mouse skills in a one-computer classroom, but there will be little influence on learning to read.

In classrooms with enough multimedia computers for groups of students to work together, it is possible to treat an area of the room as a "technology center" and have students rotate in and out of the center as needed for various activities. Five or six computers, for instance, can enable you to group students by interests, skill levels, projects, research assignments, or cooperative learning activities. The technology center operates like any other center you have created.

Because older schools were constructed before computers became more plentiful in classrooms, it has been the practice of many schools to line the computers against the classroom walls or to place them in straight lines. Although efficient in terms of installing electricity and network connectivity, these placements are the least teaching and learning friendly, especially for literacy development where interacting and sharing are common. When computers are clustered three, four, or five to a group with the backs of the computers toward one another, students can more easily interact together. Additional chairs beside the computer tables permit even more students to interact and work together.

Ideally, at some point notebook (laptop) computers will be so plentiful that schools will install dozens of Internet connections in each classroom to connect to the World Wide Web (WWW). Some schools already have moved to a wireless transmission system that allows students to carry around small computers that access the Internet through the air. As long as students stay in range of the transmitter's signal, they can carry their computers from place to place while they work on the Internet. For an example of such a system, see http://www.raytheon.com/raylink/welcome.htm.

Time Management

If the technology center approach is taken, students must be scheduled for their computer times throughout the week. A simple wall chart indicating each group's time slots is helpful. It is beneficial to rotate groups into different time slots every few days, so a single group does not always visit the technology center after lunch, for instance. With groups of five or six students working together in a classroom, 15 to 20 hours per week would be ideal for students to work at the computers.

To manage computer time efficiently, students and teachers can prepare in advance. Hardware and software should be kept in good working order with rapid replacement or repair as necessary. You can help by clarifying assignments so students are clear about their tasks in advance of using the computers. Also, you could do presearching, narrowing, and bookmarking of Web sites to limit student time spent conducting Internet searches. Students can engage in prethinking, prereading, and prewriting before going to the technology center. Students' use of journals or logs to indicate where they have found information on the Internet will help them return to it most efficiently at a later time. There is little guarantee, however, that a particular site will remain on the WWW or will retain the same information over time.

It is wise to leave at least one open time slot in the technology center each day so students who have an urgent need to find something on the Internet or work with some piece of software can do so. Also, when necessary, you should be able to use a time slot to teach students how to develop some specific understanding or skill.

Computer Management

Some schools have a student work at the same computer all the time. First, this helps students move quickly to their work area when it is their time to do so.

Second, identical software may not be found on every computer; therefore, if a student begins to work with a specific version of a program using the same computer each time, he or she can quickly continue working. This is especially important if a student's work is saved in files on the computer's harddrive rather than on floppy disks. Third, computers and keyboards often have little quirks or feel a bit different to a user, so using the same computer eliminates the need to deal with such idiosyncrasies. Fourth, having students use the same computer encourages more responsible use of equipment because it is easier to determine who has used a computer if there is damage to the hardware or software. Finally, through examining the Web browser's history or the caches in computers, teachers can determine where specific students have been on the Internet (see the textbox "Checking a Computer's History and Cache" on page 161). Some schools give each computer a name or number and tape a log sheet to the computer or the desk. Students initial the sheets and report the time when they first sit down to work. In addition, routine basic maintenance on the operating system and application software is a must.

Theme or Unit Management

In 1998, the International Society for Technology in Education (ISTE) published *National Educational Technology Standards for Students* (NETS). Some U.S. states and school districts have considered adopting the ISTE standards to guide their schools' technology initiatives. The standards are divided into six broad categories: basic operations and concepts; social, ethical, and human issues; technology productivity tools; technology communication skills; technology research tools; and technology problem-solving and decision-making skills. Within levels (grades pre-K–2, 3–5, 6–8, and 9–12) specific performance indicators are listed, disclosing the kinds of technology knowledge students can profit from learning at those levels. In kindergarten, for example, students can demonstrate their use of a mouse, keyboard, and so forth. At the high school level, students should be able to use technology in their research, writing, and communication with others. Scenarios and examples in the publication show how the standards can be used to guide classroom instruction.

As a follow up to the NETS project, a second publication was published in 1999, *National Educational Technology Standards for Students: Connecting Curriculum and Technology*. A group of educators from around the United States and representatives from several professional associations collaborated on this publication that contains examples of multidisciplinary and thematic learning activities across grade levels in the areas of English/language arts, mathematics, science, social studies, and foreign language. The resulting themes are models for helping teachers integrate technology into schoolwork in authentic ways. The themes are coded to indicate which of the ISTE NETS standards and the standards of professional organizations, such as the International Reading Association (IRA), the National Council of Teachers of English, and the National Council of Teachers of Mathematics, would be dealt with through the various activities related to the theme. For each theme or unit, a purpose is stated along with a brief description of the overriding instructional plan. Then activities, tools and resources, and assessment plans are identified.

Language arts teachers can learn several important things from the *Connecting Curriculum and Technology* publication. The English/language arts examples show methods of infusing technology into literacy activities at all grade levels. Descriptions of various projects model ways to structure similar thematic units teachers already use, and the examples are replete with ideas, URLs, and the identification of hardware and software that some teachers may not yet use.

Vignettes From Literacy Teachers

Many teachers, reading specialists, librarians, and administrators are beginning to share descriptions of their uses of technology in promoting literacy growth in their classes and schools. The following are accounts of real-life anecdotes that show a wealth of creative uses of technology as an aid to improving literacy development. Some of these examples were created by award winners and other teachers who participated in the International Reading Association's Presidential Award for Reading and Technology. Sponsored by TLC School, a division of The Learning Company, this award honors K–12 educators for their outstanding, innovative contributions to using technology in reading education. Seven U.S. regional winners, a Canadian, and an international winner are named yearly, and a grand prize is awarded for the best entry across all IRA regions. The first International Reading Association Presidential Award for Reading and Technology was awarded by then IRA President Kathy Ransom at the association's 44th annual convention in May 1999.

Examples of Literacy and Technology in Grades 1-3

Teachers in the primary grades have described various activities that indicate they are actively integrating technology into their classrooms. As you read

International Society for Technology in Education (ISTE) Standards

Shown here is an example of the themes created by ISTE in its *National Educational Technology Standards for Students* project. *Awesome Authors* was created by Barbara Ridgway, a former member of the International Reading Association's Technology, Communication, and Literacy Committee who currently teaches in the Helena Public Schools in Montana, and JoAnn Gadicke, a teacher in the Sheboygan Area School District in Wisconsin.

Awesome Authors
English Language Arts
Primary Grades Pre-K–2

Purpose
Students will (1) use spoken, written, and visual language to communicate effectively with a variety of audiences; (2) use a variety of technological and information resouces to gather and synthesize information and to create and communicate knowledge; (3) read a wide range of print and nonprint materials to build an understanding of texts and acquire new information; (4) apply a wide range of strategies to comprehend, interpret, evaluate, and appreciate texts; (5) use a wide range of writing strategies and use different writing process elements to communicate with different audiences for various purposes; and (6) apply knowledge of language conventions and media critiques to discuss print and nonprint materials.

Description
To young students, an author of a book or story often does not seem like a real person. Students will learn about an author, read stories written by that author, and communicate later with that author. They will work in small groups to learn about plot development (beginning, middle, and end), character development, story structure, and creating parallel stories. Students will be introduced to illustrations and associated copyright issues. Students will then write and illustrate their own stories, incorporating a character from one of the author's stories or generating a parallel story. Students will edit, revise, and publish their stories electronically. Parents and other students will be encouraged to read and respond to a student's published stories. Students will also be introduced to interviewing and questioning techniques. They will work with a partner, read the partner's story, and generate questions to ask the author. Videotaped author interviews will be conducted with students asking their peer author questions.

Activities	ELA Standards	Nets for Students
Preparation		

- Meet with the school library media specialist to identify and select the author to be studied. Consider doing a Web search on the author. Many authors have their own Web pages created by them or their publishers.

- Identify available resources on or about the author (e.g., video, Web sites, print, CD-ROM, software, audiocassettes, laserdiscs).

(continued)

International Society for Technology in Education (ISTE) Standards *(continued)*

Activities	ELA Standards	Nets for Students
Preparation		

- Locate and highlight the author's Web site (if available).
- Assemble a list or a collection of the author's books to use as an introduction.
- Prepare lessons on plot and character development or a lesson on story structure for students who will write parallel stories (same plot, different characters, setting, and so on).
- Prepare a minilesson sequence on techniques in interviewing, assembling questions, and reporting information from an interview.
- Plan an electronic meeting with the author (e.g., through e-mail, CU-SeeMe, a Web site, Internet chat, Scholastic Network).
- Ask in advance if the author is willing to record a story in his or her own voice.
- Prepare a minilesson on characters and plot.
- Discuss copyright and its importance when considering illustrations.
- Discuss illustrators and illustrations. Identify style, composition, color, and media used by the author or illustrator.
- Set aside time to confer with individual students about their stories.
- Prepare a minilesson on electronic publishing software.
- Alert the school Webmaster that a student project will be ready for uploading. Share your project time line with the Webmaster.
- Introduce students to the video camera and the fundamentals of recording.

Procedure:

	ELA Standards	Nets for Students
1. Introduce the class to the selected author. In the library, find books and other media about the selected author. Let the students select their own books to read, but encourage them to select one by the author.	ELA 1, 3	2, 4
2. Help the students read about the author and become familiar with the author's life and writing.	ELA 1, 3	2, 4
3. Read and view a variety of stories by the selected author and work in small groups to identify the stories' plots and character features.	ELA 1, 3, 6, 11	2, 4, 5
4. Work in small groups to create a dramatization or develop a Readers Theatre presentation based on a story by the author. Record the student presentations for viewing by the whole class.	ELA 3, 4, 5, 11, 12	1, 9

(continued)

International Society for Technology in Education (ISTE) Standards *(continued)*

Activities Preparation	ELA Standards	Nets for Students
5. Facilitate a brainstorming session so students can describe what they have learned about the author and to help you determine what students still need. Record what the students have learned about the author and his or her work. Categorize and classify what the students share by using concept-mapping software. (If possible, share what the students know with the author.)	ELA 3, 6, 7, 11, 12	1, 2, 4, 10
6. Plan a video or online conference with the author (see Tools and Resources). Use a word processor to record questions to ask the author during the electronic conference or by e-mail.	ELA 4, 5	1, 9
7. Participate in an online conference with the selected author.	ELA 8, 11, 12	6, 10
8. Students will select a character from one of the stories they have read and include the character in a short story of their own. If they want, students can write a story that parallels the author's story structure. Students will use electronic-publishing software to write and illustrate their story. Have students or adult helpers print copies of their stories for friends, family, and the library.	ELA 4, 5, 6, 11, 12	1, 2, 8, 9
9. Divide students into teams of three to develop questions and make plans to interview a peer author. Using these questions (or similar ones), provide a situation where students become a famous author. Students should take turns trying on the following roles: author being interviewed about the story he or she has written, interviewer, and cameraperson who is making sure that the camera angles are correct and that the interview is captured on video. (Ask for assistance from another adult or from an older student.) Compile all videos onto a single tape for distribution to parents and families.	ELA 8, 11	1, 2, 5, 7, 8, 9

Tools and Resources
- Concept-mapping software such as *Expression* or *Inspiration*
- Library reference materials, both print and nonprint (books, videos, CD-ROMs)
- Electronic-publishing software (*HyperStudio*, *Kid Pix*, etc.)
- Multimedia computers with electronic-publishing software
- Video camera(s), television, VCR

Web sites:
  Teacher Resources
    Go Places with Suse MacDonald (children's book author & illustrator):
      http://create4kids.com

(continued)

International Society for Technology in Education (ISTE) Standards *(continued)*

Celebrating Cultures with Tomie dePaola:
  www.memphis-schools.k12.tn.us/admin/tlapages/cultures.html

Children's Literature (reviews):
  www.childrenslit.com/home.htm

Carol Hurst's Literature Site (reviews):
  www.carolhurst.com

Authors and Illustrators on the Web (guide):
  www.acs.ucalgary.ca/~dkbrown/authors.html

Aaron Shepard's RT Page (Readers Theatre):
  www.aaronshep.com/rt

Index to Internet Sites: Children's and Young Adults' Authors & Illustrators:
  http://falcon.jmu.edu/~ramseyil/biochildhome.htm

Scholastic Network:
  www.scholasticnetwork.com

Author Sites
  Jan Brett: www.janbrett.com
  Marc Brown's Arthur site: www.pbs.org/wgbh/arthur
  Eric Carle: www.eric-carle.com
  Janet Stevens: www.janetstevens.com
  Dr. Seuss: http://randomhouse.com/seussville
  Leo & Diane Dillon: www.best.com/~libros/dillon
  Robert Quackenbush: www.rquackenbush.com
  Mike Artell: http://members.aol.com/mikeartell/page/index.htm
  Judy Blume: http://judyblume.com/home.html

Assessment

Assess the students (1) in their ability to work cooperatively in their small groups and (2) on their participation and contribution to the online author conference.

Develop a rubric to assess individual student stories. The rubric will cover mechanics, content, voice, grammar, spelling, characterization, plot, and the effective use of writing and illustrating software. Review the rubric with students before beginning the project. (Tie the levels and content of the rubric to state and local standards for writing, as well as to expectations for students.)

With students, develop a rubric to evaluate their performance during the preparation and production of peer author interviews. The rubric should address preparation, quality, appropriateness of interview questions, and basic camera usage and technique.

Credits

Barbara Ridgway, Helena Public Schools, Helena, Montana
  (bridgway@helena.k12.mt.us)
JoAnn Gadicke, Sheboygan Area School District, Sheboygan, Wisconsin
  (jgadicke@sheboygan.k12.wi.us or jgadicke@excel.net)

(continued)

International Society for Technology in Education (ISTE) Standards *(continued)*

Comments

For a long time, not much information seemed to be available on Dr. Seuss. Through the Web site, my students were able to find more biographical information. They wanted to interview him, but Geisel had recently died. With further research, they were surprised to learn just how much his foundation supports kids and reading. The class went into such a frenzy reading his books and talking about where all the money goes from buying the books that they asked the librarian to have a picture of the Cat and the Hat painted on the wall outside the library—which she did! Now that the same kids are in fourth grade, I hear them pass the library chatting about Theodore Geisel and the reading programs supported by his legacy. It has been a great way to learn about stewardship as well as the notion that good writers can support themselves—as well as some professional athletes!

Reprinted with permission from the *National Educational Technology Standards for Students: Connection Curriculum and Technology* (1999), published by the International Society for Technology in Education (ISTE), NETS Project. (The book is available from ISTE at 800-336-5191 or 541-302-3777; cust_svc@iste.org; www.iste.org. Find more information on the standards at http://cnets.iste.org.)

these accounts, note the teachers' use of themes to develop literacy as well as the use of technology to support communication, collaboration, and the locating and sharing of information.

Using a computer with early and emergent readers

Marilyn Eisenwine and Diane Hunt, first-grade literacy group teachers at Frost Elementary School in Georgetown, Texas, work in a one-computer classroom. At the beginning of the year, they made books for students to read. By the end of the year, students learned to publish their own original writing in the same types of books. At first, the teachers used a word-processing program, enlarging the font size and exaggerating spaces between words. "The spacing enables students to point and read more easily, establishing the concept of a word," they said. "Also, the text is on only one line, beginning at the top left of the page, to emphasize left-to-right directionality for those students who need extra help in this area." The books typically were six to eight pages long and were bound at the school.

Technology was also used for patterned language activities in the created books. Sentences such as "I see a ____" were used with appropriate illustrations. For a simple concept such as "I like _____," the teachers found and saved graphics of different kinds of food. When a child chose a particular food, its image was imported into a page, and the student typed in "I like _____," inserting as many letters for the name of the food as he or she could, with the teacher filling in the other letters. Students learned to type their names on the computer-generated pages, and the pages were placed into a class book for later use. The books also were taken home for parents to see.

Later in the school year, Eisenwine and Hunt created animated books on the computer using *HyperStudio*. They made stories that gave the effect of a finger pointing to each word when students clicked on the mouse. The computer also was programmed to read the word aloud when the student pointed to it, and a dog barked when students clicked on it. Again, the purpose of these basic programs was to help students learn the concept of what a word is. Later, the teachers produced animated sentences that illustrated the actions of characters in the books they made. For example, when the text reads "I can walk," a man is walking along a road to music. In another story, a frog jumps across the grass to the sound of frogs croaking, while the words say, "A frog is jumping."

The teachers acquired the program *SimpleText*, and students created longer stories that the computer read back to them. Different voices could be selected, making listening to the story several times with different voices interesting. The students "quickly learned the value of rereading their writing to be sure it said what they intended," the teachers said. *Kid Pix* was used so students could experiment with graphics and special effects. Eventually, students created and illustrated longer stories. "Ultimately, by the end of the school year, we had come full circle from writing simple storybooks for students to read to helping students publish their own books. For these emergent readers and writers, computers had been a vital tool in their journey to literacy," the teachers reported.

The new and improved Language Experience Approach

Frederic Wellington teaches first grade at Nether Providence Elementary School in Wallingford, Pennsylvania. He said, "I have combined the old Language Experience Approach with the modern-day computer. The results are wonderful!" Wellington taught phonics through the use of poetry. He read a poem that contained a specific letter pattern, and students soon discovered the target pattern and located all the words in the poem containing that pattern. Then they brainstormed to create a list of other words containing that pattern. Students typed the list on a computer and printed copies for everyone to file in their homework folders. Students also received small square cards that had beginning consonants on them and cards with the target pattern on them so they could manipulate the cards to make new words.

Wellington typed a Language Experience story while students gathered around the computer and a large screen television connected to the computer. Before starting the story, the teacher and students examined the previous day's list to see if any of the words were suitable as the setting of the story or if any could be used as story characters' names. They also brainstormed about what might happen in the story. While students created the story, Wellington encouraged them, and he had them stop from time to time to read what they had written to that point. When a story was finished, students gave it a title, and they received copies for their homework folders. The teacher used *SuperPrint Deluxe* to make large, laminated posters of stories to use in a variety of activities.

Wellington took a digital camera along on class field trips. When they returned to school, students examined and discussed the digital photographs on the computer and created Language Experience stories based on their trip. Early in the semester, the entire class helped with the story. Later, however, the teacher just printed the photos and gave them to groups of students to create stories on their own. Then Wellington placed the photos in *ClarisWorks*, adding the sentences the students had contributed. Pictures also were taken on special days such as "The Hundredth Day of School," "Clifford Day," and "Amelia Bedelia Day," and the pictures were integrated into books that could be shared with parents who had been unable to attend the events.

Building the foundation: Using technology in a primary classroom

Paula Reber is a first- and second-grade "looping" teacher at Kelly Elementary School in Lewisburg, Pennsylvania. (She teaches the same group of children for first and second grade.) She used computers, a digital camera, and *Kid Pix* to create class books that go with stories her students read in class. "For instance," said Reber, "when we read the book [Merle Peek's] *Mary Wore Her Red Dress and Henry Wore His Green Sneakers*, students wore their favorite clothing articles to school. I took pictures of the students with a digital camera and imported them into *ClarisWorks*, where we typed the words to our story following the same format used in the original book." Similar books were made for Joy Cowley's *Mrs. Wishy-Washy*, Pat Hutchin's *Rosie's Walk*, Eric Carle's *The Very Hungry Caterpillar*, and others. All the books were placed in the classroom library. "These books are some of the class favorites because of the ownership students have in creating them," said Reber.

For a unit called "All About Me," students drew self-portraits and pictures of their friends, and then they added text. They created books about the life cycles of butterflies, pumpkins, and frogs. They designed jack-o-lanterns whose faces revealed a variety of "feelings" and wrote about the feelings. The jack-o-lantern pages were placed into a *Kid Pix* slide show, and the students recorded themselves reading their pages. Students also made slide shows about digraphs and short vowel sounds.

Reber's second-grade students created multimedia projects using *Hyper-Studio*. One unit was about the solar system. Students conducted research, wrote, and illustrated reports about the various planets and constellations. They included Internet links about the solar system and downloaded images from the Internet. Near the end of the year, Reber's students, working in cooperative teams, created a Web site about their town. They took disposable cameras home with them and took photos of various stores and landmarks. They scanned the best photos and inserted them into their Web pages. They designed buttons and graphics, and proudly showed their site to parents. During a study of dinosaurs, students created a survey and e-mailed it to various listservs. From the responses, students created a spreadsheet to indicate which dinosaur was the favorite of the people surveyed.

"Perhaps the most significant project we completed was a project with a class from Brisbane, Australia," said Reber. "We exchanged stuffed animals (travel buddies) and e-mailed regularly to update each other on how the animals were doing. Students took the animals home at night and wrote in journals about their activities." This activity generated such an interest that the class decided to conduct research about Australia both on the Internet and in the school's library. Later, the class sent three travel buddies to schools in various locations in the United States. In addition, students communicated with a fourth-grade class in another school in Lewisburg several times a month via e-mail. They exchanged autobiographies with students in the Linntown Elementary School, worked on a shared writing activity together, and started leprechaun stories that the students in the other school finished. After adding graphics, both classes received complete sets of the stories.

"Using technology in the classroom has allowed my students to learn about people and places faraway and next door," said Reber. "Travel buddies are thought of as members of our classroom, and even the most reluctant reader and writer cannot wait to share the adventures that our buddies have had at their homes."

Inspiring young readers and writers: Using a Web site to enhance an author study project

Elizabeth Rohloff, teacher at Buckman Elementary Magnet Arts School in Portland, Oregon, created an author study project to help first- and second-grade students identify the beginning, middle, end, and plot of a story. Her major goal was to strengthen comprehension. Using The Children's Literature Web Guide (http://www.acs.ucalgary.ca/~dkbrown), Rohloff located author and illustrator Jan Brett's Web site (http://www.janbrett.com) and used it as the basis of the following objectives:

- to enhance the reading and writing process by responding to literature in various ways to identify plot, characters, and the beginning, middle, and end of folktales;
- to make a meaningful presentation to a group;
- to communicate with an author; and
- to learn more about the author and her process as an illustrator.

After introducing students to a variety of Brett's books, Rohloff and her class visited Brett's Web site. Rohloff demonstrated how to navigate through the site, and the students quickly discovered that they did not have many of Brett's books. In the school library, a student printed out a list of Brett's books found at the Web site, and the class created a letter asking parents to find in the local library, or from their personal libraries, those books that the school did not have. When the books became available, they were read individually and with partners. Students then decided which books to review and how they would present their reviews to others. Rohloff placed photocopies of the book covers and simple directions for accessing the site beside the computers so beginning students could find them easily. At the Web site, students listened to Brett's Hedge-A-Gram, an audio feature that is delivered by *RealAudio* describing her latest projects. (See http://www.realplayer.com for more information about *RealAudio* and *RealVideo*.)

Several students wrote questions and sent them to Brett through e-mail, and rapid replies from the author motivated students to share their books with others. Using a word-processing program and the Web site, students copied small images of book covers into their documents, added colorful backgrounds, and added text. These were e-mailed to Brett. Other students presented a play based on Brett's *The Mitten*, having downloaded animal masks from the Web site. One student created a "boot book" after reading Brett's

Armadillo Rodeo and downloading boot pictures for her classmates to illustrate. Two students created a new ending for Brett's *Trouble With Trolls*.

Rohloff's class benefited greatly from exposure to an author's Web site on the Internet. She stated,

> The immediate connections with this author's Web site did engage all levels of students in my classroom.... We heard a real author discuss her process for writing and illustrating.... Learning was integrated and fun. So much fun that the next time I plan an author study, I'll check whether there's a Web site I can use. The enthusiasm will follow.

Southern Local Primary School and technology for today and the 21st century

Tonyea Kellison teaches kindergarten through second grade at Southern Local Primary School in Salineville, Ohio. Believing that reading and writing should be learned together, Kellison engaged students in various writing activities, including using e-mail to write letters to students in other classrooms, in other parts of the United States, and around the world. Students, after receiving parental permission, communicated with their relatives through e-mail, also.

Kellison's class engaged in the "Trucker Buddy" program. A truck driver worked with the class, and students received letters and postcards from every part of the country that he visited. Students tracked his progress, wrote letters to him on a word processor, and mailed them to his home address. In addition to text, students used a drawing program to create illustrations to include in their letters, and they used a digital camera to add photos. They sent these through e-mail, and the driver e-mailed letters back to them whenever he could.

Students also published a school newspaper using the *Student Writing Center*, and they wrote and published books. Kellison said, "Most students do not want to hand print their own books any more now that they can write, type, and print them on the computer." During the school open house, students introduced themselves by writing autobiographies that included their digitized photos. Those works were displayed in the halls of the school. Students also created screensavers from frames of *QuickTime* movies about themselves. "One of the most rewarding results is the fact that the students love to write and read using technology," said Kellison. "They cannot wait to get to the lab to start a story, work on a reading lesson, or write a letter."

Classroom Internet applications with children's authors: Building "a community of authors"

Lynne Spence, a second-grade teacher at McCoy Elementary School in Aztec, New Mexico, had one non-networked computer in her classroom, yet she was able to bring the WWW to her students. The only Internet-capable computer was located in another room called the publishing center. Spence had two goals in mind:

- to integrate the World Wide Web into the established curriculum, using both online and offline activities to spark interest among students; and
- to integrate student use of computers and related technology into the curriculum by using themes and author studies and in doing so build "a community of authors."

Spence used *WebWhacker 2000* software to bring the Internet into her classroom. As mentioned, this software permits a person, while connected to the Internet, to download all or part of a Web site onto that person's computer or a disk. In this case, materials were downloaded onto a Zip drive, which holds more information than floppy disks. The Web site can then be accessed from the disk without an Internet connection. Spence featured one or two authors of children's books each month, and she integrated CD-ROMs, Internet sites of the authors, and other activities into the themes that are part of her curriculum. Student objectives were as follows:

- to learn about authors on the WWW and offline;
- to write to authors, getting e-mail addresses from the Web;
- to read CD-ROM books and do activities in the classroom related to themes and authors of the month; and
- to publish some of the students' poems and stories on the WWW.

The following authors, themes, and CD-ROMs were part of Spence's activities:

August

Arnold Lobel	Theme: Friendship	CD-ROM	*Frog and Toad Are Friends*
Kevin Henkes	Theme: Friendship	CD-ROM	*Sheila Rae the Brave*

September

Dr. Seuss	Theme: Food	CD-ROM	*Green Eggs and Ham*
		CD-ROM	*Dr. Seuss's ABC*
		CD-ROM	*The Cat in the Hat*

Month	Author	Theme	Media	Title
October	Janell Cannon	Theme: Animals—Bats	CD-ROM	*Stellaluna*
November	Bernard Most	Theme: Dinosaurs	CD-ROM	*Dinosaur Hunter*
			CD-ROM	*I Can Be a Dinosaur Hunter*
December	Chris Van Allsburg	Theme: Giving	Book	*The Polar Express*
	Shel Silverstein	Theme: Poems	Publish poems on Web	
January	Jan Brett	Theme: Animals in Winter		*The Mitten* (Download masks from Web site)
February	Jan and Stan Berenstain	Theme: Manners	CD-ROM	*The Berenstain Bears Get in a Fight*
			CD-ROM	*The Berenstain Bears in the Dark*
March	Various authors	Theme: Pioneers	CD-ROM	*American Girl's Collection*
			CD-ROM	*Oregon Trail*
April	Laura Numeroff	Theme: Animals	CD-ROM	*If You Give a Mouse a Cookie*
			CD-ROM	*Amazing Animals*
May	Tomie dePaola	Theme: Food—Spaghetti	CD-ROM	*Big Anthony's Mixed Up Magic*

Spence said,

> I believe that access to the Internet brings authors to life, makes learning fun, and fosters reading and literacy. The children have enjoyed learning about different authors. They look for these books and authors in book orders and the library. They are excited about reading and writing. When asked what they want to be when they grow up, many of them say "an author or an artist."

Winter wonderland: A thematic literature collaborative Internet project

Susan Silverman, second-grade teacher at Clinton Avenue Elementary School in Port Jefferson Station, New York, and her class hosted the "Winter Wonderland" project on the Internet (see http://members.aol.com/winter2nd). Thirty-three second-grade classes from the United States, Canada, and Russia selected books having a winter theme. The books became the basis for reading and writing activities that resulted in a variety of student-created materials. Activities were submitted to Silverman who acted as Webmaster for the project; therefore basic competency with e-mail and familiarity with using a Web browser were the only special technology skills that others were required to know. "This project is not a 'traditional' class lesson or unit of study," said Silverman. "Rather, it consists of a thematic literary collaboration among lower primary classes around the world, facilitated through online technology. The resulting experience created student/teacher, student/student, and teacher/teacher interactions that would otherwise not be possible." Because participating schools were in so many locations, it was natural for students to learn map skills during this project.

Silverman advertised the project through Classroom Connect (http://www.classroomconnect.com) and the Global School Network (http://www.gsn.org), recruiting more than the 25 schools she had initially wanted to include. Not only did her students participate in the project, but also they had the added advantage of reading and critiquing the other schools' contributions. Via e-mail, many students sent compliments about work they particularly enjoyed, and Silverman's students were very happy when they received compliments. A visit to "Mrs. Silverman's Second-Grade Class" Web site (http://www.kids-learn.org) contains examples of these students' projects and many others.

The Arctic: An interactive theme for students and teachers

Gloria Antifaiff teaches a second- and third-grade class at Connaught Community School in Regina, Saskatchewan, Canada, and created a CD-ROM about the Arctic with the help of her students. Yearly, her class studies the Arctic community as part of the social studies curriculum. Noting the difficulty she had in finding materials that were appropriate for her students' wide range of reading capabilities, she decided to create a CD-ROM using information from the Internet. Using *HyperStudio*, a digital camera, a video camera, a scanner, and the Internet, Antifaiff engaged her students in research skills, the writing process, oral presentation skills, and locating information about the Arctic. She also helped them gain knowledge of the capabilities of multimedia technology, practice Internet skills, use a digital camera, engage in snowshoeing skills, learn computer skills, and develop vocabulary.

Antifaiff's CD-ROM is organized into eight sections. "Arctic Animals" contains information, some of which students located, about 12 different animals.

Antifaiff audiotaped the information so it could be heard by nonreaders or students with limited reading abilities. "Arctic Information" consists of sections dealing with The Land, The People, Dog Sledding, The Igloo, and Did You Know, which offers short anecdotes about the Arctic. "Arctic Stories" are original stories that Antifaiff's students wrote, edited, polished, illustrated, and audiotaped. "The Arctic Map" starts with images of the world that she found on the Internet and then the view zooms in on the Arctic region. "Arctic Movies" includes the building of an igloo video that was produced by a local television station and a video of the students learning to use snowshoes in the schoolyard. "The Arctic Test" consists of 10 true or false questions. "Teachers' Ideas" contains ideas that other teachers can use to teach a theme about the Arctic. Photos taken with a digital camera illustrate items such as a snowflake project. "Arctic Resources" includes synopses of books about the Arctic. Antifaiff said, "This project went beyond the original intent of learning about another community. Literacy skills were enhanced and developed as children who could be classified as reluctant learners wanted to be part of the project."

Comments About Technology Use in Grades 1-3

From the preceding descriptions, it is clear that literacy teachers are finding creative ways to use hardware, software, and the Internet to infuse technology into their class activities. Teachers are placing original information on Web sites for their students, referring students to specific preselected sites so they can locate information efficiently, helping students question what they find on the Internet, and introducing students to authors and others so they can communicate with one another.

Modern computers have enabled students to change from being print journalists to becoming photojournalists, videographers, and animators. Speaking and listening skills are being more highly developed because of the ability students now have to share their multimedia presentations. In addition, students are responding to having their works placed on the Internet with more motivation, more pride in their productions, and interest in different times, places, and cultures.

Examples of Literacy and Technology in Grades 4-6

In grades 4 through 6, there are sophisticated themes, more complex software applications, and an increased use of electronic references. Many of the types of activities described in the primary grades continue to be pursued, but students are being encouraged to conduct much more research as they think about their own communities, people, and events around the world.

From here to eternity

Nancy McCulloch, a fourth-grade teacher at Mitchell Road Elementary School in Greenville, South Carolina, said,

> Many children did not read outside of the required materials for classes; they were not motivated to read. The school's achievement in reading and language arts, as measured by norm- and criterion-referenced tests, was dropping. In short, we were making very little progress and needed a change that would move us from "here to eternity."

Determined to improve students' literacy, McCulloch and the other teachers developed a plan emphasizing technology and its integration into all areas of the curriculum. They also developed a partnership with several local businesses, found volunteers to connect four Internet connections in each classroom, and obtained computer donations from more than 30 businesses. Within 3 months, every classroom had an Internet-capable computer.

Student objectives of the project McCulloch's school undertook were

- to operate an electronic card catalog system;
- to select and evaluate Web sites in order to research topics;
- to create and write original works;
- to be excited about reading and engage in recreational reading activities; and
- to communicate with students, authors, and authorities around the world.

The staff created a 14-station writing and Internet lab and used *Netscape, Read, Write, & Play!, Student Writing and Research Center,* and *Student Writing Center* to enable each student to complete eight book reviews during the school year. Students in the special education program used 15 reading software programs to assist in individualizing their reading. A variety of adaptive technologies were used for students with disabilities. [Note: An excellent source of information about technology for persons with visual, hearing, physical, or cognitive disabilities can be found at the U.S. Department of Energy Assistive Technologies Web site (http://cio.doe.gov/assistive). The site has links to current and emerging assistive technologies, information about governmental agency programs, and additional online resources.]

Teachers and students used digital cameras, Super Disks, Zip drives, AverKeys (a device that connects a computer to a television monitor), scanners, laserdiscs, and a CD-ROM tower to access several CD-ROMS at one time and from various classrooms. Also, they started to create their own CD-ROMs to archive student work, and they planned a CD-ROM for the Chamber of Commerce. Students published a wide variety of books, produced research projects, and corresponded with other students, authors, and authorities via e-mail. Students not only wrote eight book reviews during the school year, but also wrote monthly critiques of up to six books and published their work for contests.

McCulloch stated,

> [The students] have become perpetual authors. Students write class books with each child completing a page, school books with each class completing a page, and individual books. Children authors make their own hardback books for Young Writer's Day. Technology is so infused in our reading/language arts program that teachers cannot imagine how they taught effectively without the technology.

The Academy of Reading

Andrew McKenzie teaches fourth grade at Ernest R. Graham Elementary School in Hialeah, Florida. McKenzie started an after-school program that he named Project RASCAL (Reading After School with Computer-Assisted Learning). He used *The Academy of Reading* software to focus on phonemic awareness, auditory and visual reading skills, and reading comprehension. Students completed assignments, played educational games, and wrote poetry or descriptive essays that included clip art or other images, and they made *PowerPoint* presentations. Some students participated in the annual ThinkQuest Junior contest as they worked in groups to create original and innovative Web pages. (Note: Created by Advanced Network & Services, Inc., ThinkQuest is an annual contest designed to promote Internet-based learning. Students 12 to 19 years of age work in teams to create projects in several curricular areas on a wide variety of topics. Students in grades 4 to 6 can enter ThinkQuest Junior. Awards totaling US$1,000,000 are made, including scholarships for each student on a winning team. Visit the ThinkQuest Web site at http://www.thinkquest.org to see examples of previous award-winning projects.)

Students in McKenzie's room used digital cameras and a scanner to create their pages. They learned HTML (Hypertext Markup Language) and learned to use *FrontPage Express* for Web construction. McKenzie also had students access the Internet in order to learn terminology that is typically used in math word problems.

"Believe it or not," research projects improve literacy!

Steve Freeman teaches grades 4–6 in Washington Elementary School in Centralia, Washington. He said, "We have definitely entered an era where the amount of information available makes it necessary for us to teach not only reading and writing skills but problem solving and evaluative skills, too." His learning objectives included the following:

- to involve students with techniques and resources used in research using traditional reference books, computer software, and the Internet;
- to provide opportunities for students to use their imagination to think creatively and flexibly;
- to develop and improve higher order thinking skills; and
- to strengthen literacy skills in the areas of comprehension, structural analysis, research and reference skills, vocabulary development, communication, and presentation skills.

Freeman, who has won several awards for his use of technology in the classroom, engaged students in a "Believe It or Not" project that was placed on the school's Web site. Students chose items that interested them and followed certain guidelines (for example, a geographic location had to be included as well as a known scientific fact or information about a person of historic significance). At first, students used print-based dictionaries, encyclopedias, and other references to conduct initial research. Later they used CD-ROMs, the Internet, and other technology-based references. They collected e-mail addresses and regular mail addresses so they could write letters of inquiry to find answers to questions not found in their research.

Students used AlphaSmart computers, *The Complete National Geographic*, a scanner, and an HTML editor to construct the Web pages. They obtained permissions (including from Ripley of "Ripley's Believe It or Not") to use all copyrighted materials that appeared on their Web site (http://www.centralia.wednet.edu/title/title.html).

Students wrote about their projects, gave status reports about what they learned, and listed questions they wanted to have answered. They also listed vocabulary words that might be difficult for or new to young or limited-English proficient readers. Their projects included graphic illustrations of the object whenever possible and contained links to other appropriate sites.

Technology as a tool in a balanced literacy program

Kathleen Schmaltz is a fifth-grade teacher teaching mainstreamed learning disabled students in an inclusion class at Lewis Elementary School in Kennesaw, Georgia. Students in her class did a great deal of reading and writing during the year. Students' final drafts were produced using a word processor. They used software to create newsletters to inform their parents and others about classroom events. Other students designed and produced multimedia presentations, creating their slides on the computer. Schmaltz and Pam Thompson, her teammate, used a computer to generate vocabulary lists and other materials for their classes.

The class used integrated thematic units as the framework of their literacy program. They studied such topics as fairy tales, sharks, famous Americans, poetry, and even the Iditarod Dog Sled Race. They created and aired a daily closed-circuit newscast on the Iditarod. Schmaltz said, "Technology is incorporated into each of these units through reading and writing workshops. For example, while reading about famous Americans, students created their own virtual classroom of famous people (themselves)." Students also created multimedia presentations and "infomercials," and they followed the dog sled race on the Internet, sharing daily updates with others at the school.

Comments About Technology Use in Grades 4-6

Intermediate-grade teachers are building on the technology foundations that students are bringing to their classrooms. Students are being introduced to more complex software applications that enable them to publish, create Web sites, share ideas using audio and video, and interact with a variety of more sophisticated computer applications. Heightened creativity, particularly through writing, increased interaction among students, and the desire to create a presence on the Internet grow stronger at these grade levels.

Examples of Literacy and Technology in Grades 6-8

Students in grades 6–8 cast ballots in author award contests, visit reference sites to find answers to specific, difficult questions, and participate in synchronous events such as the space shuttle missions or the travels of famous voyagers. Vocational programs that provide information about a host of occupations appear in classrooms as do software programs that help prepare students for college (The Scholastic Assessment Test, for instance, using *One-to-One With the SAT: Home Version*). Themes become more impressive in their scope, and presentations turn into student portfolios. Students continue to work on projects such as those previously described, but as their literacy capabilities expand, students engage in more research and data analysis, interact more independently with students in other locations, and engage in various publishing ventures. They also interact more with students from other cultures and develop more sophisticated Web pages or school Web sites using Web-authoring tools. They study weather maps and specialty Web sites such as Encyclopedia Titanica (http://atschool.eduweb.co.uk/phind), and visit The Internet Public Library (http://www.ipl.org) or *The New York Times* (http://www.nyt.com). By the end of eighth grade, many students are poised to make even more progress in the use of technology to control their own learning at higher grade levels.

Technology like a pencil in the reading room

Patricia Williams teaches sixth grade at Utley Middle School in Rockwall, Texas. She stated, "Technology is like a pencil in the reading room: Students do not give a second thought as to how it works—it just does." For one unit, Williams discussed the history of storytelling and then told various stories to her class. Students searched for stories that had elements that would lend themselves to good storytelling and selected one of several versions of the Cinderella story (Rafe Martin's *Rough-Face Girl*, Penny Pollock's *The Turkey Girl: A Zuni Cinderella*, John Steptoe's *Mufaro's Beautiful Daughters*, and so on. Williams had her students make *PowerPoint* presentations about the stories to the class "that included plot, setting, characters, themes, problems, solutions, background information, country, and a comparison with the familiar version." The presentations needed to include at least eight slides, including a graphic slide, a title slide, and an author slide. Sound and animation also were required.

Students also participated in a hi-tech interdisciplinary unit called "The Raising of the Titanic." Using Encyclopedia Titanica on the Internet (see http://atschool.eduweb.co.uk/phind for this thorough site), students went on an online scavenger hunt with 10 questions about the Titanic. "Students had to read critically," said Williams, "to find three of the nine famous people on board the Titanic." They also had to find information such as Who was the only child in first or second class to die? and How many people could Life Boat Four hold and how many were actually on it? Some students wrote character sketches based on information found at the site. Some students played a character in a rendition of the raising of the Titanic that was videotaped for later analysis. For their final projects, some students created newscasts of the Titanic's sinking; others created *PowerPoint* presentations. Some students wrote reports or wrote and illustrated poems using a word-processing program. "In English class, students word processed a narrative from the point of view of a person on the Titanic. In science, students studied the ocean and its animals," said Williams.

From the Internet, students found facts for biographical reports, read online poetry written by other students as well as famous poets, created animations to illustrate two poems, and located audio and video clips to insert into their electronic presentations. Students used brainstorming techniques and *Inspiration* software to make graphic representations of their thoughts. (See the accompanying textbox about this software.) They also learned about emoticons [such as this one :) depicting a smiling face] and how they are "shortcuts" used in e-mail. "The students have to think critically to shorten their ideas and make e-mail messages summaries instead of novels," said Williams. She added, "The students have been given short quizzes via e-mail to access their knowledge of content as well as their ability to use e-mail."

Students in this technologically astute classroom created almost 400 projects, reports, and presentations. Technologies used included *Office 97*, *Publisher*, *Inspiration*, and *Netscape Communicator*. Signals were sent from a computer to a television monitor. A scanner, printer, speakers and a microphone, and a VCR and camcorder were used.

The Iditarod dog sled race, from Alaska to South Carolina

Debra Belue, the library/media specialist at O.P. Earle Elementary School in Landrum, South Carolina, describes a school project that enabled 520 kindergarten through sixth-grade students to participate in the Iditarod Race, a 1,049 mile dog sled race that is run from Anchorage to Nome, Alaska (see http://www.Iditarod.com). A local veterinarian who participated in the race encouraged Belue's school to sponsor one of the dogs on his team, so students raised US$1,000 in order to sponsor Buttons, one of the lead dogs. Student objectives of the project included those on page 196:

Inspiration

Inspiration software is a visual thinking and learning tool. Students can create outlines and semantic maps of stories or other things that lend themselves to logical organization. Concept mapping, diagramming, brainstorming, outlining, organizing, planning, and creating materials for the World Wide Web are possible uses for this program. At the *Inspiration* Web site (http://www.inspiration.com) there are sample lessons and a diagram created using the program. Also, below is an example of a semantic map created with *Inspiration* by fifth-grade students at Lawrence School in Tucson, Arizona, as part of a workshop conducted by Chris Johnson, of the University of Arizona, and their teacher, Mary Bouley.

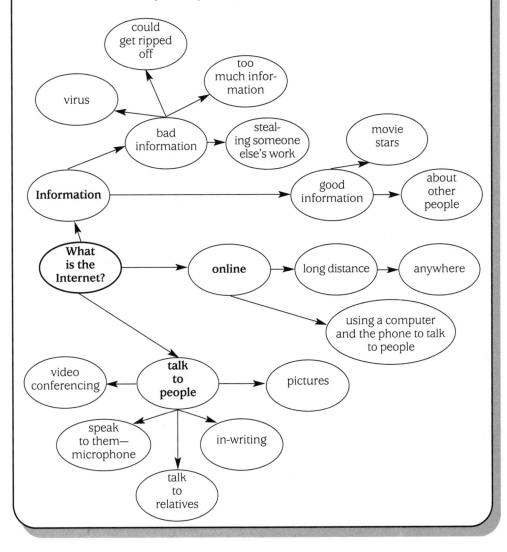

- to read and listen to literature about the Iditarod;
- to create and publish flyers, signs, and labels advertising the class "shop" (a fund-raising activity);
- to use cameras, 35mm and digital, to record events and write articles for the school newspaper;
- to use maps to track progress during the race;
- to learn to use e-mail to read and send messages; and
- to research the Alaskan terrain and the history of the Iditarod and create presentations for the classes.

Students used Internet-capable computers, desktop publishing software such as *The Print Shop Deluxe* and *Publisher*, and presentation software such as *PowerPoint*.

Because the teachers knew little about the Iditarod, they found information, ordered books and materials, and collaborated with Buttons's owner. Soon, they were reading aloud books and other materials they had found, and the students became enthusiastic about the project. To raise money to sponsor Buttons in the March event, students created a classroom "shop" and sold items for Valentine's Day. They created bookmarks, chocolate roses, and tissue paper carnations that they sold before school and at a Parent Teacher Association meeting. Using technology, they designed signs, flyers, and labels for their shop as well.

Once the race started, the dog sledder's wife sent daily reports via e-mail from her hotel room to the school. She attached pictures to the e-mail, which the students used for various tracking activities, including figuring mileage covered and the team's placement on the trail. Some of the sixth graders created visual presentations that included the pictures and research findings about the Iditarod. Belue said, "Our students in the little town of Landrum had been on the trail.... They had become pros at using technology that the previous year we did not even own. What valuable lifelong skills our students have learned while on the Iditarod Trail!"

The eye of the storm

Jennifer Rosenboom teaches sixth grade at Carlos E. Haile Middle School in Bradenton, Florida. She and Leslie Leduc, the eighth-grade science teacher, involved nearly 300 sixth- and eighth-grade students in a six-week project to explore hurricanes during the September–October hurricane season that often affects Florida. Her learning objectives, among others, were as follows:

- to give students opportunities to work with partners and learn the responsible use of the Internet in the classroom;
- to model for students, demonstrating learning strategies and study skills;
- to explore the science of hurricanes;
- to encourage parental and community involvement;
- to introduce students to fictional, age-appropriate literature relating to the theme of hurricanes (Theodore Taylor's *The Cay* was used);
- to help students produce a hurricane awareness pamphlet; and
- to help students use technology.

Students created a book of weather Web sites and concept maps of key weather terms, and they conducted research about major U.S. storms. They downloaded photographs of a hurricane and labeled its parts. Students located and categorized information. They read fictional materials that related to a hurricane theme. "Students used hurricane tracking maps to track current hurricanes, formulate charts, compare and contrast active storms, and discover patterns," said Rosenboom. In addition, Rosenboom said,

> A variety of vocabulary strategies such as Vocabulary Webs and Concept Definition Maps were used to explore weather-related terms.... The presence of Hurricane Georges in our area and the accompanying evacuation, closing of our schools, buying frenzy of necessary supplies, and hurricane preparedness measures truly provided real-life application. We could not believe this actually happened in the middle of our unit!

Student projects were completed using *HyperStudio*, *Netscape Communicator*, Cable in the Classroom (videotaped educational cable programming), video documentaries, CD-ROMs, laserdiscs, cassette tapes, a digital camera, a word-processing program, iBooks (portable Internet-capable computers, made by Apple Computers), and laptop computers.

Technical reading and writing

John Van Rossum teaches eighth grade at Chilton Middle School in Chilton, Wisconsin. Technology is used in a variety of units throughout the school year. "In the Technical Communications unit," said Van Rossum, "students analyze and create different types of technical communications that are commonly used in the workplace. Students analyze audience, purpose, style and design of business letters, memos, newsletters, reports, instruction manuals, and proposals." *TechWriter* software, which provides students with real-life examples of technical writing to edit, gave students much practice in 10 grammar skills areas. While learning to create proposals and reports, students also learned how to make *PowerPoint* presentations. Students learned to present the main points and themes of their works in ways that would interest their audience. Students "learned to emphasize and stress what they felt were the important points of their reports and proposals by analyzing what the audience most needed to know," Van Rossum said.

Students used the Internet to improve their reading and critical thinking skills in a Web page design unit. "Students studied various Web pages...and analyzed them for content, style, and design," said Van Rossum. Students "determined the purpose of the Web page and how useful the page was to their needs." Students eventually created their own Web pages, after deciding on appropriate content and evaluating other Web pages that they linked to from their own Web pages.

Students used the Wisconsin Career Information System to study career information such as salaries, educational background, and the number of jobs available in Wisconsin (http://www.cew.wisc.edu/wcis) is the URL of this fee-based project). The Career Exploration unit's culminating project was the creation of *HyperStudio* presentations showcasing students' career choices and their educational and personal long- and short-term goals.

The genre of science fiction was studied as part of a Science Fiction/Future unit. Students watched science fiction movies, read stories and novels, and created a Utopian society. Students also created term papers on topics that had to include technology. "Students studied the past and present history of technology as well as the scientific principles needed for the advancement of the technology in the future," said Van Rossum. Students also made predictions about the future of technology. Further information and examples of these projects can be seen on the Technical Reading and Writing Home Page at the school's Web site (http://www.chilton.k12.wi.us).

Jay Stailey's amazing Japanese adventure

Jay Stailey, principal of Zue S. Bales Intermediate School in Friendswood, Texas, traveled to Japan on a Fulbright grant. Before leaving he created a Web site, and, while on the trip, he updated the site every 3 days. He had these areas on the site:

1. A folktale or legend from Japan that changed every 3 days.

2. A poetry page that featured ancient and modern Japanese Tanka and Haiku poetry that changed every 3 days, also.

3. A travel update, sharing details of the journey and visits to cultural sites and schools.

4. Amazing observations and epiphanies about culture through exposure to another culture.

5. Links to Japanese culture on the Internet.

Stailey said, "They read of my adventures as well as the stories and poetry of the country in which I was traveling. It was through the wonders of modern technology that my students were able to travel with me, all the while learning about the Japanese culture through reading on the Web." Stailey added, "They kept track of their principal who was traveling in a different day, in a world very different from Friendswood, Texas. A world that was suddenly much closer to home." The site (http://www.friendswood.isd.tenet.edu/ba/japan) contains materials placed there during the principal's travels.

This activity exemplifies an exceptional use of technology that makes reading and learning about other people around the world very exciting and personal. Teachers traveling within their own states or countries could emulate this model and take their students along to places they might never learn about otherwise.

Comments About Technology Use in Grades 6-8

Middle school teachers are encouraging greater technology use to help students engage in inquiries that demand analysis of the abundant nonfiction materials that students are able to locate on the World Wide Web. The amount of technology-assisted projects and reports they create increases dramatically as students become more efficient in conducting Internet searches, collating information, and writing reports. Students also are becoming more comfortable and adept at using presentation products to share their research findings. Further, middle school students appear to be very interested in tracking and examining real-time events, and they are using increasingly sophisticated software programs to help them learn about careers and vocations. Technology-assisted projects that lead to greater literacy development in students are now helping middle school students prepare for high school and beyond.

Concluding Remarks

Teachers are creating excellent classroom projects and are using, in stimulating and educationally valuable ways, information technologies as tools to foster growth in literacy. From helping students understand the concept of "word" to helping students learn to create knowledge and present it in imaginative ways to others around the world, teachers are demonstrating how instructional technology is changing literacy instruction systemically. With powerful tools for themselves and their students to use, creative teachers will continue to be the most important variable in the classroom and in hyperspace.

Author's note

While on a sabbatical, I visited schools in southern Arizona to speak to teachers, students, technology trainers, technology workers (such as network administrators), and school administrators. My conversations and observations form the basis for information described in this chapter. My memberships on university and public school technology committees, such as the Tucson Unified School District #1 Technology Futures Team, provided the basis for additional ideas. Finally, the recounting of classroom practices supplied by entrants in the International Reading Association's first Presidential Technology Award provided more descriptions about how technology is really being infused into today's literacy classrooms.

References

The Academy of Reading [Computer software]. (1999). Ottawa, ON: Autoskill International.

Amazing Animals [Computer software]. (1997). New York: DK Interactive Learning.

American Girls Collection [Computer software]. (1995). Cambridge, MA: The Learning Company.

The Berenstain Bears Get in a Fight [Computer software]. (1995). Novato, CA: Brøderbund/The Learning Company.

The Berenstain Bears in the Dark [Computer software]. (1996). Cambridge, MA: Brøderbund/The Learning Company.

Big Anthony's Mixed-Up Magic [Computer software]. (1996). Cambridge, MA: MECC/The Learning Company.

Brett, J. (1989). *The mitten: A Ukranian folktale*. New York: Putnam.

Brett, J. (1992). *Trouble with trolls*. New York: Putnam.

Brett, J. (1995). *Armadillo rodeo*. New York: Putnam.

Carle, E. (1981). *The very hungry caterpillar*. New York: Philomel Books.

The Cat in the Hat [Computer software]. (1997). Cambridge, MA: Brøderbund/The Learning Company.

ClarisWorks [Computer software]. (1997). Santa Clara, CA: Claris.

The Complete National Geographic: 109 Years of National Geographic Magazine [Video disk]. (1998). Washington, DC: National Geographic Society.

Cowley, J. (1999). *Mrs. Wishy-Washy.* New York: Philomel Books.

Dinosaur Hunter [Computer software]. (1996). New York: DK Interactive Learning.

Dr. Seuss's ABC [Computer software]. (1995). Cambridge, MA: Brøderbund/The Learning Company.

Explorer [Computer software]. (1999). Redmond, WA: Microsoft.

Frog and Toad Are Friends [Computer software]. (1997). Beverly Hills, CA: Fox Interactive.

FrontPage Express [Computer software]. (1999). Redmond, WA: Microsoft.

Green Eggs and Ham [Computer software]. (1996). Cambridge, MA: Brøderbund/The Learning Company.

Hutchins, P. (1968). *Rosie's walk*. New York: Macmillan.

HyperStudio [Computer software]. (1999). Torrance, CA: Roger Wagner Publishing.

I Can Be a Dinosaur Hunter [Computer software]. (1996). New York: DK Interactive Learning.

If You Give a Mouse a Cookie [Computer software]. (1995). New York: HarperCollins Interactive.

Inspiration [Computer software]. (1999). Portland, OR: Inspiration Software.

International Society for Technology in Education (1998). *National educational technology standards for students (NETS)*. Eugene, OR: Author.

International Society for Technology in Education (1999). *National educational technology standards for students: Connecting curriculum and technology*. Eugene, OR: Author.

Kid Pix [Computer software]. (1993). Cambridge, MA: Brøderbund/The Learning Company.

Martin, R., & Shannon, D. (1992). *Rough-face girl*. New York: Philomel Books.

Netscape Communicator [Computer software]. (1999). Mountain View, CA: Netscape Communications.

Office 97 [Computer software]. (1997). Redmond, WA: Microsoft.

One-on-One With the SAT: Home Version [Computer software]. (1999). New York: The College Board.

Oregon Trail [Computer software]. (1991). Cambridge, MA: The Learning Company.

Peek, M. (1998). *Mary wore her red dress and Henry wore his green sneakers*. Boston: Houghton Mifflin

Pollock, P. (1996). *The turkey girl: A Zuni Cinderella*. Boston: Little Brown.

PowerPoint [Computer software]. (1996). Redmond, WA: Microsoft.

The Print Shop Deluxe [Computer software]. (1999). Cambridge, MA: Brøderbund/The Learning Company.

Publisher [Computer software]. (1996). Redmond, WA: Microsoft.

QuickTime 4 [Computer software]. (1999). Cupertino, CA: Apple.

Read, Write & Play! [Computer software]. (1996). Cambridge, MA: The Learning Company.

RealAudio [Computer software]. (1999). Seattle, WA: RealNetworks.

RealVideo [Computer software]. (1999). Seattle, WA: RealNetworks.

Sheila Rae the Brave [Computer software]. (1996). Cambridge, MA: The Learning Company.

SimpleText [Computer software]. (1998). Cuptertino, CA: Apple.

Stellaluna [Computer software]. (1996). Cambridge, MA: The Learning Company.

Steptoe, J. (1993). *Mufaro's beautiful daughters*. West Yorkshire, England: Mulberry Books.

Student Writing and Research Center [Computer software]. (1995). Cambridge, MA: The Learning Company.

Student Writing Center [Computer software]. (1994). Cambridge, MA: The Learning Company.

SuperPrint Deluxe [Computer software]. (1999). New York: Scholastic.

Taylor, T. (1969). *The cay*. New York: Doubleday.

TechWriter [Computer software]. (1985). Waltham, MA: CMI Software.

U.S. Department of Education. (1999, February). Office of Educational Technology Internet posting. Washington, DC: Author.

Van Allsburg, C. (1985). *The polar express*. Boston: Houghton Mifflin.

WebWacker 2000 [Computer software]. (1999). Draper, UT: Blue Squirrel.

CHAPTER 8

Is Technology Worth My Professional Time, Resources, and Efforts?

ERNEST BALAJTHY

Schools are being transformed by instructional technology in ways that few would have imagined 10, 20, or 30 years ago. Indeed, they have already been transformed.

In technologically cutting-edge schools across the world, students are connected

- to information sources that are up to date, varied, rich, and comprehensive; and

- to one another, across boundaries of states, nations, and continents and across language and cultural and racial groups.

Our students are technologically proficient, accustomed in their homes and schools to using the latest hardware and software. They demand that schools keep pace with the new technologies that seem to appear at ever faster rates. They recognize that technology is the wave of the present and of their futures—that economic and social leadership in the 21st century depends on our encouragement of technological prowess of our fellow citizens.

Our students also are enchanted by technology. They have simple "gee whiz" reactions to video games or special effects in movies. But more important, they recognize that technology is transforming our lives in marvelous ways. Our students recognize that they can be part of this technological future, whether in

- the field of medicine, as researchers use gene-splitting to develop new vaccines and cures for disease;

- the field of meteorology, as scientists find new ways to predict the weather that allow farmers to grow their crops more efficiently to feed an ever-increasing population;
- the fields of economics and business as complex problem-solving procedures are developed to maintain healthy economic growth; or
- the many other fields in which technology is bringing about massive transformation.

This transformation is happening in the fields of education and literacy, as well. In fact, our definition of what it means to be "literate" in today's society is evolving at a rapid rate.

- Can any student truly be literate today without a proficient understanding of how to operate computer hardware and major types of software, such as word processors, spreadsheets, and databases—so-called "computer literacy"?
- Can any student truly be literate today without the ability to navigate the Internet to find information and resources and reorganize them in personally meaningful ways?
- Can any student truly be literate today without an understanding of how to create multimedia resources—such as Web pages—of his or her own, for publication on disk or on the Web?

In an early book on instructional use of computers, Papert (1980) described the transformation in thinking that takes place as human minds interact with technology as a "mindstorm." The figurative description of this transformation as a "storm"—with all its potential for enormous power, but also with the potential for confusion and chaos—is an apt metaphor for the effects of technology on learning and thinking. Educators will spend the next years or decades—perhaps centuries—wrestling with the implications of this storm and benefiting from its power for improving students' reading, writing, listening, speaking, and thinking.

Why Should I Use Technology?

Technology Improves Instruction

An abundance of research dating from the earliest days of educational computing demonstrates that students' achievement can be improved through use of instructional technology. Those who are skeptical about the effectiveness of technology justly warn that computers are no panacea for the educational needs of the United States (Oppenheimer, 1997; Robertson, 1998). Computers can be an expensive waste of time unless teachers integrate them appropriately to meet students' needs. Informed, flexible, dedicated teachers remain the key to effective instruction.

Yet the results of research speak clearly on the issue. Seventy-eight percent of teachers report that they have seen evidence of achievement gains due to computer use. Ninety-five percent believe that the achievement of low-performing students can be enhanced by computers (Kamp, 1999). Bangert-Drowns's (1993) survey of computer-based activities for writing indicated clear benefits. Bowman (1998) reported on a project targeting the lowest performing third graders in an urban school, combining one-on-one tutoring and mentoring with computer-assisted programs that gave frequent feedback and continuous progress reports. Reading scores improved one full grade level during the 3-month project.

To obtain improved achievement, we should plan carefully by doing the following:

1. *Make sure the computer applications reflect "best practice" in teaching reading and literacy.* Reading materials should be interesting, relevant, and well written—reflecting the best of narrative and expository text available. Writing assignments should be authentic and involving. Direct instruction should be creative and motivating—but carefully designed with appropriate and immediate feedback to students.

2. *Carefully monitor software objectives for the appropriate level.* It makes no sense to have computers teach phonics skills that already have been mastered or comprehension skills that are too advanced and frustrating. Just as you target your teaching objectives to the needs of particular students, software must precisely target the ever-changing needs of students using it.

3. *Give priority to using computers in ways that allow you to expand your expectations for your students.* Simply replacing existing literacy activities with similar computer-based literacy activities will not result in achievement growth for your students. Use computers to add to the richness and rigor of your classroom literacy curriculum.

Computers Are Mindtools

An important consideration for all teachers using instructional technology relates to how to use it. Part of the answer to that question, as we have seen, has to do with improvement of instruction, with the more efficient and effective achievement of traditional curricular goals—such as improving reading achievement and writing ability.

Another important part of the answer to the question of how to use instructional technology deals with how computers can be used to transform learning and thinking. Jonassen (2000) focused his attention on the use of computers as tools, as what he calls "mindtools":

> Mindtools are computer-based tools and learning environments that have been adapted or developed to function as intellectual partners with the learner in order to engage and facilitate critical thinking and higher order learning. (p. 9)

If we are to achieve necessary educational goals for the 21st century, we need to transform our idea of what lifelong learning involves. Our students will become able to think on higher levels, critically, analytically, and creatively. They will need to make decisions, to problem solve, and to develop their own designs to achieve goals and create products. They will need to analyze and synthesize, evaluate, connect ideas, and imagine new and different options and futures. None of these are new goals for educators, but our vision of the future makes these goals even more inescapable than in the past.

Our efforts to achieve these goals can lead to our most exciting opportunities to use technology. Three important principles for a "mind tools" approach to using computers in the classroom are as follows:

1. *Use computer application software for authentic, higher level activities.* Some teachers think of only the glitzy gamelike drill software when they think of instructional technology. But common computer-tool software such as word processing, databases, and spreadsheets provide tremendous benefits. When your students build a database related to the parts of the muscular system, they carry out research and organize information as they begin to understand the structure of the content topic. Examining existing databases involves students in recognizing patterns, in analyzing their assumptions and conclusions, and in comparing and contrasting the information in the database. Constructing and using spreadsheets and computer-based semantic organization networks provide additional experiences for authentic thinking.

2. *Teach and guide students through well-organized intentional searches of the Internet, and move them toward greater independence.* Finding, criti-

cally analyzing, and organizing information from the Internet is complex, especially if the information is needed to solve an authentic problem or to help make an authentic decision. Careful guidance and monitoring is required, especially at first. As students become familiar with this new way of finding information, and as they become better able to deal with the information in informed and wise ways, they will gain greater independence.

3. *Carefully consider new applications of technology that may be quite different from traditional approaches.* Not every new computer application will necessarily help achieve goals that are important to you and your students, but keep an open mind. The time needed for your students to learn to create Web pages, and to actually carry out the creation, is formidable. However, this experience can offer opportunities for your students to engage in authentic "how-to-do-it" learning experiences that will be invaluable in future years. The reading, writing, and collaborative learning in such a project is substantial.

New Technologies Challenge Us to Rethink Our Students' Work

One of the most often-voiced concerns about educational applications of the Internet is whether students will learn to use this valuable resource in productive ways. Educators and parents must provide students with clear guidance as to appropriate use of the Internet—or indeed, of any information sources or communication forms.

Electronic media present powerful, easy-to-use tools to steal the intellectual property of others, what McKenzie (1998) called the "new plagiarism" (see textbox on page 209). McKenzie suggested that the traditional educational approach of assigning topical research has always encouraged plagiarism, because such assignments are mere information gathering and reporting exercises (for example, the assignment "Find out all you can about Ecuador and write an essay on it"). Teachers can think through student-centered assignments that involve higher level tasks, such as comparing, contrasting, making choices, and weighing information to make judgments and conclusions.

Bruce (1997) described such effects of technology on the classroom curriculum as a transactional relationship. New technologies transform literacy

Internet Acceptable Use Policies and Netiquette

Among the difficulties faced by users of the Internet is that some other users display inappropriate behavior. Partly this is due to a frontier mentality—the Internet is a new frontier and there is an appeal to its "untamed" quality. There has been no accepted standard of behavior established. Of course, even if there were established standards, there are no easy methods of policing such behaviors.

Yet there is certainly no need for educators or social leaders to give up on the Internet because of the behaviors of a few of its users. Already, state, federal, and international law enforcement agencies are enforcing standards. In addition, Internet Service Providers (ISPs), including the largest of all, America Online, are beginning to enforce standards for their clients. If nothing else, fears of lawsuits or lost business is compelling them to action.

Schools also must play a role in teaching and enforcing appropriate behaviors. It is important for teachers and administrators to think through the issues and establish policies before problems occur. The American Association of School Administrators has a Web site (http://www.aasa.org/Issues/Techplans/plansTC.htm) that links to a variety of online policy statements on "acceptable use" and on appropriate Internet behaviors (netiquette). One of the more useful is policies offered by Eugene, Oregon, public schools (http://www.4j.lane.edu/4jnet).

acquisition and literacy instruction. But at the same time, teachers transform the technologies to accomplish their objectives.

Part of the issue we deal with will have to do with reconsidering the kinds of activities we require of our students. How many students will see reading and writing assignments such as "What I Learned in the Library About the State of New Hampshire" as valid and useful when they know that hundreds of text files answering just that question are available for instant downloading from the Web?

What is meaningful learning? Our answers to that question are being challenged by today's technology. More and more, we will have to move away from the old answers—which all too often involved rote, artificial learning—and seriously consider just what we mean by the term "meaningful." Jonassen, Peck, and Wilson (1999) suggested that the learning necessary for our technological future will have five characteristics: active, constructive, intentional, authentic, and cooperative.

Technology Offers Exciting Opportunities for Critical Thinking

Free speech, with accompanying tolerance of divergent expression and tolerance of error, is a foundational value of great importance. We have long recognized the power of free speech to work for the good of all. In recent classes,

Avoiding the "New Plagiarism"

How can we simultaneously help students avoid plagiarism from the Internet and help develop their research skills and creative thinking? Our assignments need to change from simple information gathering (such as, "Tell me all you can find out about bottlenose whales") in order to require students' insightful thinking based on organized research. Here are some examples of assignments that help develop students' research skills and creative thinking.

In the Animorphs series by K.A. Applegate (published by Scholastic), a group of children are given the ability to "morph" into animals in order to fight evil alien invaders, the Yeerks. Imagine that you are given such power, to morph into a bottlenose whale. Carry out research on the Internet and in the school library that will provide you with information about bottlenose whales. Discuss which characteristics would be important to you if you were to morph into a whale. Use that information to create a multimedia presentation that combines Animorph adventure with details about life as a morphed bottlenose whale.

You have been selected by the President of the United States to serve on an advisory committee to determine whether a new Pathfinder mission should be sent to Mars. Carry out research on the Internet and in the school library that will provide you with information about the 1997 Pathfinder mission and its findings. Determine whether you believe those findings to have been worth the effort and expense of the Pathfinder mission. Use the information to provide an oral report to the class that will offer conclusions as to whether a second mission is advisable.

Karchmer (2000) reported on Susan Silverman, a second-grade teacher in New York who has offered an Internet project entitled "Stellaluna's Friends" (http://www.kids-learn.org/stellaluna), a title drawn from a children's picture book about a bat (Cannon, 1993). Students researched information about bats, then developed reports, stories, and poems about a bat that might live near them. The results were published on the class Web site. (See also Chapter 4 for a plan that uses *Stellaluna*, and Chapter 7 for more information about Silverman's activities and Web site.)

my students have studied the political novels of exiled Kenyan author Ngugi wa Thiongo. We have explored the Internet to study widely diverging views on the state of human rights in Kenya. The Kenyan Embassy's Web site and Web sites of political dissidents provide conflicting information.

The power of the Internet for good is enormous. During the attempted coup in the Soviet Union in the early 1990s, the Internet provided the outside world with vital information. Computer users in Moscow were able to provide the world with critically important information as soon as events occurred. But stories abound about the spread of unreliable information on the Internet. Such information is occasionally read by reporters and then disseminated further through traditional mass media. Stories about the supposed involvement of a U.S. Navy missile ship in the destruction of TWA Flight 800 and the disputed facts about Central Intelligence Agency distribution of drugs to African Americans are examples of how unreliable information can be spread widely as the result of Internet misuse. Internet enthusiasts sometimes defend the unreliability of its information by pointing out that even traditional media are unreliable.

In addition, the use of the Internet as a commercial advertising medium reinforces the need for us to provide our students with consumer education. Many of the most popular Web sites contain heavy commercial content. The ambitious Disney site (http://www.disney.com), for example, is well designed as a large, entertaining advertisement for Disney media products. We need to help our students learn about how marketers use a host of tactics to encourage spending on their products.

We also need to give our students instruction in the concepts underlying free speech and the open marketplace of ideas. They can learn how to sort through large amounts of information that is often unreliable and contradictory. As students become more familiar with various Internet resources, they will learn to distinguish reliable sites from unreliable, just as people today can tell the difference between the reliability of such information outlets as *The New York Times* and the tabloids. Using the Internet, valuable lessons can be created to distinguish useful from misleading information.

Another general principle of encouraging thoughtful, critical analysis deals with learning as a social activity. If learning is indeed socially mediated, then widespread use of collaborative methods, integrated with technology, offers tremendous potential. Use of such classroom devices as networked word-processing systems and long distance e-mail projects is being examined by researchers and found to have exciting potential (Fey, 1997).

Collaborative Internet Research Guide

Name _____   Topic _____

Date _____

What do we already know about our topic that will help us fulfill our assignment?

What are the questions we want to answer in our Internet research?

How can the task be divided among our group?

Notes
My Research Results   Related Results From My Group

Technology Can Help Us Meet Students at Their Appropriate Reading and Learning Levels

We understand the principle of avoiding use of traditional print materials written at students' frustration levels. For the same reason, we should carefully preview Web sites to assess their readability. A student's random surfing of the Internet on a high-interest topic such as dolphins might lead to esoteric biological research that is written for university researchers. Teacher planning time is necessary to find sites that match curriculum and learning levels of students. This is particularly important as new Web sites are constantly being created and old Web sites change addresses or become inactive.

One important new resource for teachers that will provide appropriate levels of instruction is the host of Web sites created by students for students. These sites lack the glitzy "bells and whistles" of some commercial Web sites, and quality varies considerably. With teacher oversight, students at a wide variety of reading levels can find appropriate material on many different subjects. For example, Anne Keller, a third-grade teacher from Arizona, has used annual units on African animals to have her students create research reports. The reports are posted on the Internet (http://www.havasu.k12.az.us/starline/akeller/african_animals.htm) and can be accessed by other classes to be used as resources.

Another important resource for students is electronic books (see Chapter 4 for a description and examples). Research is quite positive about the benefits of such electronic text (Anderson-Inman, 1999; McKenna, Reinking, & Labbo, 1997; McKenna, Reinking, Labbo, & Kieffer, 1999).

Students Can Learn to Find Information From a Wide Variety of Sources and Reorganize It to Make It Personally Meaningful

Successful use of the Internet by students requires that teachers provide increased instruction, modeling, and practice in dealing with multiple sources and nonlinear presentation of ideas. Warnings similar to those that have criticized educational television shows such as *Sesame Street* may have some degree of truth. Himmelfarb (1996), for example, has suggested that

> Young students constantly exposed to "multimedia" and "hypermedia" replete with sound and images often become unable to concentrate on mere "texts" (known as books), which have only words and ideas to commend them. Worse yet, the constant exposure to a myriad of texts, sounds, and images that are only tangentially related to each other is hardly conducive to the cultivation of logical, rational, systematic habits of thought. (p. A56)

Yet, the randomness and nonlinearity of the Web may offer real benefits in terms of learning style for the new postmodern generations. Research will be needed to investigate the potential effects of the Internet's unique form of accessing information.

We increasingly recognize the complexity of many important issues in our world. On one hand, the ready availability of massive amounts of textual and multimedia information on world events strengthens the possibility that we can be truly informed decision makers. On the other hand, we are greatly challenged by the need to sort through that information, differentiating what is repetitive from what is new, what is reliable from what is unreliable, and what is fact from what is opinion.

The Internet can be a tool in our classrooms to give students experiences in dealing with large amounts of divergent information on issues of interest.

Students can experience what it means to be "lost in hyperspace" (Edwards & Hardman, 1989, p. 105)—bewildered by the unmapped network of ideas on the Internet. Teachers can guide students through the thinking and researching processes necessary to find their way, to structure ideas and recognize patterns of information. McKenzie (1998) described this goal as "raising a generation of free-range students," grazing for information and knowledge on the Internet. I am not sure I completely like the analogy linking students with herd cattle, but McKenzie's description of the kind of students we want to develop is a good one: "Young people capable of navigating through a complex, often disorganized information landscape while making up their own minds about the important issues that affect their lives and their times" (p. 27).

She notes the link that is at the heart of my thesis in this chapter, as well. The same skills that students develop in well-guided activities using computers will serve them well in the tests of life, and also in the increasingly challenging state and nationally mandated achievement tests.

Our goal, after all, is not simply to teach our students to be mere consumers of information. Our goal is to lead them to be *educated* consumers of information. In his best-selling book *Closing of the American Mind*, Bloom (1987) made the important point that open-mindedness is not an ultimate educational goal, despite tendencies in our culture to establish it as such. Open-mindedness can be empty-headedness, Bloom told us, if it is used as an excuse to avoid thinking through important issues in life. The intellectual goal of an educated person should be to examine issues, to weigh the evidence critically, and finally, to take a position based on these considerations. Chall, in her developmental model of reading (1983), likewise identified the ability to think through complex issues and to establish an intellectually valid position on them as the highest stage in reading development (the stage of Construction and Reconstruction: A World View).

It has been estimated that there are more than 4 million Web sites and hundreds of millions of documents on the Internet (Nielsen, 1999). Sorting through all documents on any one topic may be a hopeless task—but it is also unnecessary. No student needs to read every book and magazine in a library to carry out substantive research on a topic. Likewise, no one needs to read every document on the Web about atmospheric pollution in order to draw firm and worthy conclusions on the topic. Teaching students to become "infotectives" (McKenzie, 1998), to do basic research on the Web, follows most or all of the same principles involved in teaching research skills using traditional print-based library books and documents (see textbox on the next page).

What Is an "Infotective"?

An "infotective" (McKenzie, 1998) is a term designed for the Information Age "student thinker capable of asking questions about data in order to convert the data into information (data organized so as to reveal patterns and relationships) and eventually into insight (information that may suggest an action or strategy)" (p. 27). In the past, teachers provided information to students to be memorized and learned. In the Information Age, students must construct meaning. To do this, they must learn traditional research skills (and the changes brought about in research tasks by electronic technologies) and how to do original thinking.

An infotective project can be organized as follows. Note that, as in all writing process approaches, the stages are recursive and students will typically move back and forth between them.

Developing the Question

Students think through the basic issues to be addressed and develop an interrelated web of questions that will drive the entire project.

Researching the Question

Students use electronic and traditional media to obtain data and information and to sort it in ways that address the questions.

Organizing the Information

Students formally organize the data to provide answers to the questions in ways that are appropriate to their audience.

Presenting the Information

Information can be presented in a wide variety of ways to the intended audience: public speech or discussion, written essays, electronic text, or multimedia.

We Can Help ALL Students, Regardless of Socioeconomic or Other Factors, Achieve Success

The general issue of providing a quality education to the disadvantaged is one of the most difficult challenges facing U.S. public education today, as is providing the disadvantaged access to instructional technology. Kamp (1999), for example, reported that 90% of schools in high socioeconomic areas have access to the Internet, but in low socioeconomic areas only 78% do. The problem is not so much that schools in disadvantaged communities have fewer computers per student. This problem can be readily solved in states that are concerned about the issue and willing to fund the changes. The problem is that advantaged students have far greater access to computers at home, where much of their time on task with computers occurs.

One attempt to provide some remedy for this situation has come from the U.S. federal government. Under the Telecommunications Act of 1996, Congress established the Universal Service Fund Education Rate (E-Rate) to support educational use of the Internet. Schools and libraries are applying for funding to underwrite the costs of Internet connections and hardware. The sheer size of this fund, $1.9 billion in 1999 (Kamp, 1999), is having a major impact in expanding student access to the Internet.

Another factor to consider in the quest to provide all students with equal, quality education is the types of software available for students from different backgrounds. Balajthy (1999) surveyed commercial software publishers whose products are designed to enhance multicultural education and found a limited but significant number of such products. Teachers of literacy can choose from a wide range of multicultural electronic texts, as well as products that are designed to support students whose first language is not English.

Equity is also an issue with educators who are concerned about technology and gender. A far too common scene in classrooms has the boys crowded around the computer table and the girls engaged in nontechnology activities. Some publishers are making efforts to develop software of interest to girls. *Let's Talk About Me* includes diaries, personality profiles, and advice from a variety of well-known women. *The Baby-sitters Club Friendship Kit* is based on the popular series. Software includes a journal, a subprogram for making stationery, an address book, and games.

Concluding Remarks

So, is instructional technology worthwhile? Should you devote a significant portion of your time and effort to integrating technology into your curriculum, or should you choose some other important avenues of creative pedagogical endeavor?

We teachers will choose to answer this question differently, and I believe that the different ways in which we reach out to our diverse student population are all part of the reason the education system is successful. Does instructional technology fit in? There is not much doubt that this question has already been answered by teachers and students alike. The proliferation of computers in schools is readily apparent. Teachers are seizing on this new technology to promote their curricular goals.

In this chapter, we have looked at a wide variety of reasons for promoting use of technology. From the issue of effectiveness to the issue of encouraging critical thinking necessary for the 21st century, all teachers will be able to find important reasons for making the time to learn about computers and to plan for their use in the classroom.

References

Anderson-Inman, L. (1999). Computer-based solutions for secondary students with learning disabilities: Emerging issues. *Reading and Writing Quarterly, 15*, 239–249.

Baby-sitter's Club Friendship Kit [Computer software]. (1996). Cambridge, MA: Creative Wonders/The Learning Company.

Balajthy, E. (1999, May). *Trends in literacy software publication and marketing: Multicultural themes*. Paper presented at the National Reading Research Center Conference on Literacy and Technology for the 21st Century, Atlanta, GA (ERIC Document Reproduction Service No. ED 424 562)

Bangert-Drowns, R. (1993). The word processor as an instructional tool: A meta-analysis of word processing in writing instruction. *Review of Educational Research, 63*, 69–93.

Bloom, A. (1987). *Closing of the American mind*. New York: Simon and Schuster.

Bowman, J. (1998). Technology, tutoring and improved reading. *English Update: Newsletter from the Center on English Learning and Achievement, 3*, 2–3.

Bruce, B.C. (1997). Literacy technologies: What stance should we take? *Journal of Literacy Research, 29*, 289–309.

Cannon, J. (1993). *Stellaluna*. San Diego, CA: Harcourt Brace Jovanovich.

Chall, J. (1983). *Stages of reading development*. New York: McGraw-Hill.

Edwards, D.M., & Hardman, L. (1989). "Lost in hyperspace": Cognitive mapping and navigation in hypertext environment. In R. McAleese (Ed.), *Hypertext: Theory into practice* (pp. 105–125). Oxford: Intellect Limited.

Fey, M. (1997). Shared writing via computer networking. *Reading and Writing Quarterly, 13*, 383–388.

Himmelfarb, G. (1996). A neo-Luddite reflects on the Internet. *Chronicle of Higher Education, 43*, A56.

Jonassen, D.H. (2000). *Computers as mindtools for schools* (2nd ed.). Upper Saddle River, NJ: Merrill.

Jonassen, D.H., Peck, K.L., & Wilson, B.G. (1999). *Learning with technology: A constructivist approach*. Upper Saddle River, NJ: Merrill.

Kamp, S. (1999). *1999 education market report, K–12*. Washington, DC: Software and Information Industry Association.

Karchmer, R.A. (2000). Understanding teachers' perspectives of Internet use in the classroom: Implications for teacher education and staff development. *Reading and Writing Quarterly*, *16*, 81–85.

Let's Talk About Me [Computer software]. (1996). New York: Simon & Schuster Interactive.

McKenna, M., Reinking, D., & Labbo, L. (1997). Using talking books with reading-disabled students. *Reading and Writing Quarterly*, *13*, 185–190.

McKenna, M.C., Reinking, D., Labbo, L.D., & Kieffer, R.D. (1999). The electronic transformation of literacy and its implications for the struggling reader. *Reading and Writing Quarterly*, *15*, 111–126.

McKenzie, J. (1998). Grazing the net: Raising a generation of free-range students. *Phi Delta Kappan*, *80*, 26–31.

Nielsen, J. (1999). User interface directions for the web. *Communications of the ACM*, *42*, 65–72.

Oppenheimer, T. (1997). The computer delusion. *Atlantic Monthly*, *280*, 45–62.

Papert, S. (1980). *Mindstorms: Children, computers and powerful ideas*. New York: Basic Books.

Robertson, H. (1998). *No more teachers, no more books*. Toronto: McClelland and Stewart.

Appendix
Software Company Addresses

Adobe Systems, Inc.
http://www.adobe.com
345 Park Avenue
San Jose, California 95110-2704
  Adobe PageMaker 6.5 Plus
  FrameMaker
  PhotoShop
  SuperPaint

Advantage Learning Systems, Inc.
http://www.advlearn.com
PO Box 8036
Wisconsin Rapids, Wisconsin
  54495-8036
  Accelerated Reader

Apple Computer, Inc.
http://www.apple.com
PO Box 4040
Cupertino, California 95015-4040
  AppleWorks
  QuickTime
  SimpleText

Autoskill International, Inc.
http://www.autoskill.com
85 Albert Street, Suite 1000
Ottawa, Ontario, Canada K1P 6A4
  The Academy of Reading

Blue Squirrel
http://www.bluesquirrel.com
170 West Election Drive
Draper, Utah 84020
  WebWhacker 2000

Brøderbund/The Learning Company
http://www.broderbund.com
One Athenaeum Street
Cambridge, Massachusetts 02142
  Arthur's Birthday Deluxe
  Arthur's Computer Adventure
  Arthur's Reading Race
  Arthur's Teacher Trouble
  The Berenstain Bears Get in a Fight
  The Berenstain Bears in the Dark
  Carmen Sandiego Word Detective
  The Cat in the Hat
  Dr. Seuss's ABC
  Dr. Seuss Kindergarten Deluxe
  Green Eggs and Ham
  Just Grandma and Me Deluxe
  Kid Pix
  Kid Pix Studio Deluxe
  Little Monster at School
  The Print Shop
  The Print Shop Deluxe
  Reading Galaxy
  Sheila Rae, the Brave
  Stellaluna
  The Tortoise and the Hare
  Where in the USA Is Carmen Sandiego?
  Where in the World Is Carmen Sandiego?
  Where in Time Is Carmen Sandiego?

Claris Corporation
http://www.apple.com
  ClarisWorks

(now *AppleWorks*; see Apple
Computer, Inc.)

The College Board
http://www.collegeboard.org
45 Columbus Avenue
New York, New York 10023
  One-on-One with the SAT

Computer Curriculum Corporation
http://www.ccclearn.com
1287 Lawrence Station Road
Sunnyvale, California 94089
  Writers Studio

Corel Corporation
http://www.corel.com
1600 Carling Avenue
Ottawa, Ontario, Canada K1Z 8K7
  WordPerfect

Creative Wonders/The Learning Company
http://www.cwonders.com
One Athenaeum Street
Cambridge, Massachusetts 02142
  The Baby-sitters Club
  Elmo's Reading
  Madeline 1st & 2nd Grade Reading
  Slam Dunk Typing

Curriculum Associates
http://www.curriculumassociates.com
PO Box 2001
North Billerica, Massachusetts
  01862-0901
  PostCards
  SuperSonic Phonics

Davidson & Associates
http://www.davd.com
PO Box 2961
Torrance, California 90509
  Kid Phonics 1

Kid Phonics 2
Kid Works 2
Spelling and Grammar

DK Interactive Learning
http://www.dkinteractive.com
95 Madison Avenue
New York, New York 10016
  Amazing Animals
  Dinosaur Hunter
  I Can Be a Dinosaur
  I Love Spelling

Edmark
http://www.edmark.com
PO Box 97021
Redmond, Washington 98023
  Bailey's Book House
  Destination: Pyramids
  Imagination Express
  Let's Go Read! An Island Adventure
  Let's Go Read! An Ocean Adventure

Entrex Software, Inc.
http://www.entrex.org
PO Box 30029, Sanich Centre Postal
  Outlet
#104-3995 Quadra Street
Victoria, British Columbia, Canada
  V8X 5E1
  Sugar & Snails

Fox Interactive
http://www.foxinteractive.com
2121 Avenue of the Stars, Suite 400
Los Angeles, California 90067
  Frog and Toad Are Friends

Great Wave Software
http://www.greatwave.com
5353 Scotts Valley Drive
Scotts Valley, California 96066
  DaisyQuest
  Daisy's Castle
  Reading Mansion

Grolier Interactive, Inc.
http://gi.grolier.com
90 Sherman Turnpike
Danbury, Connecticut 06816
Grolier Multimedia Encyclopedia

HarperCollins Interactive
http://www.harpercollins.com
10 East 53rd Street
New York, New York 10022
If You Give a Mouse a Cookie

Herzog Keyboarding
http://www.herzogkeyboarding.com
1433 E. Broadway
Tucson, Arizona 85719
Herzog Keyboarding

Houghton Mifflin
http://www.hmco.com
120 Beacon Street
Somerville, Massachusetts 02142
Curious George Learns Phonics
Spelling Spree
The Ribbit Collection

Inspiration Software, Inc.
http://www.inspiration.com
7412 SW Beaverton
Hillsdale Hwy, Suite 102
Portland, Oregon 97225-2167
Inspiration

Icon Technology Limited
http://www.iconsupport.demon.co.uk
Church House
Church Street
Carlby Lincs., United Kingdom PE9
4NB
TechWriter

Knowledge Adventure
http://www.knowledgeadventure.com
4100 W. 190th Street
Torrance, California 90504
JumpStart 1st Grade Reading
JumpStart Typing
Kid Works Deluxe

Lawrence Productions
http://www.voyager.net/lawrence/
software
1800 South 35th Street
Galesburg, Michigan 49053-9687
The New Katie's Farm

Leap Into Learning, Inc.
http://www.leapintolearning.com
PO Box 803
Evanston, Illinois 60204
Leap Into Phonics

The Learning Company
http://www.learningco.com
One Athenaeum Street
Cambridge, Massachusetts 02142
Africa Trail
Amazon Trail
American Girls Collection
The Art Lesson
Bilingual Writing Center
MayaQuest Trail
Oregon Trail
Reader Rabbit's Interactive
Reading Journey
Storybook Weaver
Storybook Weaver Deluxe
Student Writing and Research
Center
Student Writing Center
Yukon Trail

MECC/The Learning Company
http://www.mecc.com
One Athenaeum Street
Cambridge, Massachusetts 02142
Big Anthony's Mixed-Up Magic
Odell Down Under
Opening Night

Paint, Write & Play!
Spellevator Plus
Spelling Toolkit Plus
Spellbound
Super Solvers Spellbound
Word Munchers
Word Munchers Deluxe

MetaCreations Corporation

http://www.metatools.com
6303 Carpinteria Avenue
Carpinteria, California 93013
Art Dabbler
Painter

Microsoft

http://www.microsoft.com
One Microsoft Way
Redmond, Washington 98052
Excel
Front Page
FrontPage Express
Internet Explorer
MS Kids
Office 97
Office 2000
PowerPoint
Publisher
Word

Mindplay

http://www.mindplay.com
160 W. Fort Lowell
Tucson, Arizona 85705
Math Magic

Mindscape/The Learning Company

One Athenaeum Street
Cambridge, Massachusetts 02142
Mavis Beacon Teaches Typing

Multimedia Design Corporation (The Learning Company)

One Athenaeum Street

Cambridge, Massachusetts 02142
mPower

Netscape Communications

http://www.netscape.com
501 R. Middlefield Road
Mountain View, California 94043
Netscape Communicator
Netscape Navigator

RealNetworks, Inc.

http://www.realnetworks.com
1111 Third Avenue, Suite 2900
Seattle, Washington 98101
RealAudio
RealVideo

Roger Wagner Publishing

http://www.hyperstudio.com
1050 Pioneer Way, Suite P
El Cajon, California 92020
HyperStudio

Scholastic

http://www.scholastic.com
555 Broadway
New York, New York 10012-3999
Favorite Greek Myths
*If Your Name Was Changed at Ellis
  Island*
Malcolm X: By Any Means Necessary
The Math Shop Series
SuperPrint Deluxe
Titanic
WiggleWorks Plus

Simon & Schuster Interactive

http://www.simonsays.com
  interactive
1230 Avenue of the Americas
New York, New York 10020
Let's Talk About Me
*Richard Scarry's Best Reading
  Program Ever*

Skills Bank/The Learning Company

One Athenaeum Street
Cambridge, Massachusetts 02142
*CornerStone Reading
    Comprehension*

Spyglass, Inc.

http://www1.surfwatch.com
1240 E. Diehl Road
Naperville, Illinois 60563
SurfWatch

Sunburst Communications, Inc.

http://www.sunburst.com
101 Castleton Street
Pleasantville, New York 10570
*EasyBook Deluxe
Expression
M-ss-ng L-nks
Sunbuddy Writer
Tiger's Tales
Type to Learn
Web Workshop*

SRA/McGraw-Hill

http://www.sra-4kids.com
McGraw-Hill
2 Penn Plaza, 9th Floor
New York, New York 10121
PAWS in Typing Town

Troll

http://www.troll.com
100 Corporate Drive
Mahwah, New Jersey 07430
*Young Abraham Lincoln: Log-
    Cabin President
Young Harriet Tubman: Freedom
    Fighter
Young Helen Keller: Woman of
    Courage
Young Jackie Robinson: Baseball
    Hero
Young Orville & Wilber Wright:
    First to Fly*

Author Index

Page references followed by *f* indicate figures.

Rupley, W.H., 51, 55, 73, 74
Russell, J.D., 43, 73

S

Scardamalia, M., 110, 132
Schwartz, J.E., 33, 39
Schwartz, Judah L., 86
Scruggs, T., 79, 104
Selfe, C., 107, 131
Seuss, Dr., 51, 52*f*, 53, 74, 76, 81, 185
Sexton, M.A., 59, 73
Shannon, D., 201
Sharmat, M.W., 132
Sharp, Jean, vii, 106–132
Shiah, R.L., 79, 104
Siegel, L.S., 55, 75
Silverstein, Shel, 186
Simont, M., 132
Smaldino, S.E., 43, 73
Smith, A., 65, 74
Smith, N.B., 55, 74
Smith, S.H., 146, 158
Snow, C.E., 54, 74
Spinelli, J., 146, 158
Stabenau, J., 139, 158
Stahl, S., 79, 103
Steptoe, J., 193, 202
Stine, H.A., 80, 105
Stoodt, B.D., 146, 158
Strong, M.W., 79, 105
"Study Shows Technology Achievement Link", 79, 105
Sullivan, Jane E., vii, 106–132

T

Taylor, Mildred, 86
Taylor, R., 79, 103

Taylor, T., 197, 202
Thurlow, Richard, vii–viii, 19–39
Tierney, R.J., 80, 105
Torgesen, G.E., 47, 75
Torgesen, J.K., 44, 48, 49, 59, 72, 73, 75
Twain, Mark, 81

U

Underwood, G., 81, 105
Underwood, J., 81, 105
U.S. Department of Education, 168, 202

V

Vacca, J.L., 66, 68, 75
Vacca, R.T., 66, 68, 75
Valmont, W.J., viii, 2–18, 137, 158, 160–202
Van Allsburg, C., 186, 202
Vandervelden, M.C., 55, 75
Vitosky, Lisa, 121

W

Wagner, R.K., 47, 73
Watkins, J.H., 80, 104
Wepner, Shelley B., viii, 2–18, 76–105
White, E.B., 86
Willis, W., 149, 154, 158
Willson, V.L., 55, 74
Wilson, B.G., 208, 216
Wilson, L., 79, 105
Wood, Audrey, 125
Wood, Don, 125

Subject Index

Page references followed by *f* indicate figures.

ANIMORPHS, 210

APPLE COMPUTER, INC., 163, 197, 219

APPLEWORKS (COMPUTER SOFTWARE), 14, 17, 219

APPLICATIONS: with authors, 185–186; best practice, 205; classroom, 185–186; computer, 139–148, 205; cross-curricular, 148–155; innovative, 126–127; instructional, 21, 25*f*; Internet, 185–186; mindtools approach to, 207; plan of action for, 21, 25*f*; priorities for, 205

THE ARCTIC (CD-ROM), 187–188

ARCTIC (THEME), 187–188

ART(S): Web sites for, 144, 145*f*

ART DABBLER (COMPUTER SOFTWARE), 154, 157, 222

THE ART LESSON (COMPUTER SOFTWARE), 76, 102, 155, 157, 221

THE ART TEACHER CONNECTION (WEB SITE), 145*f*, 154

ARTELL, MIKE, 178

ARTHUR'S BIRTHDAY DELUXE (COMPUTER SOFTWARE), 81, 98, 102, 219

ARTHUR'S COMPUTER ADVENTURE (COMPUTER SOFTWARE), 81, 98, 102, 219

ARTHUR'S READING RACE (COMPUTER SOFTWARE), 76, 81, 98, 102, 219

ARTHUR'S TEACHER TROUBLE (COMPUTER SOFTWARE), 14, 17, 36, 39, 76, 81, 98, 102; address, 219

ASK JEEVES FOR KIDS (WEB SITE), 128

ASSESSMENT, 167–168; journal "haves assessment," 26–35

ASSISTED LEARNING, 160

ATLAPEDIA ONLINE (WEB SITE), 141, 145*f*

ATLASES, ELECTRONIC, 140–141, 141*f*

ATM (AUTOMATED TELLER MACHINE), 13, 27

AUDIOTAPES, 136–137

AUTHOR STUDY PROJECTS, 183–184; Awesome Authors (theme), 175–179; classroom Internet applications, 185–186; community of authors, 185–186; instructional plan for, 98*f*, 98–99; Web sites, 78, 93–94

AUTHORS AND ILLUSTRATORS ON THE WEB (WEB SITE), 178

AUTHOR'S CHAIR, 107

AUTOSKILL INTERNATIONAL, INC., 219

AVERKEYS, 190

AWESOME AUTHORS (THEME), 175–179

B

THE BABYSITTERS CLUB (COMPUTER SOFTWARE), 215, 216, 220

BAILEY'S BOOK HOUSE (COMPUTER SOFTWARE), 54, 72, 220

BALANCED LITERACY PROGRAM, 192

G

H

INTERNET-BASED LEARNING, 190

I-SEARCH, 119–120; instructional plan for teaching informational-text writing with, 119–120, 120*f*

ISP (INTERNET SERVICE PROVIDER), 21

ISPs. *See* Internet Service Providers

ISTE. *See* International Society for Technology in Education

J

JAPAN: Jay Stailey's amazing Japanese adventure (Web site), 198–199

JARGON, 21

JOURNALS: to create plan of action, 35–38; "haves assessment" with, 26–35; teacher, 21, 22*f*–25*f*

JUMPSTART 1ST GRADE READING (COMPUTER SOFTWARE), 58–60, 73, 221

JUMPSTART TYPING (COMPUTER SOFTWARE), 112, 131, 221

JUST GRANDMA AND ME DELUXE (COMPUTER SOFTWARE), 76, 81, 82*f*, 103, 219

K

KEYBOARDING, 109–113; Alpha Smart keyboards, 111; improving, 36

KEYPALS (E-MAIL PENPALS), 78

KID INFO...ATLASES (WEB SITE), 145*f*

KID PHONICS 1 (COMPUTER SOFTWARE), 58, 73, 220

KID PHONICS 2 (COMPUTER SOFTWARE), 57, 58, 68, 73, 220

KID PIX (COMPUTER SOFTWARE), 134, 154, 158, 180, 181, 201; address, 219

KID PIX STUDIO DELUXE (COMPUTER SOFTWARE), 14, 18, 101, 104, 121, 131; address, 219; personal responses to *Tar Beach* with, 121, 123*f*

KID WORKS 2 (COMPUTER SOFTWARE), 220

KID WORKS DELUXE (COMPUTER SOFTWARE), 54, 73, 116, 131, 221

KIDPUB (WEB SITE), 129

KIDPUB PUBLISHER'S PICKS (WEB SITE), 129–130

KING BIDGOOD'S IN THE BATHTUB (WOOD AND WOOD): student solutions to, with *HyperStudio*, 124, 125*f*

KITT PEAK, 16

KNOWLEDGE ADVENTURE, 221

K-W-L, 5, 81, 95, 97

L

LANGUAGE EXPERIENCE APPROACH, 180–181

LASER DISCS. *See* Video discs

LAWRENCE PRODUCTIONS, 221

LCD (Liquid Crystal Display) projectors, 126, 169

Leap Into Learning, Inc., 221

Leap Into Phonics (computer software), 50, 53, 73, 221

Learning: assisted, 160; computer-assisted, 190–191; content of, 160; Internet-based, 190; meaningful, 208; Standards of Learning (Virginia state), 110–111; technology to help meet students at appropriate levels of, 211–212; by today's children, 9–10. *See also* Literacy learning

Learning adentures, 83–85

Learning adventure (unit), 94–95, 95*f*

The Learning Company, 174, 221. *See also* Brøderbund; Creative Wonders; MECC; Mindscape; Multimedia Design Corporation; Skills Bank

Lessons: on spreadsheets (seventh grade), 149, 150*f*; transportation (third grade), 138, 138*f. See also* Instructional plans

Let's Go Read! An Island Adventure (computer software), 54, 56, 57*f*, 60, 73, 220

Let's Go Read! An Ocean Adventure (computer software), 56, 73, 220

Let's Talk About Me (computer software), 215, 217, 222

Letter knowledge development, 46–52

Letter-name learning software, 53–54

"Liberty! The American Revolution" (videotapes) (Public Broadcasting System), 154

Library collections: digitizing, 6

Library of Congress (Web site), 8, 145*f*

Library of Congress-Selected Civil War Photographs (Web site), 145*f*

Linear reading, 7

The Lion King (Web site), 83

Listservs, 146–148

Literacy: balanced program, 192; best practice in, 205; content area, 133–158; definition of, 204; enhancement of, 78–80; modern day classroom, 3–4; research projects to improve, 191–192; teacher vignettes, 174–199; and technology, x, 78–80, 174–188, 188–192, 193–199

Literacy curriculum, 1–39

Literacy learning: with technology, 5–8; technology to support, 2–18; what we know about, 5

Literary genres, 97*f*, 97–98

Literature, responding to: through bookmaking, 120–121, 121*f*; through creative problem solving, 124, 125*f*; through illustration, 121, 123*f*; with *Kid Pix Studio Deluxe*, 121, 123*f*; through memoir, 117–118, 118*f*; through plays, 122, 124*f*; through story retellings, 115, 116*f*

MINDTOOLS, 205–207; computers as, 206

MINDTOOLS APPROACH: to Internet searches, 206; principles for, 206–207; to software, 206

THE MITTEN (COMPUTER SOFTWARE), 186

MODERN DAY LITERACY CLASSROOM, 3–4

MODERN LANGUAGE ASSOCIATION: style formats (Web site), 163

MORRIS K. UDALL-A LIFETIME OF SERVICE TO ARIZONA AND THE UNITED STATES (DIGITIZED COLLECTION), 6

MOSAIC (COMPUTER SOFTWARE), 12, 14

MOUSE SKILLS, 36

MPEG3 (MP3) PLAYERS, 28

mPOWER (COMPUTER SOFTWARE), 133, 142, 154, 158, 222

"MRS. SILVERMAN'S SECOND-GRADE CLASS" (WEB SITE), 187

MS KIDS (COMPUTER SOFTWARE), 158, 222

M-SS-NG L-NKS (COMPUTER SOFTWARE), 86, 101, 104, 223

MULTIMEDIA, 117, 212

MULTIMEDIA DESIGN CORPORATION, 222

N

NASA (NATIONAL AERONAUTICS AND SPACE ADMINISTRATION): Human Spaceflight Web site, 145*f*; Shuttle Web site, 153; Solar System Internet Project, 64–65, 65*f*

NATIONAL COUNCIL OF TEACHERS OF ENGLISH, 174

NATIONAL COUNCIL OF TEACHERS OF MATHEMATICS, 174

NATIONAL EDUCATIONAL TECHNOLOGY STANDARDS FOR STUDENTS (NETS) (ISTE), 173

NATIONAL EDUCATIONAL TECHNOLOGY STANDARDS FOR STUDENTS: CONNECTING CURRICULUM AND TECHNOLOGY (ISTE), 173–174, 175–179

NATIONAL ENDOWMENT FOR THE HUMANITIES, 94

NATIONAL GEOGRAPHIC'S MAP MACHINE (WEB SITE), 141, 145*f*

NET NANNY (WEB SITE), 161

NETIQUETTE, 208

NETS. *See National Educational Technology Standards for Students*

NETSCAPE COMMUNICATIONS, 222

NETSCAPE COMMUNICATOR (COMPUTER SOFTWARE), 194, 197, 201, 222; checking computer's history and cache with, 161

NETSCAPE NAVIGATOR (COMPUTER SOFTWARE), 12, 33, 36, 37, 39, 144, 158, 189; address, 222; sample screen, 37*f*

THE NEW KATIE'S FARM (COMPUTER SOFTWARE), 84, 94–95, 104, 221

NEW PLAGIARISM, 207, 210

THE NEW YORK TIMES (WEB SITE), 193, 210

development, 43, 45*f*; spelling, 62, 63–64; teacher journals for, 21, 22*f*–23*f*; teaching and learning goals that might be accomplished with, 89; types of, 43; to use or not to use, 89–90; varieties of, 33; vocabulary, 67–69; Web sites for, 92; word-processing, 113, 142. *See also specific programs*

in mathematics instruction, 148–151; new, 207–208; opportunities for critical thinking with, 209–210; in primary classroom, 181–182; rationale for using, 5–8, 78–80, 108, 204–215; for reading development, 80–89; in reading room, 193–194; for research, 155; skill-development units using, 46, 47*f*; standards for, 173, 175–179; to support word recognition, spelling, and vocabulary acquisition, 42–75; for today and 21st century, 184; types of, 80–89; for writing development, 106–132

TLC School, 174

Tools: technological, 136–148; for writing, 109–126

Toon channel, 11

The Tortoise and the Hare (computer software), 98, 105, 219

Touch typing, 111

Trail series (computer software), 84

Training materials, self-guided, 30

Transparencies, 136

Transportation (lesson) (third grade), 138, 138*f*

Travel buddies, 182

Troll, 81–82, 223

"Trucker Buddy" program, 184

Tubman, Harriet: books about, 100; Web sites about, 100, 100*f*

Tucson Unified School District (TUSD) #1 Technology Futures Team, 168–170

Tutorial software, 56

TWA Flight 800, 210

Type to Learn (computer software), 111–112, 132, 223

Typing, touch, 111

U

Udall, Morris K., 6

Uniform Resource Locators (URLs), 37, 144

United States (unit) (seventh grade), 143, 143*f*

Units: Arctic, 187–188; Career Exploration, 198; Fables, 97*f*, 97–98; learning adventure, 94–95, 95*f*; management of, 173–174; phonemic awareness, 50–53, 51*f*; phonics, 59–61, 60*f*; "The Raising of the Titanic," 193–194; Science Fiction/Future, 198; skill-development, 46, 47*f*; Slavery, 99*f*, 99–100; spelling, 64–65, 65*f*; Survival, 100–102, 101*f*; U.S. states (seventh grade), 143, 143*f*; vocabulary, 69–71, 70*f. See also* Instructional plans

Universal Service Fund Education Rate (E-Rate), 215

The University of Arizona: Morris K. Udall–A Lifetime of Service to Arizona and the United States (digitized collection), 6; The Papers of Senator John J. Williams (digitized collection), 6

University of Delaware: Morris K. Udall–A Lifetime of Service to Arizona and the United States (digitized collection), 6; The Papers of Senator John J. Williams (digitized collection), 6

The University of Tulsa McFarlin Library Reference Center (Web site), 145*f*

URL (Uniform Resource Locator), 37, 144

U.S. Department of Energy Assistive Technologies (Web site), 190

THE WHITE HOUSE FOR KIDS (WEB SITE), 145*f*

WIGGLEWORKS PLUS (COMPUTER SOFTWARE), 14, 18, 88, 105; address, 222; types of reading material used, 88

WILD WORLD OF WORDS (INTERNET SITE), 64

WILLIAMS, JOHN J., 6

WINDOWS ON MATH (VIDEO DISC PROGRAM), 149, 158

WINDOWS ON SCIENCE (COMPUTER SOFTWARE), 152, 158

"WINTER WONDERLAND" (INTERNET PROJECT) (WEB SITE), 186–187

WIRELESS CONNECTIONS, 172

WISCONSIN CAREER INFORMATION SYSTEM (WEB SITE), 198

WORD (COMPUTER SOFTWARE), 15, 33, 39, 109, 132, 148, 158; address, 222

WORD MUNCHERS (COMPUTER SOFTWARE), 222

WORD MUNCHERS DELUXE (COMPUTER SOFTWARE), 14, 18, 69, 70, 222

WORD PROCESSING, 114–115

WORD RECOGNITION, 42–75

WORD TURTLE (GAME), 64

WORDPERFECT (COMPUTER SOFTWARE), 114, 132, 220

WORD-PROCESSING SOFTWARE, 113, 142

WORLD WIDE WEB (WWW), 7, 12, 128, 144, 172; beginnings of, 14; integration into curriculum, 185; navigating, 144

WRIGHT FLYER ONLINE (WEB SITE), 133

WRITERS STUDIO (COMPUTER SOFTWARE), 119, 132, 220

WRITERS WORKSHOPS, 107

WRITING: IN CYBERSPACE, 128–130; development of, 106–132; instructional plan for teaching with I-Search, 119–120, 120*f*; technical, 197–198; tools for, 109–126

WRITING WORKSHOPS, 109, 127

WWW. *See* World Wide Web

Y–Z

YAHOOLIGANS! DIRECTORY (WEB SITE), 95

YOUNG ABRAHAM LINCOLN: LOG-CABIN PRESIDENT (COMPUTER SOFTWARE), 82, 105, 223

YOUNG HARRIET TUBMAN: FREEDOM FIGHTER (COMPUTER SOFTWARE), 82, 100, 105, 223

YOUNG HELEN KELLER: WOMAN OF COURAGE (COMPUTER SOFTWARE), 82, 105, 223

YOUNG JACKIE ROBINSON: BASEBALL HERO (COMPUTER SOFTWARE), 82, 105, 223

YOUNG ORVILLE & WILBUR WRIGHT: FIRST TO FLY (COMPUTER SOFTWARE), 82, 105, 223

YUKON TRAIL (COMPUTER SOFTWARE), 84, 105, 221

ZIP DRIVES, 190